In Pursuit of Virtue

The Moral Theology and Psychology of
Ibn Hazm al-Andalusi
[384 - 456 AH   994 - 1064 AD]

with a translation of his book

Al-Akhlaq wa'l-Siyar

Muhammad Abu Laylah
A.M., M.A. Al-Azhar University (Cairo)
Ph.D, Exeter University (England)

Published by
TA-HA PUBLISHERS LTD.
1, Wynne Road
London SW9 0BB

© Copyright Ta-Ha Publishers Ltd. 1411/1990

Reprinted: 1998

Published by:

Ta-Ha Publishers Ltd.

1, Wynne Road

London SW9 OBB

website:http://www.taha.co.uk/

email: sales@taha.co.uk

Editing and Production by Bookwork, norwich

British Library Cataloguing in Publication Data

Laylah, M. Abu

   In pursuit of virtue.

   1. Al-Akhlaq wa'l-Siyar Arabic

   I. Title II. The moral theology & psychology

   297-209

   ISBN 0 907461-76-X

Printed and Bound by: De-Luxe Printers,

London NW10 7NR.

website: http://www.de-luxe.com

email: printers@de-luxe.com

DEDICATION

Ibn Hazm dedicated his book to the benefit of all mankind.

Here I follow his example in dedicating this book to all my fellow-men, particularly to the very rich, who are in danger of forgetting life's true values, and to the very poor, who may not realise that they can be rich in the things that matter. Money is not everything, there are greater treasures available for all.

The world is for everybody, but heaven is only for the pure in heart, the virtuous and most pious.

TABLE OF CONTENTS

IBN HAZM: A MAN FOR OUR TIME

A FOREWORD BY IAN RICHARD NETTON

It gives me great pleasure to introduce this translation by my former student, Dr. Muhammad Abu Layla, of Ibn Hazm's most important work on ethics. Ibn Hazm is truly a man for our own times. The age in which he lived, studied and wrote is not dissimilar in many respects from that in which we ourselves live and work today: wars, revolutions and upheavals of various sorts tore at the fabric of his society in much the same way as they do at the fabric of the international order now. In both ages the situations requiring a positive ethical and moral response were - and are - varied and many. Ibn Hazm tried to provide an answer to some of the questions: How should I properly interact with my fellow man today? What must do to live at peace both with him and with God?

Ibn Hazm was, however, much more than a narrow moralist. As a jurisprudent, politician, philosopher, poet and scholar of comparative religion, to mention just a few of his activities, he resembles an Erasmus in the range of his interests and the breadth of his scholarship. (It is a particular pleasure for me to note here that Ibn Hazm's work in the last-mentioned field of comparative religion has been well-chronicled and documented both by Dr. Abu Layla himself (for the Christian aspects) and his wife Dr Nurshif Rif'at (for the Judaic side) in their doctoral theses presented to, and accepted by, the University of Exeter.

Nonetheless, it is to Ibn Hazm as the man of ethics and man of morals that Dr Abu Layla directs our attention in this book. In his article on "Ibn Hazm" in the New Edition of the *Encyclopaedia of Islam*(vol. III, pp. 790-799), the author R. Arnaldez repeats E. García Gómez' description of the age in which Ibn Hazm lived as the "most tragic moments of Muslim Spain" and "the decisive crisis of Islam in Andalusia." Ibn Hazm clearly perceived the possibilities in such circumstances for evil and vice, as well as the potential inherent in a stronger man to plunder and ruin a weaker. Yet, in

Arnaldez's words, he "confronted all these inconstancies of man and society as a man passionately convinced of the truth, and all his researches led towards a truth supported by incontrovertible evidence with incontestable proofs. This Truth is the God of Islam, Who is the foundation of all the other truths." All this is at the root of the thinking about ethics in Ibn Hazm's *Kitâb al-Akhlâq wa'l-Siyar*. Arnaldez stresses that action is at the heart of Hazmian morality but it is "an action purged of any internal motive and entirely determined by the thought of God."

Dr Abu Layla, in his article "Ibn Hazm's Influence on ChristianThinking in Research" (*Islamic Quarterly*, vol. xxxl:2 (1987), pp. 103-115) has rightly called our attention to the impact which Ibn Hazm must have had on both Jewish and Christian thinkers of his own and later ages. Abu Layla notes:

> Ibn Hazm's reputation in the religious world was clearly great, but it is to be remembered that he was also an active politician, and furthermore, from an actively political family. As such, Ibn Hazm moved in circles wider than those of normal academics. His political life ensured that he became widely known as a man conspicuous for his talents and convictions. This is an important fact in terms of the transmission of his ideas, for it gave him access to people of all types. In other words, his political activity heightened his profile in the world at large and increased awareness of him beyond academia. The channels of Ibn Hazm's influence flowed into all areas of life.

Abu Layla concludes that "Ibn Hazm's influence on the Christian thinkers of his day" must be much more than mere surmise or possibility. Given the probable breadth of that influence, is it far-fetched to suppose that works such as that which is translated in this volume achieved a much greater circulation than is generally supposed, not only in Muslim but also in Christian and Jewish circles as well? The task remains for the future socio-historian of Islamic ethics to assess the possible degree that Hazmian ethics may have influenced and shaped the development of Judaic and Christian ethics in the High Middle Ages in Western Europe. It is an intriguing thought.

In the translation which follows in this volume, which is the first translation of the *Kitâb al-Akhlâq wa'l-Siyar* into English, Dr Abu Layla has rendered a signal service to the non-Arabic reader, opening up the riches to other specialists in the general ethical field who have no Arabic as well as providing a fluent guide to the general reader who is curious to gain some insight into the mind of one of medieval Spain's greatest Muslim thinkers.

Ian Richard Netton
University of Exeter
January 1990

PREFACE

This book constitutes the first attempt to give a compre-hensive account and analysis of Ibn Hazm's moral views and psychology. It contains the first complete translation into English of Ibn Hazm's work *al-Akhlâq wa'l Siyar*, or *Morality and Behaviour.*

We have also gathered together maxims and statements of Ibn Hazm's ethical code, scattered throughout his works, with the aim of presenting a coherent picture of his moral views and psychology. Moreover, some of Ibn Hazm's moral poetry has been translated, since it completes the picture.

During the time of writing this book I encountered many difficulties, and I can personally testify to the true power of the moral teachings in this book. I drew enough strength from them to persevere with this work. Ibn Hazm's most important lesson is that everyone can be happy, whether pen-niless or millionaire.

I owe a great debt of gratitude and appreciation to Mrs Hazel Mary Harvey, M.A. (London), who was an invaluable assistant in producing this work. She helped in checking the French translation and also acted as a stylistic adviser.

Mr David Harvey, M.A. (Oxford), drew my attention to the relevant works of Greek philosophy. This book could not have seen the light of day so soon without their help, and I thank them both most sincerely.

Thanks are also reserved for Dr Richard Hitchcock, the Head of the Spanish Department, University of Exeter, for his useful suggestions and advice, and Dr Ian Netton, the Head of the Arabic and Islamic Department at the same university, for encouraging me to compile this volume, and his thorough reading of the text. I would like also to thank Dr. Ali M. Ghamdi, Director of the Islamic Cultural Centre (London) for his encouragement and support. I also thank Mr. Husin Abbara for the valuable comments and suggestions he made. I would like also to thank Mrs Jenny Hickman, Secretary of the Curriculum and Resources Centre in the School of Educa-tion, University of Exeter, for her patience and careful typing of this work. I would also like to offer my thanks and gratitude to Mr. A. Siddiqi in showing great interest in publishing this book.

Many friends deserve my heartfelt gratitude for encouraging me and for their practical help during a particularly difficult time. I therefore pray to Allah most earnestly to give them the best reward.

Finally, it is beyond my capability to express my gratitude and debt to my wife Nurshif Rif'at, Ph.D. (Exeter), for her scholarly suggestions and unstinting support and encouragement throughout.

INTRODUCTION

Morality is the basis of our existence. It is the firm foundation for a just society. It enables each of us to achieve a happy life. Morality is the necessary food for the soul; it provides its staple diet; and a healthy soul creates a healthy body. That is why Allah has sent Prophets and Messengers, disciples and pious reformers, to remind us of our basic need for healthy souls and correct behaviour. The Prophet Muhammad clearly defined his own message as a continuation and completion of the moral messages brought by the Prophets before him. Today, more than ever, we are in urgent need of ethical principles. In the Qur'an, God speaks to everybody, saying that, *"He will never change the outward condition of people unless they themselves change the inward condition of the soul"* [Qur'an 13:11].

Scientific progress has brought countless benefits, but these benefits are equalled in number by new problems and moral dilemmas in the fields of warfare, of sexual relations, of personal life, etc. Science naturally deals only with the material aspects, with material means and material solutions.

Life is not material only, but also spiritual. Islam caters for all the fields of human existence. Islam does not admit of any kind of separation between the material and the moral, or mundane and spiritual life. Islam teaches that spiritual and material forces must work together and that the Muslim should work hard and spare no effort to develop and reconstruct life on sound moral foundations. Islam is the only religion to take account of the two sides of life: the material and spiritual. Islam provides the most needed balance without which life loses its stability and its desirability.

Science alone can hardly provide solutions to the new metaphysical problems which it produces. Moreover, scientific advances have seduced us from devoting time to our moral duties. Every minute of our day we are assailed by the newspapers, magazines, radio, television; we are programmed to react in regulated ways, to follow the fashions, to update our cars and household equipment - we form the consumer society with all its hectic activity and disgraceful wastefulness. We do not leave ourselves time to reflect on our lives and on our lifestyle. We have no time for morality and ethics. We are constantly tempted by the charms of the material world and worldly achievements. We seek instant gratification and the charm of the new. As a result, the crime rate increases every day, even every minute. Our time is in dire need of the wisdom of the ancients. We need their religion and their morality, which they themselves inherited and which they can pass on to us if we have ears to hear.

Morality is not something finished or changing. It is part of human predisposition. Times change and we change with them but we should not reject all the old values, nor should we accept every new invention. A thing is not bad merely because it is old. A thing is not profitable merely because it is newly invented. This is clear if we look at the evidence of our own nature, and of the nature of the earth on which we live. The earth is the same and yet it is in unceasing motion. The air is the same as that breathed by the first man on this planet, but continually renewed and always to the same formula.

Our need and urge to eat to keep alive is unchanged since the time of Adam and Eve; although we may have different preferences in food, the basic chemical constituents remain the same, dictated by the needs of our bodies. Some may eat with knife and fork, some with chopsticks, some with their hands, but we are all satisfying the same basic requirement for nourishment. Similarly, an intake of morality and ethics is very necessary to everyone in some form or another. Moral remedies always bring healing and beneficial effects to both individual and society.

This book is about Islamic morality but it is not directed only at Muslims but to all human beings. In my view, morality is the common ground on which all people can come together. There is nothing else better suited to unite different peoples. There is little disagreement between nations about moral principles. Islam is not in conflict with any manifestation of wisdom and morality. Islam confirmed morality even that of pagan peoples, recognized it and adopted it as part of its own moral code. Islam has confirmed moral precepts, which were of divine origin, from Jews and Christians. The

Qur'an clearly praises anyone who practises morality among the Jews and Christians as well as Sabaeans who display good deeds and honest practice.[1]

That is why in the book as well as the translated text here you will find moral sayings taken from Indian, Greek, Persian, Jewish and Christian sources. Wisdom knows no boundary; it is not indigenous to one people.

The translated text is Ibn Hazm's most important treatise on morality and psychology. This is the first translation of it to appear in English, although it has previously appeared in two other European languages, Spanish and French.

I have previously translated Ibn Hazm's criticism of the New Testament and Christian dogma; my wife Nurshif Rif'at has translated his major book, *al Fisal*, on Jews and Judaism.[2]

Ibn Hazm's book on morality is a unique work. It contains the fruits of more than sixty years of experience and learning, failure and success, participation in public life, periods of imprisonment and exile, and periods of political ministry. He wrote 400 books, covering all the branches of scholarship known in his time; this shows that he must have read many times this number of books, have conversed with many scholars, spent long hours in debate, meditation and writing.

The book here translated was the last of his books; it is the crown of his efforts, the distillation of his experiences. Knowing this, we can judge the importance of this text, and the great value we should place on it. Its contents are extremely useful, and necessary for the health of our souls, bodies and minds. This book will purify our consciences, relieve our hearts and help us to find a good and happy life on earth, and happiness in the world to come.

Ibn Hazm is a great man in every way by any standards. He has a magnanimity which comes across to his reader. We feel his power on us as we read. We do not have to be a fellow Muslim to reap the benefit of his advice. His influence extended beyond his own religion and his own time and his own linguistic area. He was a pioneer of comparative reli-

---

1. See e.g., 2:62, 5:82-85.
2. See below, p. 16.

gion.[1] His views on psychology do not conflict with the discoveries of modern science and can benefit us today. He laid
the foundation of experimental psychology. He was the first
scholar to write a whole chapter on the roundness of the
earth.[2]

In my article about the Braille alphabet for the blind, I
pointed out that Ibn Hazm mentioned a similar system used
in al-Andalus centuries before Louis Braille. Ibn Hazm's
teacher's grandfather had a blind son who could not read
until his father made letters moulded in tar which could be
read with the finger-tips.[3]

Ibn Hazm in modern scholarship

In the 20th century the world of scholarship awakened to
the importance of Ibn Hazm. Many books of his were discovered, and published with critical introductions. Quite a few
of his writings were translated into various languages, either
entire or in extracts. Many scholarly books and articles were
written about him, in a great many languages. Interest in
him is still growing and I have the feeling that it will continue to grow.

Ibn Hazm is a Muslim scholar of the West, remarkable in
every way. He lived in al-Andalus at a time when it was a
world centre of civilization and culture, attracting scholars
from everywhere. Many scholarly Arabic and Islamic works
had been translated into Latin, at a time when Latin was the
common language of the Christian empire. Works on theology, philosophy, astronomy, medicine, pathology, morality
and, above all, the Qur'an itself were translated into Latin
and thus made available to the European world. The transla-

1. See Muhammad Abu Layla, "An introduction to the life and work of Ibn
Hazm (II)", *The Islamic Quarterly*, vol. 29, number 2, (London, The Islamic
Cultural Centre, 1405 AH, 1985 AD) pp. 165-172, also Muhammad Abu
Layla, "Ibn Hazm's influence on Christian thinking in Research", *The Islamic Quarterly*, vol. 31, number 2, pp. 103-115.
2. Ibn Hazm, *al-Fisal fi'l Milal wa'l Ahwâ' wa'l Nihal* (Cairo, Subayh, 1384 AH
- 1964 AD) vol. 2, pp. 95-101.
3. "Ibn Abd al-Warith al-Andalusi al-Mukhtari: al-Haqiqi li Braille", *al-Muslimoon*, vol. 2, number 33, London, 1985, p. 19.

tions were produced not only by scholars but also by kings and churchmen.[1] The most famous of the Christian kings who showed great interest in Eastern culture was Alfonso the Wise of Castille. Alfonso ordered a translation into Spanish to be made of the books of maxims by the Arabic scholars, Hunayn ibn Ishâq (193 - 260 AH; 808-873 AD) and al-Mubashshir ibn Fâtik (c. 494 AH; 1100 AD).[2]

Alfonso paid no attention to Ibn Hazm although he is of equal standing to these scholars. Solomon ben Gabirol (437 AH; 1045 AD), the Jewish moralist who was influenced by Ibn Hazm, was known to the Latin world.[3] The Jewish convert to Christianity, Petrus Alfonsi, wrote his *Disciplina Clericalis*, which is a compendium of Arabic and Islamic wisdom but without making any reference to Ibn Hazm.

Asín Palacios deserves credit for translating Ibn Hazm's book *al-Fisal* into Spanish for the first time. His first volume covers Ibn Hazm's life and works. Palacios greatly regretted the neglect of Ibn Hazm and placed him on the same level as such well noted Andalusian philosophers as Ibn Bajja (Avempace) (d. 533 AH; 1138 AD), Ibn Gabirol (Solomon Avicebron) (d. 463 AH; 1070 AD), Ibn Rushd (Averröes) (520-595 AH; 1126-1198 AD) and Ibn Maimon (Maimonides) (530-601 AH; 1135-1204 AD), and in addition he considered the author of *al-Fisal* a gifted theologian, jurist, poet, moralist, literary man, and a pioneer of comparative religion.[4]

Asín Palacios' translation is good in general but there are some points to be noted about it. In some cases he failed to understand Ibn Hazm's idiomatic and highly sophisticated style and elliptic expressions. For example, he understood "the son of Noah" and "the father of Abraham" as two *kunya*

1. Muhammad Abu Layla, "Ibn Hazm's influence on Christian thinking in Reserach," pp. 103ff.
2. Petrus Alfonsi, *The Disciplina Clericalis*, translated and edited by Eberhard Hermes, translated into English by P. R. Quarrie (London and Henley, Routledge and Kegan Paul Ltd, 1977) p. 6.
3. See N. Rif'at, *Ibn Hazm on Jews and Judaism*, (Ph.D. thesis, Exeter University, 1988), pp. 181f.
4. *Abenhazam de Cordoba, y su historia crítica de las ideas religiosas*, (Madrid 1927-1932), vol. 1, pp. 5f; see also Muhammad Ibrâhîm al-Kittânî, *Hall Aththara Ibn Hazm fî'l Fikr al-Masîhî*, (Morocco, Majallat al-Bayyina al-Maghribiyya, 1962), no. 1, pp. 68-87.

titles. Moreover, he says that they were related to the Prophet Muhammad, not realizing that they referred to the two prophets, Abraham and Noah.[1]

He also felt that specialist theologians would be able to refute all Ibn Hazm's arguments, but had to warn non-specialists that they would need to consult certain modern works to find the answers.[2] In 1916 Asín Palacios also translated Ibn Hazm's *al-Akhlâq wa'l Siyar* as shall be mentioned in its context later.[3]

Palacios' translation of *al-Fisal* has indeed drawn the attention of Western scholars in general, and the Spanish in particular, to Ibn Hazm. Albornez, for example, says that he visited Asín Palacios when he was translating *al-Fisal* and says: "I felt the great and growing importance of this Spanish Muslim character, a figure without parallel." He was impressed with Ibn Hazm's ideas about civil war and he admits to being influenced by them. Albornez wrote and lectured about Ibn Hazm.[4] This is just one example of Ibn Hazm's continuing influence on scholars, and shows the high esteem in which he is held by those who have read him.

Albornez also says that "Ibn Hazm was a theologian, philosopher, jurist, scholar, philologist, historian, poet, man of letters, psychologist, moralist, and not just a thinker but also a man of action. He was both a politician and an idealist. He can be regarded as the equal of any of the greatest of the thinkers and poets of the Middle Ages. If he had written in Latin or Greek his name would be as well known as Dante or St. Thomas Aquinas."[5]

While we are on the subject of scholarly work about Ibn Hazm, the renowned orientalist Ignaz Goldziher gives much attention to Ibn Hazm; in one of his important articles

---

1. See al-Tâhir Makkî's notes on Asín Palacios' translation of *al-Fisal* in Makki's introduction to Ibn Hazm's *al-Akhlâq wa'l Siyar fî mudâwât al-Nufûs*, (Cairo, Dar al-Ma'arif, 1981), p.66; also Ibn Hazm, *al-Fisal*, vol. 4, pp. 32-35.
2. Asín Palacios, *Abenhazam*, vol. 2, pp. 45-52.
3. See below p. 121.
4. See al-Tâhir Makkî, *Dirâsât 'An Ibn Hazm wa Kitâbu Tawq al-Hamâma*, (Cairo, Dâr al-Ma'ârif, 1401 AH; 1981 AD), pp.140f; also Muhammad 'Abd Allah 'Inân, *Duwal al-Tawâ'if Mundh Qiyâmihâ Hattâ al-Fath al-Murâbiti*, (Cairo, al-Khanji, 1389 AH; 1969 AD), p. 431.
5. See al-Tâhir Makkî, *Dirasat 'An Ibn Hazm*, p. 139.

"Proben Muhammedanischer Polemik gegen den Talmud" [Samples of Muhammdan Polemic Against the Talmud], he translated about six pages of the second volume of *Kitab al-Fisal* into German.[1] His translation is thorough, but not always completely accurate. For example, he omits some important references cited by Ibn Hazm from the Talmud and other Jewish sources; sometimes his translation is so free that it is inaccurate.

Ignaz Goldziher and Martin Schreiner wrote in detail on Ibn Hazm's Zahiri doctrine. Goldziher's book, *The Zahiris, Their Doctrine and Their History,* deserves a special word of approbation,[2] although he seems to overemphasize Ibn Hazm's literalism and hardly penetrates to its intellectual aspect.

Goldziher in his *Vorlesungen über Islam* [Lectures about Islam] at Heidelberg 1910 pays great attention to Ibn Hazm and his works, and writes at length about his literalist system, his theology and Biblical criticism. Specifically he devotes one lecture to Ibn Hazm's book on ethics and morality. He described the work as "a series of maxims relating to morals and the conduct of life, arranged in chapters." Goldziher also concerns himself with Ibn Hazm's own character as described by the author, "his qualities and defects... the arrogance which ruled him... for a time, but from which he was delivered by self-discipline. His intolerance, his propensity to bitter criticism of his fellow-men, and his ill-humour he ascribes to an enlargement of the spleen resulting from an illness."[3]

D.S. Margoliouth says that Ibn Hazm's "studies in the Pentateuch led him to anticipate some of the objections urged

---

1. *Jeschurun,* (Lemberg, 1872), vol. 8, pp. 91-102.
2. *The Zahiris, their Doctrine and their History,* trans. and ed. by Wolfgang Behn, (Leiden, E. J. Brill, 1971); and Schreiner, *"Beitrage zu Geschichte der Theologischen Bewegun in Islam",* Z.D.M.G., vols. LII and LIII (1899); also 'Abd al-Majîd al-Turkî, *Polémiques entre Ibn Hazm et Baqi sur les principes de la loi musulmane: essai sur le litteralisme Zahirite et la finalité Malikite,* (Alger: Etudes et Documents, 1973); and 'Abd al-Majîd al-Turkî, *Théologiens et juristes de l'Espagne Musulmane, aspects polémiques,* (Paris, Editions G.P. Maisonneuve et Larose, 1982).
3. Ignaz Goldziher, "Ibn Hazm" in James Hastings (ed.) *The Encyclopaedia of Religion and Ethics* (Edinburgh, T & T Clark, 1908), vol. 7, pp. 70-72.

by modern critics, e.g. J. W. Colenso."[1]

R. Dozy observes: "Ibn Hazm was ultimately to be hailed as the most learned man of his age, and the most fertile writer that Spain ever produced."[2] Dozy, as well as F. Wustenfeld,[3] and Pons Boigues[4] dealt with Ibn Hazm in his capacity as a historian.

R.A. Nicholson stresses Ibn Hazm's universality and the depth of his learning in the branches of knowledge cultivated by Muslims.[5]

M. Sharif made a study of Ibn Hazm as a literalist philosopher. He particularly noted his prolific mind, which worked from different languages, and used genealogical tables, etymology and epistemology in his investigations. M. Sharif concentrates particularly on what *al-Fisal* shows us of Ibn Hazm's philosophy. He stresses that Ibn Hazm was a rationalist, and that his theories of apriorism resemble those of Kant (d. 1219 AH; 1804 AD) but preceded them by seven and a half centuries.[6]

In 1982, A. Chejne published his translation of Ibn Hazm's *Risâla fi Marâtib al-'Ulûm* [An Essay on the Hierarchy of the Sciences], with a good critical assessment. In his introduction Chejne studied the position of sciences in al-Andalus and Ibn Hazm's place in the intellectual history of Islam, and his views on education and learning. He regards Ibn Hazm as a humanist par excellence and one of the intellectual giants of Islam.[7] In this book A. Chejne devoted one paragraph only to Ibn Hazm's *al-Akhlâq wa'l Siyar*. He says: "The treatise falls into the category of ethics, but it also forms an integral part of belles-lettres (*adab*) in that it instructs and moralizes. How-

1. See "Old and New Testament in Mohammadanism" in James Hastings, *The Encyclopaedia of Religion and Ethics*, vol. 9, p. 482.
2. *Spanish Islam*, translated by F. G. Stokes, (Pakistan, Karimsons, 1976), p. 577.
3. *Die Geschichtschreiber der Araber und ihre Werke*, (Gottingen, 1882), p. 202.
4. *"Das obras importantisimas de Aben Hazam"* en Homenaje a Menendez y Pelayo, (Madrid, 1899), Ensayo, pp. 130-138.
5. *A Literary History of the Arabs*, (Cambridge, Cambridge University Press, 1930), pp. 426f.
6. *A History of Muslim Philosophy*, (Germany, Allgauer Heimatverlag GMbH, Kempten, 1963), vol. 1, pp. 281f.
7. *Ibn Hazm*, (U.S.A. Kazi Publications, 1402 AH; 1982 AD).

ever, its sober execution lacks the elements of humor and entertainment which ordinarily are found in belletristic writings. His personal views on numerous subjects drawn from first hand experience are presented austerely, with a religious emphasis on the way to attain happiness in this world and in the Hereafter."[1]

George F. Hourani concerned himself with Ibn Hazm's ethical views; he wrote a useful article on "Reason and Revelation in Ibn Hazm's Ethical Thought". Hourani does not study Ibn Hazm's ethical concepts in its wide dimension, but only "his answers to fundamental questions of modern philosophical ethics: the meanings of ethical concepts, the sources of our knowledge of them and of values in practice, the theory of moral motivation."[2]

Hourani draws his material from Ibn Hazm's three major works, *al-Fisal fi al-Milal wa'l Nihal*, *al-Ihkâm fi Usûl al-Ahkâm* and *al-Akhlâq wa'l Siyar*. He also drew heavily upon the scholarly writings and investigations of the distinguished orientalists Goldziher, Asín Palacios, Cruz Hernandez, and Arnaldes.[3]

The same author finds it worthwhile to draw his reader's attention to Cruz's mistake in "including wisdom among the four cardinal virtues listed by Ibn Hazm, and in saying that the Greek *Sophrosune* is specified by him as 'generosity'. The two latter are listed separately as *'iffa* and *jûd* respectively, and wisdom is not mentioned."[4]

Modern Arabic scholars have shown great interest and paid much attention to Ibn Hazm and his works, e.g. 'Inân wrote a good deal about Ibn Hazm as a historian, describing his perception of history by saying that: "Ibn Hazm is a phenomenon of his time in his acuteness of mind, his perceptiveness in research and in the depth of his thought ... Ibn Hazm is a great historian in every sense of that term. He was a rare example. He belongs among those whose judgment of their

1. *Ibn Hazm*, p. 133.
2. *Islamic Philosophical Theology*, ed. by Parviz Marewedge (U.S.A., State University of New York Press, 1979), p. 142.
3. Ibid, pp. 142f.
4. "Reason and Revelation in Ibn Hazm's Ethical thought", p. 164 (F.N.8)

contemporaries is totally reliable, and therefore invaluable."[1]

Zakariyya Ibrâhîm wrote a book about Ibn Hazm as a prolific thinker, emphasizing his pioneering role in the comparative study of religion and his influence upon later thinkers.[2]

Tâhâ al-Hâjrî as well as 'Abd al-Karîm Khalîfa dealt with Ibn Hazm's literary and poetic output.[3]

Shaikh Abû Zahra wrote a sizeable volume studying Ibn Hazm's jurisprudence and juridical career, in the light of other schools of jurisprudence. He paid special attention to Ibn Hazm's social and sociological views, which are still of interest at the present time.[4]

Ibn Hazm's social views emphasize liberal principles; he defended the human rights of slaves and respected and valued the labourer. Land ownership, in his view, should be restricted to those who could cultivate it, and landowners should not rent land for growing or building purposes. He supported the idea of free education, freely available. Aspects of his belief have a socialist character. His views on women were liberal, and he argued that, contrary to the common idea among Muslims, women were no more likely to commit sins than men. Women had the right to lead, with the exception of holding office as Caliph.[5]

Besides his edition of Ibn Hazm's *al-Mufâdala bayna al-Sahâba* and *Mulakhkhas Ibtâl al-Qiyâs*, Sa'îd al-Afghânî composed a book on Ibn Hazm as a linguist and philologist.[3]

1. *Diwal al-Tawâ'if* pp. 431ff.
2. *Ibn Hazm al-Andalusi al-Mufakkir al-Zâhiri al-Mawsû'i*, (Cairo, al-Dar al-Misriyya lil Ta'lif wa'l Tarjama, 1966).
3. Tâhâ al-Hâjrî *Ibn Hazm sûra Andalusiyya*, (Cairo, Dâr al-Fikr al-'Arabi, 1954); and 'Abd al-Karîm Khalîfa *Ibn Hazm al-Andalusi Hayâtu wa Adabu*, (Beirut, al-Dâr al-'Arabiyya/'Amman, Maktabat al-Aqsa, n.d.).
4. Muhammad Abû Zahra, *Ibn Hazm Hayâtu wa 'Asru Arâ'u wa Fiqhu*, (Cairo, Dâr al-Fikr al'Arabî, 1954.)
5. See Muhammad Abu Layla, *An introduction to the Life and Work of Ibn Hazm (I)*, The Islamic Quarterly, vol. 29, number 2, p .85; for further information on the subject of Islamic attitude towards slaves see Mustafa al-Shak'a, *Islam Bila Madhâhib*, Cairo, al-Halabi, 1977), pp. 70-84.
3. *Nazarât fî'l-Lugha 'Inda Ibn Hazm al-Andalusi*, (Beirut, Dâr al-Fikr, 1969); *Ibn Hazm al-Andalusi wa Risâla fi al-Mufâdala Bayna al-Sahâba*, (Beirut, Dâr al-Fikr, 1969); and *Mulakhkhas Ibtâl al-Qiyâs wa'l Ra'y wa'l Istihsan wa'l-Taqlîd wa'l Ta'lîl*, (Damascus, 1960).

Umar Farrûkh's work *"Ibn Hazm al-Kabîr"* is a general account of Ibn Hazm and his works. It draws heavily on Ibn Hazm's autobiographical information, with little analysis. In his book, Farrûkh takes issue with some eminent orientalists concerning Ibn Hazm's criticism of the Bible.[1]

A. Uways composed a lengthy book about Ibn Hazm as a historian, genealogist and biographer. In this book more attention is given to Ibn Hazm's views on politics, sociology, economic socialism and civilization in general.[2]

Mahmûd A. Himâya wrote a sizeable book about Ibn Hazm and his methodology in the study of religions.[3]

Ihsân 'Abbâs and al-Tâhir Makkî edited some of Ibn Hazm's remarkable works as shall be seen in the context of *al-Akhlâq wa'l Siyar's* edition.[4]

Academic Works

There are some academic writings on Ibn Hazm and his works; the most important of all are the following:

1. P. Ernst Algermissen's doctoral thesis *Die Pentateuchzitate Ibn Hazm's Ein Beitrag zur Geschichte der arabischen Bibelubersetzungen* (Münster, 1933) is a solid and useful piece of work, restricted to the question of Ibn Hazm's quotations from the Pentateuch and their possible textual sources. This thesis fills a gap in Ibn Hazm's scholarship, answering an often posed question as to the text used by Ibn Hazm when quoting from the Bible.

2. M. Abu Layla's thesis *The Muslim View of Christianity With Special Reference to the Work of Ibn Hazm*, submitted to the University of Exeter (England) (1404 AH; 1983 AD) is the first modern work to deal with Ibn Hazm's attitude towards Christianity comprehensively and using an analyt-

---

1. *Ibn Hazm al-Kabîr*, (Beirut, Dar Lebanon lil Tiba'a wa'l-Nashr, 1980).
2. 'Abd al-Halim Uways, *Ibn Hazm al-Andalusi wa Juhûduhu fî'l Bahth al-Târikhi wa'l Hadarî* (Cairo, Dar al-I'tisâm, n.d.).
3. *Ibn Hazm wa Manhajuhu fî Dirâsat al-Adyân*, (Cairo, Dâr al-Ma'ârif, 1983).
4. See below p. 119f.

ical approach. This thesis provides encyclopaedic information about Ibn Hazm's criticism of the New Testament and the Christian dogma.

3. Nurshif A. R. Rif'at's doctoral thesis, *"Ibn Hazm on Jews and Judaism"*, submitted to the University of Exeter (1408 AH; 1988 AD). This thesis constitutes the first serious attempt to give a comprehensive account and analysis of Ibn Hazm's attitude to Jews and Judaism. N. Rif'at holds Ibn Hazm as the most comprehensive and reliable source on this subject. The thesis deals with the references to the Jews and Judaism in the Qur'an and Muslim tradition providing a survey and analytical study of these references, and the varying relationship between Jews and Muslims; it also analyses Ibn Hazm's criticism of the Old Testament, especially the Pentateuch. It provides a survey of Jewish sects and Rabbinical writing and a discussion of Jewish sectarian belief and attitudes.

CHAPTER I

IBN HAZM'S MILIEU

We know from Ibn Hazm's own writings that he lived in al-Andalus in times of great political turmoil. He describes the confusion of the civil war, he names his outstanding contemporaries, and he himself clearly played a great part in the political and intellectual life of the period. In particular, he participated in public debates with Jews, Christians and Muslims, and he was an authority in every branch of knowledge. It is therefore surprising that his name is mentioned in return by only a very few of these contemporaries; though of course it is possible that the civil war itself brought about the destruction of many records.

There are only a few pages about Ibn Hazm in contemporary Arab sources, but then about a century after his death two Jewish writers mentioned him: Ibn Daûd (died c. 576 AH; 1180 AD) referred to his argument with Ibn Negrila,[1] and Salomo ben Adereth (633 - 710 AH; 1235 - 1310 AD) wrote in Hebrew a refutation of Ibn Hazm's theories on the Pentateuch,[2] but, unfortunately, apparently without having read Ibn Hazm's own writings. However, Ibn Hazm's own writings supply us with autobiographical details.

In modern times scholars of both east and west have shown a great interest in Ibn Hazm's achievements. The twentieth century is an age of specialists in almost every field of human endeavour and any student of history is often struck by the breadth of knowledge and learning which the great men of the pre-specialist world show. Their intellectual interests ranged easily across subjects which now seem quite incompatible with one another. Among the great polymaths of the Islamic world Ibn Hazm has a distinguished place.

Ibn Hazm was more, however, than simply a representative of an age in which science and the arts were closely

1. Abraham Ibn Daûd, *The Book of Tradition*, *(Sefer Ha-Qabbalah)*, ed. and trans. by Gerson D. Cohen, (Philadelphia, The Jewish Publication Society of America, 1967), p. 277.
2. R. Salomo b. Abraham b. Adereth, *Sein Leben und Seine Schriften...* (J. Perles, Breslau, Schletter, 1863), pp.1-24.

intertwined. His writings show a mind passionately engaged in all he undertook; persistent yet fresh. If we look at him in the context of medieval Spain he is the most outstanding figure of that country at that time, the most knowledgeable and lively scholar. He is the most accomplished and stubborn debater, inexhaustible in discussion of important topics. Ibn Hazm was an active politician, a creative author, a great historian, a jurist and many other things. In al-Andalus there may have been others who resembled him in one field, but he alone was eminent in all these fields, and has left many manuscripts of his works. If you were restricted to one person as a source to tell you everything about Islam, he would be your choice. He provides knowledge in every field, he is an encyclopaedia in himself, but, unlike an encyclopaedia, he does not give dry summaries but enthusiastic detail. He is a man of letters and a poet, a jurist and a historian, rationalist and theologian, philosopher and moralist, logician and teacher, educationalist, theorist, physician and genealogist, biographer and autobiographer. Ibn Hazm is an active politician and lawyer; he is a pioneer of comparative religion; he is a speaker and preacher, grammarian, philologist and linguist, psychologist and sociologist. Above all, he is sincere, devout, he writes what he believes to be right, and presents his criticism with great care and precision.

A Bedouin was once woken in his tent by a man from Seville singing to the moon a verse he had memorized from his King al-Mu'tamid Ibn 'Abbâd's poetry:

> Set your heart at peace,
> Stop its fluttering.
> Make it settle;
> Stop being driven along by your thoughts.
> Sorrow and carefulness, what can they
> bring back to you?[1]

The Bedouin was so moved by its beauty that he could not believe that a man could compose such verses and have

---

1. Ibn al-Abbâr, *Al-Hulla al-Siyrâ'*, ed. by Husayn Munis, (Cairo, Matba'at Lajnat al-Ta'lif wa'l-Tarjama wa'l-Nashr, 1963), vol. 2, p. 58.

time to be a good king as well. What would he have thought of Ibn Hazm's multifarious activities and achievements? According to Abu 'Abd Allah al-Humaydi (d. 488 AH; 1095 AD), Ibn Hazm was a great poet, without rival in this field, never lacking inspiration, able to compose spontaneously, in every genre.[1]

There has been a noticeable shift recently in the Spanish attitude to the part played by Islam in their own medieval history. The Muslims who lived in their midst in the Middle Ages are now seen to be part of their national heritage and acknowledged as contributors to the history of Spain. Previously the focus was on the conflict between the Arabs and the Spanish, Islam and Christianity. Nineteenth-century nationalism set the Cross in front of the Crescent, glorying in the defeat of the latter. Serious Spanish scholars are now searching for indigenous blood in their Muslim forbears. The conclusion that they reach, that the Arabs who entered the Iberian peninsula were small in number, amounting to thousands not millions, that most of them married local women, free women or slaves, means of course that the two populations were integrated to a great extent.[2] We should therefore bear in mind that the founders of Muslim civilization on Spanish soil were not all of pure Arab blood, but intermingled with the Jews and Spanish.[3]

We shall not take long here to go into further detail about this trend in modern Spanish scholarship, but we welcome it - and its conclusions - to some extent. It is a great step forward for Islam to be regarded not as synonymous with Arabs, since it is a religion which has spread wider than its Arab beginning. This is why it is now better to use the term

1. *Judhwat al-Muqtabas fi dhikr wulât al-Andalus*, (Cairo, al-Dar al-Misriyya lil Talif wa'l-Tarjama, 1966).
2. See Angel Gonzales Palencia, *al-Shi'r al-Andalusi wa Ta'thîru fi'l-Shi'r al-Urubbi*, a lecture delivered in the Spanish Institute, (Colombia, New York), and later was published in the *Modern Spanish Journal*, first year, number 2, January 1935, and translated into Arabic by al-Tahir Makki in his book, *Dirâsat Andalusiyya*, (Cairo, Dar al-Ma'arif, 1980), pp. 193ff.
3. See Angel Gonzales Palencia, *al-Shi'r al-Andalusi*, pp.193f; and Sanchez Albornoz, *Ibn Hazm Qima Aspaniyya*, quoted and translated by al-Tahir Makki, *Dirâsat 'An Ibn Hazm wa kitâbu Tawq al-Hamâma*, pp. 139f.

"Spanish Muslims" than the term "the Arabs in Spain". One result: a year ago a Spanish Muslim contacted me and told me about an institute which has been set up in Spain. It is called the Institute for the Promotion of Islam and Peaceful Cooperation. This is very different from the years of contention and hatred, when the clergy preached war on the Moors. There are many old enmities in the world which serve no useful purpose. We should work for a world of peace and understanding.

Another result of this new attitude is that in 1963, the city of Cordoba erected a lifesize statue of Ibn Hazm in front of al-'Attarin Gate [the Gate of Perfumers], which led to the place where he was born and brought up - *Balat Mughith* - it was also the way by which he went to the chief mosque to pray and to teach. The Spanish now take a pride in Ibn Hazm as a son of their soil (and a tourist attraction).

Ibn Hazm's genealogy

A few words about Ibn Hazm's genealogy: Two genealogies have survived, a long one and a short one. The long one came from Ibn Hazm himself and goes back to his ancestor Yazîd, who was a Persian by origin, and converted to Islam at the time of his namesake, Yazîd Ibn Abi Sufyân. Nothing further is known about this ancestor, and the information we have is unverifiable. The historians tell us that Ibn Hazm's great great great great grandfather Khalaf was the first of his family to come to Spain and to settle there. His grandfather Sa'îd was the first to establish the family home in Cordoba. But Ibn Hayyan insists that the great grandfather, Hazm, was the only known ancestor of Ibn Hazm and was a humble man from among the Spanish citizens of Labla.[1] We will not dwell

---

1. See e.g., 'Ali Ibn Ahmad Ibn Hazm, *al-Taqrîb li Hadd al-Mantiq*, in *Rasâ'il Ibn Hazm al-Andalusi*, ed. by Ihsan 'Abbas, (Beirut, al-Mu'asasa al-'Arabiyya lil Dirâsat wa'l-Nashr, 1983), p. 93; Sa'id Ibn Ahmad, *Tabaqât al-Umam*, introduced by al-Sayyid Muhammad Bahr al-'Ulum, (Baghdad, al-Najaf, al-Maktaba al-Haydariyya, 1967), p. 98; al-Humaydi, *Judhwa*, p. 308; Muhyi al-Dîn 'Abd al-Wâhid al-Marrakushi, *al-Mu'jib fî Talkhîs Akhbâr al-Maghrib*, ed. by Dozy, (Leiden, E. J. Brill, 1881), p. 32; and Muhammad Abu Layla, *The Muslim View of Christianity With Special Reference to the Work of Ibn Hazm*, pp. 1ff.

longer on this genealogy. It is enough to know that Ibn Hazm was a Muslim who was at least the fourth generation resident in Spain, and his mother and other female ancestors may have been Spanish. He himself said about the Umayyad Caliphs that every one of them was fair haired, taking after their mothers, so that this had become a hereditary trait with them.[1] Ibn Hazm himself never travelled outside al-Andalus. Whatever he was, Arab Qurayshite,[2] Turkish,[3] Greek,[4] Spanish, or if he perhaps had some Jewish[5] or Christian blood[6] in his veins, what interests us is the man as he was, the man as a thinker.

Early life and intellectual milieu

Ibn Hazm, whose full name is 'Ali Ibn Ahmad Ibn Sa'îd Ibn Hazm, lived in the period between 384 - 456 AH (994 - 1056 AD). His father Ahmad, the remarkable scholar and vizier, brought him up in an aristocratic way. In his childhood he was only allowed the company of women, and perhaps a few male guards. He learned the Qur'an, calligraphy, poetry and the elements of languages other than Arabic, such as the Romance language, which was current in official and Muslim quarters.[7] From the very beginning of his life Ibn

1. Ibn Hazm, *Tawq*, pp. 48f.
2. See Suhayr Abu Wâfiya's introduction to Ibn Hazm's *al-Usûl wa'l-Furû'*, ed. by Muhammad 'Atif al-Irâqi, et al, (Cairo, Dâr al-Nahda al-'Arabiyya, 1978), vol. 1, pp. 8ff.
3. See the title page of al-Sulaymaniyya Codex of Ibn Hazm's book *al-Fisal*, in Raghib Basha's library in Turkey, numbered as 815 and 816.
4. See the Italian orientalist Gabrieli, referred to in Abu Layla, *The Muslim View of Christianity*, p. 3.
5. See e.g., R. Dozy, *Spanish Islam*, pp. 575ff; R. A. Nicholson, *A Literary History of the Arabs*, p. 426; and S. M. Imamuddin, *Some Aspects of the Socio-Economic and Cultural History of the Muslim Spain (711 - 1492 A.D.)*, Leiden, E. J. Brill, 1965), p. 149.
6. See e.g., Dozy, *Spanish Islam*, pp. 575ff; Edward Sell, *Islam in Spain*, (Vepery, Madras, Diocesan Press, 1929), pp. 104f; and M. Abu Layla, *The Muslim View of Christianity*, p. 3.
7. Al-Nubahi, *Târikh Qudât al-Andalus*, (Beirut, al-Maktaba al-Tujariyya lil-Tiba'a wa'l-Nashr, n.d), pp. 99ff.

Hazm was troubled by palpitations of the heart.[1]

He studied under the great scholars of the time. A glance at their names shows that they varied widely in character, interests and specializations. Among them was the traditionalist Ibn al-Jassûr (d.401 AH; 1010 AD), who taught Ibn Hazm when he was about fifteen years old. The historian and man of letters, Ibn al-Fâradi (d.404 AH; 1013 AD); the Maliki jurist Ibn Dahhûn (d.431 AH; 1039 AD); Abu al-Khiyâr Sulaymân Ibn Muflit the Zâhiri jurist (d.426 AH; 1034 AD); the philologist Ibn 'Abd al-Wârith (d.4th Century AH; 10th Century AD) and Ibn al-Kattâni (d.420 AH; 1029 AD), who taught Ibn Hazm philosophy, logic and natural sciences.[2]

While still young, Ibn Hazm attended the official meetings of the Caliphs, their secretaries of state, their judges, scholars and the leading personalities of their society.[3] This gave him confidence and experience so that he did not hesitate later to express his opinion and ideas, in no matter what field. History records two great incidents: the first is his appearance in the presence of the Hâjib 'Abd al-Malik Ibn Abi 'Amir in the year 399 A.H. (1008 AD), where he heard the poet Sa'îd al-Lughawi (d.410 AH; 1019 AD) reciting a poem. The poet was so impressed by Ibn Hazm's obvious admiration that he gave him a copy of it in his own hand as a memento.[4] The second incident is when he appeared with his father when Hisham the Second was falsely declared to have died. He was an eye-witness of the latter's false funeral, and has left an account of it. At the time of the false declaration he was still young, perhaps about fifteen years old.[5]

Ibn Hazm occupied the post of minister three times, and

---

1. Ibn Hazm, *Tawq*, pp. 79f; see also Abu Layla, *The Muslim View of Christianity*, pp. 5ff.

2. Ibn Hazm, *Tawq*, see e.g., pp. 102f, 140, 155, 157, 166; Abu 'Abd Allah Shams al-Din al-Dhahabi, *Siyar al-Nubalâ'*, ed. by Sa'id al-Afghani, (Beirut, Dar al-Fikr, 1969), pp. 6f.

3. Ibn Hazm, *Tawq*, p. 49; and al-Humaydi, *Judhwa*, p. 63.

4. Al-Marrakushi, *al-Mu'jib*, pp. 22f; al-Humaydi, *Judhwa*, p. 241.

5. Ibn Hazm, *al-Fisal*, vol. 1, p. 47; see also Abu al-Hasan 'Ali Ibn Bassâm, *al-Dhakhîra fi Mahâsin Ahl al-Jazîra*, ed. by Ihsan 'Abbâs, (Beirut, Dâr al-Mustashriq, 1922), part 1, vol. 1, pp. 91ff; and Abu Layla, *The Muslim View of Christianity*, p. 337.

was also thrown into prison at least three times.[1] His engagement in scholarly and political activities and natural thirst for knowledge never prevented him from marriage and fathering children. It is known that he had three sons, whom he educated and taught.[2] Abû Râfi' al-Fadl, one of Ibn Hazm's sons, left an account of the number of his father's works. Abû Râfi' himself became a historian of the state of Banu 'Abbâd.[3]

Ibn Hazm left to us, to the Muslim world and to the whole world of scholarship, a camel-load of books, amounting to an estimated four hundred volumes, a total of about eight thousand pages.[4] This is despite the fact that he was plagued by various illnesses, was actively engaged in politics, suffered the threat of imprisonment, exile and separation from his family, nor did he live to a great old age. He was only just over seventy when he died.[5] Nearly all his books were written in his own hand. We should remember that the slave-girls taught him calligraphy in his childhood home. He continued to read and write until the last year of his life.

I should like to warn against anyone imagining that Ibn Hazm was a mere scribbler, a transcriber of other people's ideas, since he has left such a huge number of books. Ibn Hazm has never been accused of this. On the contrary, he has been criticized for being too creative, and for stepping out of line as regards orthodox scholarship and belief.[6] His very

1. Ibn 'Abd Allah Yaqut, *Irshad al-Arîb*, (Beirut, Dâr al-Mustashriq, 1922), vol. 12, p. 237; Lisân al-Din Ibn al-Khatîb, *al Ihâta fi Akhbâr Gharnâta*, ed. by M. A. 'Inân, (Cairo, al-Khanji, 1397 AH; 1977 AD) vol. 4, p. 115; and Abu Layla, *The Muslim View of Christianity*, pp. 9ff.
2. See Ibn Hazm, *al-Taqrîb*, pp. 345f; and Abu Layla, *The Muslim View of Christianity*, p. 9.
3. Al-Marrâkushi, *al-Mu'jib*, p. 33; Ibn Hazm, *al-Taqrîb*, p. 347; and Abu al-Qâsim Khalaf Ibn Bashkuwâl, *al-Sila*, (Cairo, al-Dar al-Misriyya lil Ta'lif wa'l-Tarjama, 1966), part 2, p. 464.
4. Al-Marrâkushi, *al-Mu'jib*, p. 33; and M. Abu Layla, *An Introduction to the Life and Work of Ibn Hazm* (II), *The Islamic Quarterly*, vol. 29, number 3, pp.83f.
5. See Ibn Hazm, *al-Akhlâq*, pp.130, 203 and 210; Ibn Hazm, *al-Taqrîb*, p. 346; M. Abu Layla, *The Muslim View of Christianity*, p. 6.
6. See e.g., *Risâlatan Lahu Ajaba fîhima An Risâlatayyn Su'ila fîhima Su'âl Ta'nîf* in Ibn Hazm, *al-Radd 'Ala Ibn al-Nighrila al-Yahûdi wa Rasâ'il 'Ukhra*, ed. by Ihsan 'Abbâs, (Cairo, al-Madani, 1960), pp. 86ff; and al-Humaydi, *Judhwa*, p. 309.

productiveness was a cause for him to be attacked by his opponents. Unfortunately not all of his books have survived. Many are lost. Some were publicly burned as a mark of punishment. This happened by a command of al-Mu'tamid Ibn 'Abbâd in Seville. Ibn Hazm commemorated this incident in a short stanza of four lines, in which he says that he does not worry at all that his books are destroyed since their contents are stored in the treasure chest of his memory.[1] This is evidence of his indestructible spirit; it is also interesting evidence of the fact that he memorized all his books. Unfortunately in the history of al-Andalus as elsewhere, there have been incidents of books having been burned.[2] But fortunately for us and also for Ibn Hazm, some of his most important books have survived. *His Encyclopaedia of Comparative Religion and the History of Religion - al-Fisal fi'l-Milal wa'l Ahwâ' wa'l Nihal* is now available in various editions (these are not good editions; they await critical attention). His lengthy book on comparative law, *al-Muhalla*, and his great work, *al-Ihkâm fî 'Usûl al-Ahkâm*, are both available and are widely used by scholars everywhere. And how could we overlook his unique book on love and lovers, *Tawq al-Hamâma -The Ring of the Dove*, in which he reveals many important facts about himself as a man and poet, his colleagues and friends, and particularly about the women of al-Andalus. In this context it is useful to note that Ibn Hazm's poems in *Tawq al-Hamâma* show a sense of high chivalry, enthusiasm, and dignity. This book can be read in many different Arabic editions and also in many other languages. Ibn Hazm's books on history, his biography of the Prophet Muhammad, books on logic, ethics, his treatise on various subjects, are available at the present time.

Ibn Hazm's books are a witness to his great learning and depth of knowledge. He says of himself that he was born with a longing for fame and victory. He considered it a defect of character and set himself to cure himself of it. He succeeded in ridding himself of these longings and devoted himself

---

1. Yaqût, *Irshâd*, vol. 12, p. 252.
2. Ahmad Ibn 'Idhâri, *al-Bayân al-Mughrib fi Akhbâr al-Andalus wa'l-Maghrib*, ed. by Colin and E. Provençal, (Leiden, E. J. Brill, 1951), vol. 4, p. 59.

to scholarship.[1]

Ibn Hazm's views on science, learning and scholarship

Ibn Hazm provided us with a very useful categorization of the different types of literary works. He said that there are seven reasons to write a book. First, a writer may have something original to say. Secondly, he may complete something which has been left incomplete. Thirdly, he may put right something that is seen to be wrong. Fourthly, he may clarify and explain a mysterious or complicated matter. Number five, he may shorten another person's work that is too long, without omitting anything vital. Six: he may collect information from various separate sources. Seven: he may assemble things that have been scattered like beads, and thread them together again. He says that these are the only categories in which scholars and perceptive people can write.[2] Ibn Hazm classifies his own book on logic in the fourth category, namely books which explain a difficult matter and clarify its terms.[3] The subject of logic was already worked out before his time; he did not add to it but explained it; however, in so doing he also corrected some erroneous ideas which people held about it, and, as he collected his information from various sources, it also overlaps with the latter categories. Authors all belong to these seven categories and can only be judged and declared better or worse according to their industry in digesting information. One man may be an expert in a very restricted field.[4] Ibn Hazm goes on to say that anyone who merely copies another person's work, merely juggling the order and not adding anything or correcting it or explaining it more clearly, or anyone who merely adds something unnecessary or even substitutes something correct for something incorrect - is a man ignorant and careless, without shame or self-respect.[5]

---

1. Ibn Hazm, *al-Akhlâq*, pp. 131f.
2. Ibn Hazm, *al-Taqrîb*, pp. 103f.
3. Ibid.
4. Ibid, p. 104.
5. Ibid, pp. 103f.

Having listed all the categories of possible books, acceptable and unacceptable, he says that truth cannot be obtained except by laborious research, and laborious research entails a great deal of reading in all religions, searching out sayings, theories, hearing the evidence of other parties and subjecting it to careful examination, looking at the nature of things and also studying the opinions, religions, sects, schools of thought, and matters of controversy of many peoples, and reading their texts.[1] Ibn Hazm differs from those Muslims who forbade the reading of all books but the Qur'an and *Hadith*, taking these as their only source of knowledge. Ibn Hazm countered their argument by saying that in the Qur'an Allah speaks of the atheists who say that the world has no end,[2] and the Zoroastrians who believe in two gods,[3] and the Trinitarians who believe in three;[4] Allah mentions them in order to show the contradictions and negations contained in their doctrines. Ibn Hazm said that it was essential for the searcher after truth to read the Qur'an, its interpretation, linguistics, and laws, and the *Hadith* of the Prophet, the history of peoples ancient and contemporary, geography, astronomy and the biography of the Prophet, which provides a model of good behaviour which brings benefits in this world and the next; but above all, the searcher after truth should have a full knowledge of the original languages from which the books were translated, in order to be sure that he understands the true sense of the works.[5]

It is important to note Ibn Hazm's call to scholars to learn languages besides that of the Qur'an, and not to depend only on translations. This indicates that he himself must have known some foreign languages. In my previous writings about Ibn Hazm I have suggested that he knew other languages. Here I should like to add some solid evidence for this suggestion. In his book on logic, Ibn Hazm criticizes the translators, using such phrases as "this is the word used by

---

1. Ibn Hazm, *al-Taqrib*, p. 344.
2. 17:49; 36:79; 45:24.
3. 22:17.
4. 5:72-73.
5. Ibn Hazm, *al-Taqrib*, p. 344.

the translators, and it is confusing."[1] In another place he says, "For this, we have translated it."[2] Moreover, and even more important, he says, "You should know that in the Arabic language the question 'By what?' and the question 'By which?' may be similar and interchangeable, having the same meaning since anyone who has mastered the Latin language would be able to distinguish between these two concepts in enquiries, because Latin uses a different word for the general and for the choice of alternatives."[3] This indicates that he knew Latin. Why does Ibn Hazm not state clearly which other languages he himself knew? It is possible that his pride in the Arabic language was so great that he did not think it anything to boast of that he also knew Hebrew, Greek and Latin. We do not suggest, however, that Ibn Hazm's knowledge of other languages is the reason for his remarkable success. Ibn Khaldûn, the great historian and philosopher, knew only Arabic, but his own works are known throughout the world.

Ibn Hazm never rejects any science which helps man. He promoted logic at a time when it was not welcomed by orthodox Muslims. He applied his literalist theories to doctrinal matters both Islamic and non-Islamic. He applied logic to all kinds of scholarship and science, to religion as well as grammar, philology, poetry, medicine and chemistry, engineering and astronomy. It helps experts in all these fields to define their terminology, to set up analogies, etc.[4]

Ibn Hazm gives his definition of *'ilm*, knowledge: he says that anything you know is called *'ilm*, knowledge. This includes the science of commerce, needlework, shipbuilding, agriculture, horticulture, building and construction works, etc, and all useful things necessary for life. He attacks those Muslims who oppose some branches of knowledge, some sciences, saying that they have no bearing on the Qur'an or on Islamic rites. He points out that the Prophet Muhammad

1. Ibn Hazm, *al-Taqrîb*, p. 112.
2. Ibid, p. 256.
3. Ibid, p. 109.
4. Ibid, p. 102; see also Hajjî Khalîfa, *Kashf al-zunûn*, (Tehran, al-Maktaba al-Islamiyya, 1387 A.H.), vol. 2, p. 1860.

commanded us to study medicine.[1]

Ibn Hazm believes that knowledge or science should serve humanity; it is not a luxury, a useless hobby, studied merely for self-satisfaction. He criticizes those who study logic and go no further. He says that they are like people who have the means to build but never do build anything.[2]

Ibn Hazm follows here the traditional Aristotelian concept of logic: "...because logic was thought to be, not one of the substantial parts of philosophy, like metaphysics or natural philosophy or ethics, but rather a method or discipline useful as a tool in all enquiries, whatever their subject-matter."[3] For this reason the *Organon* heads the list in the traditional ordering of Aristotle's works.[4] In Ibn Hazm's view, surveying is useful because it helps to locate water; civil engineering helps to lift heavy loads and develop useful machines. He does not encourage the study of astronomy, because in his view it brings no practical achievements. It requires long years of experiment and observation over several generations since the orbit of one planet can take 10,000 years.[5] If Ibn Hazm lived in our time he might change his mind since such great strides have been made in space technology. But it is certain that Ibn Hazm, the great reformer and debater, would criticize Russia and America in their use of this science for destructive purposes; they only want to win superiority.

Ibn Hazm would be very unhappy about the separation of science and religion. He believed that all branches of knowledge depend on each other.[6] He continually stresses

---

1. Ibn Hazm, *Risâla fî Marâtib al-'Ulûm*, in *Rasâ'il Ibn Hazm al-Andalusi*, ed. by Ihsan 'Abbâs, (Beirut, al-Mu'asasa al-'Arabiyya lil Dirâsat wa'l-Nashr, 1983), p. 80, Ibn Hazm's *Risâla fî Marâtib al-'Ulûm* translated into English by A. Chejne, pp. 82ff and 193ff. See also Muhammad Ibn Yusuf al-'Amiri, *al-I'lâm Bimanâqib al-Islâm*, ed. by Ahmad A. Ghurâb (Cairo, Dâr al-Kitâb al-'Arabi, 1967), pp. 84-97 and F. Rosenthal, *The Classical Heritage in Islam*, (U.S.A., University of California Press, 1975), pp. 63ff.
2. Ibn Hazm, *Marâtib al-'Ulûm*, p. 89.
3. J. L. Ackrill, *Aristotle the Philosopher*, (Oxford, Oxford University Press, 1981), p. 79.
4. Ibid.
5. Ibn Hazm, *Marâtib al-'Ulüm*, p. 68.
6. Ibn Hazm, *al-Taqrîb*, p. 102.

the morality inherent in things, the morality of man, the morality of knowledge. That is why his discussion of knowledge is part of his book on morality.[1]

Ibn Hazm is in favour of encyclopaedic learning, knowing something about every branch of knowledge. This time he is quoting one of his teachers, Yunus Ibn 'Abd Allah Ibn Muhammad, known as Ibn al-Saffâr, the chief judge of Cordoba, who told him that if a person takes some knowledge from each branch he will be able to feel at home in any society and join in any discussion.[2] This theory must have greatly influenced Ibn Hazm, who later became a veritable encyclopaedia, yet he also advises students to keep quiet about matters that they do not understand.[3] Ibn Hazm realizes that there are differences between people with regard to ability and natural aptitude for learning. If someone is not able to keep up with every branch of knowledge, he should specialise in one and leave the rest to others; the result is a community, a scholarly collective that knows everything. As in building a house, it is necessary to have some workers to carry the stones and bricks, someone to paint, a carpenter to fit the window frames; all the specialist workers together create the house.[4] This theory can be applied to scholarly matters, and also to life itself. Everyone should make his contribution to the life of the community. He quotes his teacher Abu 'Abd Allah Ibn Muhammad Ibn al-Kattâni, who told him and the other students, "Look at the loaf of bread in your hand. How many hands have prepared it for you - the sower who sowed the seeds, the reaper, the miller and so on and so on."[5]

In Ibn Hazm's view, every person should study the subject for which he has a natural inclination. He says, for example: "Anyone who has a natural inclination towards a branch of knowledge, even if it is inferior to other branches, should not abandon it, or he would resemble someone who plants coconuts in Andalusia or olive trees in India, where they

---

1. See Ibn Hazm, *al-Akhlâq wa'l-Siyar*, pp. 102ff.
2 Ibn Hazm, *Marâtib al-'Ulûm*, pp. 71f about Yunus Ibn 'Abd Allah; see al-Humaydi, *Judhwa*, pp. 384f.
3. Ibn Hazm, *Marâtib al-'Ulûm*, p. 80.
4. Ibn Hazm, *Marâtib al-'Ulûm*, p. 83.
5. Ibid.

would give no fruit."[1]

He says that we should not offer to teach those who are not worthy of it.[2] Here he does not mean that knowledge is only for the elite, distinguished by money and position. This would be wrong, since Ibn Hazm does not attribute superiority to breeding or class. He himself preached the cause of free education.[3] He meant that knowledge should be spread among those who are prepared to learn and who possess certain virtuous qualities. He says that nothing does more harm to knowledge than the outsiders who enter its field and think that they know everything and can do good, when in fact they are ignorant and corrupt. He stresses that we should instil knowledge according to the ability of the students.[4] He obliged the student to travel in the quest for knowledge if there is no opportunity to study in his own area.[5] In Ibn Hazm's view, knowledge is not measured only by its material results, but also its spiritual benefits. Scientists should not work apart from God; knowledge is a gift from God, freely available to all, but God can take it back at any time. For example, a philosopher may face a situation which makes him forget all his wisdom, and maybe lose all his intelligence. Many read greatly and achieve little; others read less and are able to create a great deal. The best knowledge, in Ibn Hazm's view, is that which brings you close to God.[6]

Ibn Hazm as a Man, Thinker and Jurist

Ibn Hazm was inventive, and interested in many things. He adopted, and defended, the theory that the earth is

1. Ibn Hazm, *al-Akhlâq*, p. 105.
2. Ibid, p. 104.
3. Ibn Hazm. *al-Akhlâq*, pp. 104; and Ibn Hazm, *al-Taqrîb*, pp. 345ff.
4. Ibn Hazm. *al-Akhlâq*, pp. 107f.
5. Ibn Hazm, *al-Talkhîs Li Wujûh al-Takhlîs* in *al-Radd 'Ala Ibn al-Nighrila*, p. 160; and M. Abu Layla, *The Muslim View of Christianity*, p .16.
6. Ibn Hazm, *al-Akhlâq*, pp. 105ff. See also Abu Tâlib Muhammad Ibn Abu al-Hasan al-Makkî, *Qut al-Qulûb* (Beirut, Dar Sadir, n.d.) vol. 1, pp .339ff and Muhyi al-Dîn Ibn al-'Arabi, *Rasâ'il, Risâla Ila al-Imâm Fakhr al-Din al-Râzi*, (Haydarabad, Deccan, Dâ'irat al-Ma'ârif al-'Uthmâniyya, 1367 A.H.; 1948 A.D.), pp .6ff.

round.[1]

In his book *al-Taqrîb*, Ibn Hazm recorded that his teacher's father invented a system of raised letters for blind readers similar to Braille's.[2]

He discussed not only jurisprudence and religious matters but also music. His observations on music are very important and accurate.[3] But, he does not encourage the study of alchemy and magic, agreeing with Ibn Khaldun (d.809 AH; 1406 AD) in this.[4] In Ibn Hazm's view the claim of the alchemists that the elements could be changed was nonsensical and a waste of time.[5] Of course he could have no idea of the discoveries of modern physics.

Ibn Hazm's cheerful nature and also his ready wit and creativity are illustrated by his explanation of the nature of poetry. He said that a poem without lies and exaggeration is not poetry. He gives two examples. First:

> Night is night, day is day, mule is mule, ass is ass, cock is cock, pigeon is pigeon and resembles it in that both are birds and have beaks.[6]

A poet who produced this would be the subject of scorn and laughter. But a poet who dug up lies and exaggeration would produce acceptable work:

> The pain and weeping grow accustomed to lodging in his body. Love whittles him away to the point of invisibility. He is invisible even to our thoughts, except as a thought. He is even harder to see than a thought. We have heard his weeping from nearby. You seek the person where the sound of weeping comes

1. Ibn Hazm, *al-Fisal*, vol. 5, p. 144.
2. Ibn Hazm, *al-Taqrîb*, p.192; see also Abu Layla, "Ibn 'Abd al-Wârith al-Andalusi al-Mukhtari' al-Haqîqî li Braille", *al-Muslimoon*, vol. 1, number 32, p. 19.
3. Ibn Hazm, *Marâtib al-'Ulûm*, p .60.
4. Ibid, pp. 68ff.
5. Ibid.
6. Ibn Hazm, *al-Taqrîb*, pp. 354ff.

from. It is not his strength that keeps him
alive, but the fact that pain made him melt
away so completely that death could not find
him.[1]

Ibn Hazm should be an example to us, as a scholar and as
writer. He was obviously widely-read. He showed a curious
mind from an early age. When he heard one of the slave-girls
in his father's house sing a stanza, he would know the name
of the poet who had written it.[2] When he listened to a good
poet his face immediately reflected his enjoyment, as mentioned in the context of Sa'id. He preferred nothing to the
search for knowledge and the spreading of it.[3] He himself
wrote a poem saying that it was the ambition of his lifetime
to learn and to spread knowledge. Once an idea for a poem
had lodged in his mind he followed it through to the end,
cutting himself off from his surroundings until it was complete and written down.[4]

When Ibn Hazm found himself the target of criticism
from the Maliki jurists and students, in Valencia and Cordoba, he devoted himself to jurisprudence and spent three
years in its study under eminent jurists, only then declaring
himself ready for debate.[5] Ibn Hazm was in his element in
public debate and even, as stated, studied law to be able to
argue with the jurists on their own ground.

When he comes upon a good idea which helps to solve a
religious or scholarly problem, he gets very excited and
enthusiastic, happier even, according to Ibn Hazm, than the
day he left al-Mutbaq prison.[6] He always studies for a reason;
he is always looking for answers. He read the Hebrew Torah,
the Septuagint and was acquainted with the Samaritan Torah,
so as to be able to debate knowledgeably with the Jewish
learned. He studied the entire Old Testament, with the exception of the five minor prophets. Ibn Hazm holds up a faithful

---

1. Ibn Hazm, *al-Taqrīb*, pp. 354ff.
2. Ibn Hazm, *Tawq*, pp. 145f.
3. Al-Humaydi, *Judhwa*, p. 310.
4. Ibn Hazm, *Tawq*, pp. 145f.
5. Al-Dhahabi, *Siyar*, p. 29.
1. Ibn Hazm, *al-Taqrīb*, pp. 346.

mirror to the multi-cultural society in which he lived. He provides invaluable and interesting information about the Jews.

It is evident that Ibn Hazm himself had a very large collection of books which covered all branches of knowledge. In debate he used to tell his critics, "I have such-and-such a book which you hold dearly" or "Here is the book, come and check."[1] He also read from the library of the Caliph al-Hakam, and read over fifty letters written by the Caliph al-Nasir to his officials,[2] and sought information in the meetings of the court and of the mosque, from public meetings and gatherings. He collected information from the written word and the spoken, from men and from women. He debated and lectured in the synagogue, and perhaps also in the church.[3]

As you will realize by now, Ibn Hazm was not a dried-up scholar but a complete man who threw himself into life. We can build up a picture of him. He suffered from heart palpitations in his childhood, dry eyes and an enlarged spleen, and lost his mother, then his brother, sister-in-law and finally his father. As a consequence of the bloody civil war which broke out in Cordoba in 399 AH (1009 AD)[4] he lost his house and belongings. His friends, the slave-girls of his father's house, were scattered hither and thither. He suffered other disappointments and trials as we have seen already, but he did not go under, he did not regard himself as a victim; he learnt from these experiences. He did not stop criticizing the corrupt rulers and their demagogues.[5] He antagonized all the conflicting parties in al-Andalus, scholars and politicians alike. Ibn Hazm does not lose himself in the midst of his traumatic experiences. He stands firm. How could he forget his father's advice? - "If you want to live as a rich man, be

1. Ibn Hazm, *Risâlatan lahu... in al-Radd 'Alâ Ibn al-Nighrila*, pp. 103, 105, 107.
2. Ibn Hazm, *Jamharat Ansâb al-'Arab*, ed. by 'Abd Al-Salam Harun, (Cairo, Dar al-Ma'ârif, 1962), p. 100; and Ibn Hazm, *Naqt al-'Arûs*, ed. by Shawqi Dayf, (Cairo, Cairo University, *Majallat Kulliyyat al-Adab*, December, 1951), p. 52.
3. Ibn Bassâm, *al-Dhakhîra*, part 1, vol. 1, pp. 132 and 163ff; and Ibn Hazm, *al-Fisal*, vol. 2, pp. 103f; see also Abu Layla, *The Muslim View of Christianity*, p. 10.
4. Ibn Hazm, *Tawq*, pp. 147, 153, 154.
5. Ibn Hazm, *Risâlat al-Talkhîs li Wujûh al-Takhlîs*, in *al-Radd 'Alâ Ibn al-Nighrîla...*, pp. 45f and 173f.

prepared to accept a change to an inferior position at any moment."[1] Is it not a great thing that such a man as Ahmad Ibn Hazm, the second highest man in al-Andalus, advises his son that he should be prepared to accept a fall in position at any time? It is more usual for rich men to advise their sons to protect their fortunes and to add to them.

Ibn Hazm loves peace and justice. He spoke against the civil war, being fully aware of its bad effects. He said, "It stops the blossom coming to fruit."[2] From his childhood Ibn Hazm is always conscious of God's presence in his life, controlling it. He may attend a meeting for amusement but never hesitates to correct intolerable behaviour. He defends women and protects their rights, and would talk to them without restriction, although he never made love to any except his wife. He joked and was pleasant, but in moderation.[3] He admitted to having faults; he said, "I have an inclination to make jokes, but I try to control it and not annoy people when I make a joke."[4] But lack of humour is a sign of narrow-mindedness and arrogance and equally to be avoided.[5]

Ibn Hazm loves children and he criticizes the Book of Joshua [7:18-26] in which Joshua gives orders that Achan son of Carmi should be stoned to death and his cattle and children should be burned. In Ibn Hazm's view the children have no guilt, and the cattle have no sin - why should they be killed?[6] He defends the rights of slaves, and the right of everyone to a free education.[7] Ibn Hazm knew the weakness of human nature, and the strength of temptations. Concerning the sins and faults which emerge from physical temptations, and which inhibit faith and doctrine, we find that Ibn Hazm is tolerant and forgiving. He is sympathetic with men who love women, even with men who love boys. He has an exact knowledge of the temptations of women and of men,

---

1. Al-Humaydi, *Judhwa*, p. 126.
2. Ibn Hazm, *al-Akhlâq*, p. 129.
3. Ibn Hazm, *Tawq*, p. 171.
4. Ibn Hazm, *al-Akhlâq*, p. 130f.
5. Ibid.
6. Ibn Hazm, *al-Fisal*, vol. 2, p. 3.
7. See Abu Layla, *The Muslim View of Christianity*, p. 18.

the appointments and lovers' meetings; nevertheless he over-looks many such things, because they are human. He does not criticise but asks Allah's forgiveness on them to wash away their sins.[1] He does not draw a sanctimonious contrast between his own piety and their behaviour. He is humble and does not speak from an ivory tower. Abu 'Abd Allah ibn Kulaib of Kairouan asked Ibn Hazm what he should do with his lover, should he see her? Ibn Hazm's answer was "You should try to cheer up your spirit by seeing her, even if she does not want to see you."[2] Ibn Hazm regards such faults as temporary, that, like a sickness, can be cured. We have already said that Ibn Hazm respected women, rejecting the ideas current at the time that women were more liable to cor-ruption than men. In his view a woman could be a prophet-ess, such as Mary and Sarah, who spoke to the Angel; they could be rulers, though not as high as the rank of Caliph. In his book *Naqt al-'Arûs* he gives us this information: "A woman called Thamal al-Qahramâna sat as a judge during the time of al-Muqtadir. In her presence sat the judges and jurists with her."[3] Ibn Hazm passes no comment here, show-ing that he was not disturbed by the fact that a woman acted as a judge. In the same book there is quite a lot of informa-tion about women and their role in history.[4]

In his book *al-Fisal*, Ibn Hazm mentioned two Jewish scholars, whom he declared to be great, sincere and truth seekers.[5] Ibn Hazm referred also to Saadia Gaon (269-331 AH; 882-942 AD), as a great theologian,[6] and acknowledged the ability of Ibn al-Nighrîla (383-448 AH; 993-1056 AD), as the most accomplished scholar and debater among the Jewish community.[7]

Ibn Hazm praises Ishmael Ibn Yunus al-'Awar (the One-Eyed), the Jewish physician who, according to him, was a skilful and expert physiognomist, who held the theory of the

---

1. See e.g., *Tawq*, pp. 65, 79, 80, 96, 97.
2. *Tawq*, pp. 73f.
3. Ibn Hazm, *Naqt*, p. 84.
4. Ibid, pp. 68ff.
5. Ibn Hazm, *al-Fisal*, vol. 1, p. 123.
6. Ibid, vol. 3, pp. 121 and 125.
7. Ibid, vol. 1, pp. 107 and 103.

equivalence of proofs.[1] According to Ibn Hazm this means "It is impossible for one system so to triumph over another system, or for one theory so to vanquish another that truth will shine forth clearly and unmistakably, distinct from error beyond any doubt. Rather, it may be that the proofs for any one theory are as valid as those for any of the other theories. They say that whatever is established through dialectics may be destroyed by dialectics."[2]

Ibn Hazm's argument against the theory of the equivalence of proofs enables us to discover more about the background and the course of scepticism and relativism as one aspect of the path that led to the philosophy of Ibn Rushd[3] (Averröes (520-595 AH; 1126-1198 AD)). In this context, Ibn Hazm refers to another Jewish thinker, Ismâ'îl Ibn al-Qarrâd,[4] who propagated a universal religion.

Ibn Hazm has a critical eye when he looks at society. He first analyses his own nature, mentions his own defects of body and mind, and how he has overcome them.[5] He then criticises the society of his time, the religious leaders and thinkers belonging to different religions. But do not think that he only spotted their faults and was blind to their good qualities. His criticism of the Jewish people and Judaism does not need stressing. Ibn Hazm criticised the Christians as severely as he did the Jews, but he admitted that the Christians were also a great nation, possessing philosophers and wise men in spite of their belief in the Trinity.[6] His arguments with the Christian chief judge of Cordoba, about the sensual pleasures in Paradise, were productive and peaceful.[7] Ibn Hazm is also the greatest political critic of the petty kingdoms, and also a great defender of the people's rights. He says that the society of his time was sinking into unlawful

1. Ibn Hazm, *Tawq*, p. 35, and Ibn Hazm, *al-Fisal*, vol. 5, pp. 193f.
2. Ibn Hazm, *al-Fisal*, vol. 5, pp. 193f; see also M. Perlmann, "Ibn Hazm on the Equivalence of Proofs," *The Jewish Quarterly Review*, vol. 40.
3. E. Gilson, *Reason and Revelation in the Middle Ages*, (New York, 1938), pp. 37ff; see also M. Perlmann, "Ibn Hazm on the Equivalence of Proofs", p. 279.
4. Ibn Hazm, *al-Fisal*, vol. 5, p. 193.
5. Ibn Hazm, *al-Akhlâq*, pp .129f.
6. Ibn Hazm, *al-Fisal*, vol. 5, p. 187.
7. Ibid, vol. 2, pp. 77f.

matters, and in his view this was due to the corrupt rule of the petty kings. The petty kings took poll-tax from Muslims as well as Jews and Christians. For political reasons they strengthened the position of the Jews and made them tax-collectors. They exacted heavy taxes from the people on their cattle, farms, commercial undertakings, their herds of sheep and sales of honey, and everything that could be sold in the market. Some of these rulers allowed Muslims in some areas to sell wine in order to collect more taxes from them.[1] Ibn Hazm calls these people, the petty kings, "usurpers"[2] who had taken the land by force and were kept in power by hypocrites and opportunists.[3] Ibn Hazm sees all this as contrary to Islam. Islam does not approve of oppression, or of requiring more of a people than they can deliver, otherwise the state will not work towards the prosperity of the people.

Ibn Hazm stresses the internal weakness of the petty kings, and their political ineptitude. He says that they would even worship crosses if they knew that the worship of crosses would benefit them. They already took the help of Christians against their co-religionists. In his criticism, Ibn Hazm gives us a vivid picture of the farms and markets of al-Andalus, and what the people were growing on their lands. From him we know for example that in Larda they mined gold.[4] Ibn Hazm's description of his country is like a physician's description of a dying person. Despite this, Ibn Hazm does not deny all good qualities to the petty kings.

He wrote a book about the merits of al-Andalus,[5] which shows a degree of patriotic feeling.

Ibn Hazm as Critic and Debater

The Arabs and Muslims laid the foundation of literary

1. Ibn Hazm, *al-Talkhîs li-Wujûh al-Takhlîs*, in *al-Radd 'Alâ Ibn al-Nighrîla*, pp. 175f.
2. Ibid, p. 177.
3. Ibid.
4. Ibn Hazm, *al-Talkhîs li-Wujûh al-Takhlîs*, in *al-Radd 'Alâ Ibn al-Nighrîla*, pp. 173f.
5. Ibn Hazm's book *Fadâ'il al-Andalus wa Ahliha*, ed. by Salâh al-Dîn al-Munajjid, (Beirut, Dar al-Kitab al-Jadid, 1387 AH; 1968 AD).

criticism before Ibn Hazm. Criticism was their touchstone, used to check and evaluate their poetry and linguistics. They applied a critical eye to the *Hadith* literature. This gave birth to activities known as *mustalah al-Hadith*, "the terminology of *Hadith*", and *al-Jarh wa'l-Ta'dîl* ," "authentification and rejection". There are many books of criticism of theology, poetry, rhetoric and literature. But criticism went beyond the world of books. It also took the form of debates between logicians and linguists, public debates, sometimes in the presence of the Caliph himself.[1]

Several schools of criticism are known to have existed, dealing with theology, philosophy and logic. This massive literature was known to Ibn Hazm; he assimilated it and benefited from it, as is clear from his own works. But there was still room for his own contribution, an empty space for him to put his feet, waiting for him to create something new. He built up his own theory of criticism unlike those that had gone before.

He sets out his guiding principles of criticism. In his view, the wise man should accept what is proven, and reject what is unproven. It is not for us to force tongues to declare defeat when the argument is over, but we should oblige our souls to accept the outcome and our tongues to acknowledge it. True evidence cannot be contradictory: a thing cannot be both wrong and right. If something is proved right you should accept it and abandon your previous opposition. "Do not refrain from accepting it for one hour." If you find something confusing, you should clarify it and not rely on your opponent being unaware of it, because someone else may raise it in his presence later. When the truth is on your side, do not bother about the people, however many they are, or how reputable, or high-ranking. Truth ranks higher and takes precedence over everything else, and deserves all our venera-

1. See Ibn Ishaq's *Sirat Rasûl Allah*, translated by A. Guillaume (London, Oxford University press, 1980) pp. 270ff; A. Mingana (trans.) *The Apology of Timothy the Patriarch before the Caliph al-Mahdi*, (Cambridge, Heffer and Sons Ltd, 1928); Abu 'Ali 'Amr al-Sakuni, *'Uyûn al-Munâzarat*, ed. by Sa'd Ghurab (Tunis, Tunis University Press, 1976), pp. 212f, 218 and 232f; and M. Abu Layla, *Faith Meets Faith*, edited by Gavin D'Costa, (London, BFSS RE Centre, 1988), p. 23.

tion. In declaring the truth, he says, "Do not worry about the rank of the people. A superior person can still be wrong, unless he is infallible like the Prophets. If this superior person had seen the truth as you have seen it, he would have immediately taken it up. If not, he is not as great as he seems."

Ibn Hazm himself was quick to admit that his opponent was right if the argument proved it.[1] He said, "Do not be misled by the many correct points that someone can make - he may then make a mistake in something very obvious, after arguing correctly about very complicated and abstruse matters."[2]

Nothing distinguished Ibn Hazm more than his critical ability and insight. The basis of his theory may be defined as follows:

1. Analysis and study of the text per se.
2. Close attention to linguistic form.

Ibn Hazm is sharply sensitive to nuances of language. He himself was a great logician and linguist. He was able to coin terms for all the many subjects he dealt with. He lays so much emphasis on the function of the words that he will only accept what is in the text, and rejects what is additional commentary from critics. He also used translation to examine whether a passage had a real meaning capable of being transferred to another language.[3]

He criticized commentators who used unnecessarily complicated phrases.[4] He also criticized authors who used too many metaphors, as in the Psalms of David.[5] He gave his own comments on translations, especially in the field of the Torah, and logic.[6] He frequently argued with Jewish and

1. Ibn Hazm, *al-Taqrîb*, pp. 337f.
2. Ibid.
3. 'Alî Ibn Ahmad Ibn Hazm, *al-Ihkâm fî Usûl al-Ahkâm*, ed. by Ahmad Shâkir, reprinted and published by Zakariyya 'Ali Yûsuf (Cairo, Dâr al-I'tisâm, n.d.) Part 1, vol. 1, pp. 1ff.
4. Ibn Hazm, *al-Fisal*, vol. 1, pp.1ff and Ibn Hazm, *al-Taqrîb*, pp. 1ff.
5. N. Rif'at, *Ibn Hazm on Jews and Judaism*, pp. 258-72.
6. See F.N. 4 previous page; also N. Rif'at, *Ibn Hazm on Jews and Judaism*, pp. 221f.

Christian scholars about the significance of a single word.

He employs history in his criticism, looking at internal and external circumstantial factors that may have affected the text.[1] He accepts the obvious meaning of a word and rejects far fetched interpretations. In his view the latter lead to dispute and eventual corruption and distortion, and lead us away from the main purpose of the author, whether Prophet or lawyer. However, he does not hesitate to go beyond the obvious meaning of a word if there is evidence that it is necessary as in the matter of the divine attributes in the verses which paradoxically appear to be anthropomorphic.[2]

His theory of criticism depends on collecting a wealth of textual evidence. This is the basis of the beliefs of the Zahiri school.[3] In his criticism of the Torah we find him quoting more than seventy-five passages.[4] He himself kept closely to the text accepted and acknowledged by his opponents. He displayed the internal contradictions in the text under discussion. He compared the texts against such other texts as were available to him.[5]

It is possible to reconstruct his critical views but we shall give here a brief account of the method of his criticism and debate in the field of literary criticism, religious dialogue and controversy.

In one of my articles I have talked about the objectivity of Ibn Hazm's method, particularly in his book *al-Fisal*:

> This is revealed in several ways, but most importantly in the soundness of his quotations and his use of reliable source material. Ibn Hazm's concern for objectivity is demonstrated by his willingness to discuss seriously his theories with eminent scholars of different

---

1. See Ibn Hazm, *al-Fisal*, e.g. vol. 1, pp. 119ff, 147ff; vol. 2, pp. 108ff, also N. Rif'at, *Ibn Hazm on Jews and Judaism*, pp. 277ff.
2. See M. Abu Layla, *The Muslim View of Christianity*, pp. 19ff.
3. Ibid.
4. Ibn Hazm, *al-Fisal*, vol. 1, p. 147.
5. See M. Abu Layla, *The Muslim View of Christianity*, pp. 154-248 and N. Rif'at, *Ibn Hazm on Jews and Judaism*, pp. 220-294.

faiths, especially the Christian and Judaic.[1]

As a theologian he not only developed the *Zâhiriyya* (literalist) doctrine devised by Dâwûd ibn 'Alî al Isfahânî (d.270 AH; 883 AD), at a time when Spain was dominated by the Malikite school of thought, but he also championed the cause of comparative religion, producing the encyclopaedic five-volume *al-Fisal* which investigates the entirety of religious life known in Spain at the time.[2] There is nothing of the ivory tower in this vast enterprise. Ibn Hazm knew religious persecution at first hand and his insistent demands that scholars should investigate religion with exactitude and without prejudice sprang from personal experience. He himself was a model of the value of active debate with men of other faiths as well as Muslims and during a brief period spent in the atmosphere of religious toleration in Alméria engaged in active debate with Jews and Christians; debate which he recorded in faithful and fascinating detail in *al-Fisal*.

It was this contact with men of different belief that seems to have influenced his minute investigation of the Christian Gospels. It is instructive to reflect how few are the theologians who have been willing to study the scriptures of other religions in a genuine attempt to understand precisely how and why they differ. Ibn Hazm's researches into the Gospels were, in one respect, the fruits of his own intense personal faith in Islam. His analysis of inconsistencies between the four Gospel stories - conducted, it must be remembered, in the 11th century - bear a remarkable similarity to 19th and 20th century historical biblical criticism undertaken by Christian scholars. Such studies are now quite acceptable, but the establishment of this modern method of investigating the Christian scriptures met with fierce opposition when it was introduced.[3] In this context, Ibn Hazm was eight centuries ahead of his time.

However, although Ibn Hazm's investigation of the Gospels was highly personal he, like other Muslims, found

1. M. Abu Layla, *An Introduction to the Life and Work of Ibn Hazm* (II), *The Islamic Quarterly*, vol. 29, number 2, p. 169.
2. See M. Abu Layla, *The Muslim View of Christianity*, pp. 19ff.
3. See M. Abu Layla, *The Muslim View of Christianity*, pp. 72-195.

sanction for it in the Islamic scriptures. Unlike Christianity, aspects of Islam positively encourage the believer to consider the sacred texts of other faiths. The Qur'an contains references to both Judaism and Christianity, acknowledging their existence while declaring that they have departed from their original genuineness and harmony with Islamic doctrine. Furthermore, the question of comparative doctrine occupied Muslims as different canonical schools in their faith were established and such questions were easily transferred to other religions. We should not forget, either, the close proximity in which Muslims lived with other religious communities, a factor experienced in Almería by Ibn Hazm. Close contact led to intellectual curiosity about non-Muslim patterns of belief and Muslim administration of non-Muslims necessitated some knowledge of the practices of Jews and Christians.[1]

Ibn Hazm's work, both his extant writing and the contemporary debate he records in *al-Fisal*, testify to the value of a genuine scholarly interest in other religions. In Ibn Hazm's case the study of the Gospels actually strengthened his conviction that the Christian scriptures had suffered distortion during their transmission and interpretation, and his conviction that the Christian doctrines of the Trinity and Resurrection were late developments and could not be supported from the Gospels.[2] This strengthening of his own faith, however, never led him to an easy dismissal of Christianity. His work stands as a plea for better religious understanding based on a serious approach to the structure of other faiths. Verbally he shows impatience, and at times scorn for what he sees as the lack of authority in those texts his Christian contemporaries hold dear, but the pattern of attack in his writing is the attack of a scholarship that ultimately takes the opposition seriously.

---

1. See M. Abu Layla, *The Muslim View of Christianity*, pp. viiif and H.A.R. Gibb, *Arabic Literature, An Introduction*, (Oxford, Oxford University Press, 1974), p. 115.
2. See M. Abu Layla, *The Muslim View of Christianity*, pp. 358ff and M. Abu Layla, *Faith Meets Faith*, p. 32.

Ibn Hazm's criticism and arguments

Here we give a few examples of Ibn Hazm's criticism and arguments. In *al-Fisal*, Ibn Hazm refers to his debates with the Chief Judge of Cordoba. These meetings are examples of the direct transmission of Ibn Hazm's thought. The Christian judge who repeatedly attended the latter's classes, discussed with him the nature of sensual and physical pleasure in the afterlife. The judge objected to Ibn Hazm's position concerning the subject whereat he replied:

> Jesus said to his disciples at the Last Supper,
> "I tell you, I will not drink of this fruit of the
> vine from now on until that day when I drink
> it anew with you in my Father's Kingdom."
> (Matthew 26:29)

Ibn Hazm supported this with a reference to Luke 16:19ff. This reference concerns the story of the rich man and Lazarus. Lazarus, who suffered misfortunes in his lifetime, goes to Paradise and receives comfort there, whilst the rich man is sent to hell. When, in the torment of hell-fire, the rich man looked up and saw Abraham with Lazarus by his side, he called to Abraham to send Lazarus to dip the tip of his finger in water and to cool his tongue with it, he being in agony in the fire. Ibn Hazm used the reference to the cooling of the tongue to demonstrate that physical pleasure, as in the relief of tormented senses, is indeed possible in the afterlife - be it in Paradise or Hell. (Ibn Hazm expanded this argument elsewhere in *al-Fisal* with reference to Mark 14:25, Luke 22:28 and Genesis 3:19 and 18:21).[1]

The Chief Judge with whom Ibn Hazm debated and the times of his debates are not identified in *al-Fisal*. However, research undertaken by the present author reveals that the judge was called Asbigh Ibn 'Abd-Allah ibn Nabîl, who became a judge by the order of al-Hakam, who also dismissed him for his arrogance in 363 AH; 973 AD. Concerning

---

1. M. Abu Layla, *Ibn Hazm's Influence on Christian Thinking in Research, The Islamic Quarterly*, vol. 31, number 2, p. 111.

the date, the debate must have taken place between 418-422 AH, 1027-1030 AD, a time which coincides with the end of Ibn Hazm's political activity.[1] It is also evident that at this time Ibn Hazm wrote a long, controversial poem attacking a Muslim renegade, who initiated the attack on Islam and Muslims.[2]

Such face-to-face confrontation, as with the Chief Judge of Cordoba, extended into the melée of theological debate and the major theological disputes of the day. Of particular significance in this context is the participation of Ibn Hazm in the genealogy debate. This important issue concerned the disparities between Matthew and Luke in their account of genealogy. Ibn Hazm objected to a Christian interpretation of the disparities, derived from Africanus (c.160 - c.240) that they illustrated a legal and natural account of descent. This particular view was held by a contemporary Christian and was refuted by the author of *al-Fisal* who asked how such a solution could be arrived at when the actual form of the genealogy does not permit a two-fold distinction.[3]

This debate was of particular relevance to Ibn Hazm who was himself a great genealogist. His concern with these contradictions was not merely pedantic or historical, but was quite clearly within the context of the divinity of Christ. With this in mind, Ibn Hazm saw the divinity of Christ as untenable. His objection was based on the genealogy of Christ as traced through the paternal line. This he regarded as misplaced and indeed ultimately wrong, for he held that if any line of descent was to be ascribed to Jesus it could only be through his mother.[4]

Involving the divinity and status of Christ, this issue was one of the central areas of theological debate and dispute. The status of Ibn Hazm's voice in this debate must, according to historical evidence, have been extremely high. He was, it is to be remembered, not only a supremely gifted academic, but also the only man in the Iberian peninsula to enter theologi-

---

1. Ibid.
2. Ibid.
3. See M. Abu Layla, *The Muslim View of Christianity*, pp. 154ff.
4. Ibid.

cal dispute on matters of such importance.[1]

Among the biblical passages condemned by Ibn Hazm as immoral and therefore false, is Genesis 12:13, in which Abraham advised Sarah to say that she was his sister so that Pharaoh would not kill him and take her for a wife. Ibn Hazm is even more incensed about Genesis 20:11-13, where Abraham states that Sarah actually was his sister. The author of *al-Fisal* had argued with Samuel Ibn al-Nighrila Halevi on this matter. The Jewish scholar told his Muslim opponent that the word "sister" in this passage can also mean in Hebrew a kinswoman. Ibn Hazm riposted by referring to Genesis 20:12; the phrase which he emphasizes is: "It is not from my mother's side, but she is a daughter of my father." This clearly states that Sarah was his half-sister. Ibn Hazm maintains that the least that can be said about this passage is that it allows abrogation; in other words if Abraham's wife were indeed his half-sister, the position does at least open the way for the change in marital laws later introduced by Moses. Rabbi Solomon ben Isaac Rashi (432-499 AH; 1040-1105 AD) seems to accept that Sarah was indeed Abraham's half-sister, and explains it as the accepted practice of the time.[2]

Ibn Hazm also wonders how Sarah could have attracted the King of Gerara [Genesis 20:1-14], when she was so old. He took her after she had given birth to Isaac in her nineties. She herself told the angel that she was old and barren. After the baby was born she would have been even older and certainly more tired.[3]

Ibn Hazm concludes his critical examination of the Pentateuch by referring to Deuteronomy 34:5-6, where it is mentioned that Moses died and was buried and nobody knew where his grave was. Ibn Hazm finds that this passage provides evidence to support his argument against the Bible, that it is history written by human agents, not a revelation

1. See al-Humaydî, *Judhwa*, p. 309; also M. Abu Layla, *Ibn Hazm's Influence on Christian Thinking*, p. 112.
2. Ibn Hazm, *al-Fisal*, vol. 1, p. 107; see also N. Rif'at, *Ibn Hazm on Jews and Judaism*, pp. 226f.
3. Ibid.

from God. It is impossible that such a passage was revealed
to Moses during his lifetime. It might be justified as a fore-
telling, were it not that the whole passage is in the past
tense.[1] It is important to note that the ancient Jewish tradition
in its extreme form states that "Moses wrote the whole Pentateuch, including a (prophetic) account of his own death and
of the events immediately following", or even in its more
moderate form (mentioned in the Talmud), it says that
"Moses wrote everything except the concluding section of
Deuteronomy, which was written by Joshua."[2] In this context
it is useful to refer to the Spanish Jesuit, Benedict Pereira
(c.1535 - 1610 AD), who maintained that "there was a considerable number of additions made to the Pentateuch".[3] It is to
be noted that Benedict Pereira may have been influenced by
Ibn Hazm's work.

Here we give one more example of Ibn Hazm's debate,
but this time with a fellow Muslim scholar. Once Ibn Hazm
debated with a poor jurist, Sulaymân ibn Khalaf al-Bajjî
(d.474 AH; 1081 AD), and he won the argument. The poor
jurist began to excuse himself, saying, "I had to study at
night, reading by the light of the lamp of the market-guards."
Ibn Hazm replied, "I was disadvantaged too; I had to read
from gold and silver discs, resting on footstools." The point
he was making is that the possession of wealth may be as
much a hindrance as poverty is.[4]

Ibn Hazm was a phenomenal memorizer. He was famous
for it in his own time and afterwards. Even his enemies and
critics always acknowledged that his learning was vast and
deep.[5] Despite the great amount of information stored in his

---

1. Ibn Hazm, *al-Fisal*, vol. 1, pp. 146f; also N. Rif'at, *Ibn Hazm on Jews and Judaism*, p. 246.
2. See D. Guthrie et al (ed.), New Bible commentary *Moses and the Pentateuch* by J. W. Wenham (Oxford, Oxford University Press, 1985), p. 42; also N. Rif'at, *Ibn Hazm on Jews and Judaism*, p. 246.
3. See Edward J. Young, *History of the Literary Criticism of the Pentateuch*, in New Bible commentary, p. 34; see also Spinoza, *Risala fi'l Lahut wa'l Siyasa*, translated by Hasan Hanafi and Fu'ad Zachariyya (Cairo, al-Hay'a al-Mis-riyya al-'Amma li'l Ta'lif wa'l Nashr, 1971), pp. 265ff.
4. Yaqût, *Irshâd*, vol. 5, p. 88.
5. Al-Humaydî, *Judhwa*, p. 309; al-Dhahabî, *Tadhkîrat al-Huffâz*, (Hyderabad, Dâr al-Ma'ârif al-'Uthmâniyya, 1958), part 2, vol. 2, p. 1148; and al-Dhahabî, *Siyar*, p. 28.

mind he was a great creative author. Here I do not agree with Ibn Khaldun that too great a store of memorized poetry and literature inhibits the personal muse.[1] Ibn Hazm and Imam al-Shâfi'î, who were great memorizers and poets, can disprove Ibn Khaldûn. Some later scholars have observed that because Ibn Hazm was such a great *Hâfiz*, memorizer, he made some mistakes, sometimes confusing the narrators in *Hadith* literature.[2] This criticism has some basis. For example, Ibn Hazm mistakenly counted the book *Shi'r Quma* as a Talmudic writing.[3] He ascribed to John Chrysostom (the Golden Mouthed) (c. 347- 407 AD), the idea that the tree on which Jesus hung was the same tree from which Adam ate.[4] I could not find it among the known writings of John. He mistakenly ascribed the book *al-Intisâr wa'l Radd 'Alâ Ibn al-Râwandî al-Mulhid* ... by Abû al-Hasan 'Abd al-Rahîm al-Khayyât (d.300 AH; 912 AD) to Abû Bakr ibn al-Bâqillanî (d.403 AH; 1014 AD), the author of *Kitâb al-Tamhîd*.[5] Ibn Hazm says that after the Jews came from Babylon no Prophet arose among them, while in fact Haggai was a Prophet and Zachariah was also a post-exile Prophet.[6] But he may have his own reasons for excluding these prophets. Perhaps he regarded them as minor figures with no message to convey.

Ibn Hazm the critic explained how to lead the public, how to correct them, how to enter debate with others, how to start a conversation: the debater should seek to establish the truth tactfully and wisely, help his opponent to arrive at the truth and not drive him away from it; he should not exploit any lapses or confusion on the part of his opponent, but help him to understand. When we enter into conversation with someone, we should not express agreement with wrongdoers. If we do so we shall regret it later. Do not argue with your friends or your contemporaries. This will make enemies and

---

1. 'Abd al-Rahmân Ibn Khaldûn, *Muqaddima*, ed. by 'Alî 'Abd al-Wâhid Wâfî, (Cairo, Dâr Nahdat Misr, third edition, n.d.), vol. 3, p. 1315.
2. Shihâb al-Dîn Abû al-Fadl Ibn Hajar, *Lisân al-Mizân*, (Beirut, al-'Alami, 1971), vol. 4, pp. 198f; and al-Dhahabî, *Siyar*, pp. 140f.
3. Ibn Hazm, *al-Fisal*, vol. 2, p. 16.
4. Ibid, vol. 2, p. 75.
5. Ibn Hazm, *al-Fisal*, vol. 5, p. 60.
6. Ibid, vol. 2, pp. 7f.

may lead to legal action, and brings no benefit. Faced with a choice, a man should always choose God and the truth.[1]

Anyone who gives advice and warnings should employ gentleness and wisdom. He should use gesture wisely, smiling not frowning; he should try not to give direct advice or warning, but look as if he is just expressing his own opinion. He should be brief and to the point and know when to stop. In his attacks on wrongdoers he should not confront them directly, but praise those who act rightly so that the wrongdoers may take an example from them.[2]

An adviser and preacher should show good intention. Good intentions are the basis of every action in Islam. Here Ibn Hazm is holding up the Prophet Muhammad's method as the ideal; indeed it is the method used by all the Prophets when trying to convert others.[3] Arab men of letters have written at length on the same subject. It has been reported that the Prophet Muhammad said "We Prophets of God are by nature slow to speak." That is why the words spoken by Muhammad are not too many to be counted or too many to be memorized as an aid to good behaviour.[4]

In this context a speaker should not repeat himself again and again. Once Ibn al-Sammâk asked his slave-girl (who had been listening to him) "What do you think of my speech?" She said "It would be more beautiful if you did not repeat yourself." He said, "I say things twice so that everyone will understand." The slave-girl said, "Before the people who haven't understood understand it, the ones who did understand will be bored."[5]

In a divided twentieth-century world we could, perhaps, learn a lesson from the theology of Ibn Hazm. It is sad to con-

1. Ibn Hazm, *al-Akhlâq*, pp. 154 and 162.
2. See ibid, p. 193.
3. See Ibn Hazm, *al-Akhlâq*, pp. 162 and 193; also Ibn Hazm, *Jawâmi' al-Sîra*, (Cairo, Maktabat al-Turâth al-Islâmî, 1982), pp. 32ff; Abû al-Fidâ' Ibn Kathîr, *Shamâ'il al-Rasûl*, ed. by Mustafa 'Abd al-Wâhid, (Beirut, Dâr al-Ma'rifa, 1386 A.H.; 1967 A.D.), pp. 57ff; and Muhammad Ibn 'Abd Allah al-Khatîb al-Tibîizî, *Mishkât al-Masâbih*, ed. by M. N. al-Albani, (Beirut, al-Maktab al-Islâmî, 1399 AH; 1979 AD), vol. 3, pp. 1600-1686.
4. See Ibn Qutayba, *'Uyûn al-Akhbâr*, (Cairo, Dâr al-Kutub, 1343 AH), vol. 2, p. 170; also Ibn Kathîr, *Shamâ'il*, pp. 69-71.
5. Ibid, p. 178.

sider just how much ignorance exists concerning the most deeply-felt religious pre-occupations of the people of the world. The fiercest intolerance is often the result of ignorance and the failure to try to understand. A highly-specialized age does not have to be an age which dismisses the values of debate and persuasion.

Ibn Hazm never showed himself willing merely to live in peaceful co-existence with men of other faiths. The energy with which he argued with his opponents, his remarkable attention to every detail of analysis, and the firmness with which he maintained his own doctrinal position indicate an active and demanding search for the truth. The Muslim-Jewish and Christian dialogue described in *al-Fisal* is informed by this search, a search that is not incompatible with tolerance but which shows a real willingness to understand and investigate.

Ibn Hazm as a psychologist

Ibn Hazm was a skilled psychologist and sociologist. He was politically active. He showed great concern not only for scholarship but also for public affairs and practical leadership. His views on the role of politicians and public servants are of great significance. His suggestions are constructive and wide-ranging, so much so that we cannot cover them all here.

There has been no serious study of Ibn Hazm's theories on psychology. Those who have studied his book on love and lovers have given some account of his views on psychology, but not enough to give a complete picture of him as a psychologist. Psychology, after all, is the precise observation and analysis of human behaviour and activities, and is therefore not a science which can be studied in seclusion. It involves mixing in society and keeping company with all kinds of persons. Human society itself is the research material for sociologists and psychologists.

Ibn Hazm himself is sensitive and perceptive by nature. The environment in which he grew up helped him to develop his critical and analytical faculties. His long stay as a child and youth in the harem among women of different nations and cultures made him extraordinarily observant of differences. He is perhaps at his best when he analyses female psychology, both free and enslaved.[1]

Ibn Hazm's contact with the Caliph and leading personalities in the state helped him to understand the psychology of ministers and officials. He unveiled their interior world, stripping them of their badges of office and showing them as humans. He analysed the psychology of his friend Muhammad Ibn Abi 'Amir who was quick to change friends and quickly bored with any surroundings.[2]

When you read Ibn Hazm's book on love and lovers you are continually reminded that he is a psychologist and sociologist. He spoke of lovers' schemes, their dreams and daydreams. He analysed the feelings of all kinds of people, kings and public officials, the lower classes and humble people. He also threw light on the psychology of Christians and Jews, their thoughts and beliefs. He studied their allegiances and traditions in the light of their psyche. He studied the psychology of the debaters and of the common people. We say this in order to indicate the range of Ibn Hazm's interest in psychology. It is again too wide a matter to be dealt with fully here; but we will illustrate it with a few specific points. Our examples concern anxiety, intelligence and the emotions. But before we deal with these matters we should emphasize that Ibn Hazm was a man of action with a message to deliver; for him psychology was a means to an end, not study for study's sake.

Ibn Hazm spoke of anxiety, regarding it as the main cause of disturbance and distress. He laid special emphasis on this aspect of psychology, as is clear from the book here translated. Generally, Ibn Hazm regarded psychology as a branch of medicine, the branch which deals with the soul and with morality.[3]

With regard to intelligence, Ibn Hazm believed that some are born intelligent and others acquire intelligence. According to him intelligence is a gift from God, not hereditary and

---

1. See Ibn Hazm, *Tawq*, pp. 40, 79, 92f; 147f.
2. Ibid, pp. 104f.
3. Ibn Hazm, *Marâtib al-'Ulûm*, p. 238.

not environmentally conditioned.[1] We can see children of outstanding intelligence born to mentally defective parents, or mentally defective children born to extremely brilliant parents. Ibn Hazm illustrates his view that intelligence is a gift from God by pointing out that God can take it from anyone at any time, by taking away his mental capacities or his reason.[2]

Concerning the emotions, Ibn Hazm supplies an unusual and useful image: human nature is like a globe, where the lines around it can meet their opposites at the poles. So a man can be so happy that he cries; and extreme love can turn to extreme hate.[3]

Ibn Hazm speaks of false pride. He asked a man "Why are you so proud?" The man replied, "I am nobody's slave." Ibn Hazm pointed out that most of the people around were likewise not slaves; moreover, some of the people in authority over him were in fact slaves. Freedom was here equated with arrogance and overweening pride. Ibn Hazm noticed the psychology of this, and how such people imagine that they would have been great rulers and great scholars, if they had only had the opportunity.[4]

Al-Muhâsibî (died 243 AH; 857 AD) has a similar story. A proud rich heir believed that he was freeborn, but a man came who was able to prove that the heir's dead parents had been his slaves, and the heir's property actually belonged to him.[5] The moral of this story is that one should not boast and be proud of something that may be taken away. God is the true owner of all and we should be grateful to hold things in trust. Material things, by their nature, are not lasting.

It is interesting to note in this context that a proud person always thinks that what he has is good, and what others have is bad. A man who is proud of his work does not strive to improve it.

---

1. Ibid, p. 235.
2. Ibn Hazm, *al-Akhlâq*, pp. 202ff.
3. Ibid, pp. 235f.
4. Ibn Hazm, *al-Akhlâq*, pp. 220ff.
5. See *al-Ri'âya li Huqûq Allah*, (ed. by M. Smith, (London, 1940), E. J. W. Gibb Memorial Series, N.S., xv, p. 252) quoted in Franz Rosenthal, *The Muslim Concept of Freedom*, (Leiden, E. J. Brill, 1960), p. 114.

Ibn Hazm's moral interpretation of history

Ibn Hazm uses history as a resource for the training of the soul. He studies history according to his own method and philosophy. This is clear in his works on history both long and short. We will restrict ourselves here to examining how he uses history in his book on morality.

Ibn Hazm regards history as a continuous succession of events. The present stands in the centre between past and future. Man cannot shake off his history. He is firmly embedded in it. History is not a dead record of people who no longer exist, but a storehouse of information and guidance. We should make good use of history and follow the good examples and avoid the actions which have brought ruin to individuals or nations in the past.

He sets out his principles very clearly when he says that we analyse the good and the bad in historical events in order to know which example to follow.[1] In other words, God in the holy books speaks of some individuals of higher moral stature and piety; others were immoral and irreligious. God spoke of them not to record history but to provide examples for us. For example, in the Qur'an Pharaoh, the Egyptian king, was pictured as an example of arrogance, disbelief and tyranny, and Moses as an example of patience and steadfastness. Jesus was pictured as an example of obedience, modesty and love of God; Solomon as an example of wisdom; Joseph and his brothers as an example of the evil effects of envy; Qarun, a rich Jew, as an example of arrogance and overweening pride; Lukman as an example of a wise father who taught his son how to hold faith in God and His omniscience; the people of Lot, who practised homosexuality in their community, destroyed by God; the people of Noah, destroyed by God's flood; Mary is a good example of obedience to God; God supplies her with food and drink when the people desert her.[2] To sum up, the prophet Muḥammad is seen as an

---

1. See *al-Akhlâq*, p. 195.
2. See e.g. Qur'an 10:83; 11:97; 20:24; 26:44; 29:39; 10:84; 18:66; 19:51; 6:85; 4:172; 19:29ff; 21:79; 27:15,16; 12:1ff; 28:76ff; 31:12ff; 11:27ff; 71:1ff; 3:21ff; 19:16ff; also Ibn Hazm, *al-Fisal*, vol. 4, pp. 30ff.

example of all good merits.[1] Ibn Hazm takes history as a resource-bank of human wisdom.

Ibn Hazm's political views in relation to morality

Ibn Hazm has a knowledge of politics from both sides, practical and theoretical. He had personal experience of holding office; and his father and his father's friends had held public office while he was growing up. As far as the practical side of politics goes we cannot pinpoint any political achievements by Ibn Hazm. Even when he served as prime minister to the friend of his youth, 'Abd Al-Rahmân ibn Hishâm known as al-Mustazir (411 AH; 1023 AD), the fact that he was imprisoned several times, the short period of his ministry, his fugitive life from city to city, are evidence of his failure in politics. This was due to the disturbed conditions of the time. He was not a person to change his policies to suit the crowd. He was adamant in clinging to what he believed to be right. He reacted quickly to events. One of his biographers explained his failure in public office as being due to his preoccupation with scholarly debate.[2]

However in the theoretical side of politics, Ibn Hazm was a master. He wrote of the function of the Caliphate and the Caliph;[3] he wrote social criticism; he wrote about the rulers of his own time. There are some ideas of political theory in every book that he wrote. In his book *al-Fisal* he pointed out the necessity of appointing a ruler to lead the nation. The ruler does not have to be the best man in the nation, but he does have to be just, and to rule according to the word of God. He criticized and rejected the Shi'ite idea of the infallibility of the imam, and also their belief in heredity.[4] In his book on morality and behaviour, he speaks of the absolute importance of justice, the catastrophic destruction and confu-

---

1. See Ibn Hazm, *Jawâmi' al-Sîra*, p. 32.
2. Al-Maqqâri, *Nafh al-Tîb min Ghusn al-Andalus al-Ratîb*, ed. by Ihsân 'Abbâs, (Beirut, Dâr Sâdir, 1968), vol. 1, p. 489.
3. Ibn Hazm, *al-Fisal*, vol. 4, pp. 106ff.
4. See ibid, vol. 5, pp. 3ff.

sion caused by civil war.[1]

Ibn Hazm listed ten rankings that can be achieved in the hereafter. The first is for the scholar who teaches people and educates them, and acts according to his own teaching. Without scholars, religion would die away; they are the heirs of the Prophets. The second rank is reserved for rulers who are just. A just ruler benefits equally from the advantages that he brings to his people; he shares in the rewards that result. Even while he sleeps he is earning profit equal to the amount earned by the workers that he has enabled to find employment. In the *Hadith*, the messenger of God says that those rulers who act justly will sit on a footstool of light, by the right hand of God.

The third ranking is assigned to those who strive to follow God's way and fight His enemies. The fourth ranking is for those who plant trees and other useful sources of food. Anyone who ever picks food from a tree that they have planted will bring them reward. Ibn Hazm tells of a man who pulled up a vine that his daughter had just planted, saying that we were not created to plant things. Ibn Hazm says that he was a very foolish man, out of step with nature and his duty. Ibn Hazm's message is that we should strive actively to improve the world, and the provision of food for others will take our sins away.

The other rankings in the hereafter are, briefly, apportioned for avoiding the capital sins, such as killing; for avoiding magic; for repentance; the eighth is reserved for those who stand in the middle of the road, between paradise and hellfire, and so on.[2]

Ibn Hazm refers again and again to the *fitna*, civil war and decay, when society falls into confusion, and men do not know for whom they should fight, and people listening to a debate would shift sides for no reason other than that they liked shouting and cheering. The petty kings were at war with each other, in a civil war which divided the country to the point that there were no victors and no defeated. No single authority provided leadership; there were many conflict-

1. Ibn Hazm, *al-Akhlâq*, pp. 128, 140, 216f.
2. Ibn Hazm, *al-Radd 'Alâ Ibn al-Nighrîla*, p. 150.

ing parties.[1] Elsewhere, Ibn Hazm informs us that there had been four rival Caliphs at one and the same time.[2] Our author's keen observation is illustrated by his comment on the blossom, which symbolizes the life and beauty of the world destroyed by warfare. The noble and aristocratic Ibn Hazm chooses blossom for his image to show that war destroys not only the produce of the countryside but also its beauty.[3]

It is interesting to point out that in an ancient Arab poem ascribed to Imru' al-Qays a war before it starts is compared with a young girl decked in ornaments who attracts the young and inexperienced. But when fighting rages and burns over the country, it is like an old woman no longer capable of attracting admirers; her hair is thin and all her beauty has gone and she inspires no one by her odour to kiss her or embrace her. Ibn Nighrila, the most learned Jewish scholar of Ibn Hazm's time, wrote a very similar poem in Hebrew.[4]

As has been referred to above, he speaks of heavy taxes, the abuse of power, etc. Ibn Hazm's advice to politicians and people in public service is of central importance:

> Do not take power unless you know how to set it aside again. Otherwise you will harm yourself and your behaviour will be detestable.[5]

It should be remembered that Ibn Hazm himself had held ministerial posts several times, retiring voluntarily afterwards, in order to devote himself to scholarship. He is therefore able to speak from personal experience, not only from

1. See Ibn Hazm, *al-Radd 'Alâ Ibn al-Nighrîla*, pp. 45f; also Ibn Hazm, *al-Akhlâq*, pp. 127f; Ibn Hazm, *al-Fisal*, vol. 5, pp. 193ff; and Ibn Hazm, *Tawq*, pp. 147f.
2. *Naqt al-'Arûs*, pp. 83f.
3. See Ibn Hazm, *al-Akhlâq*, p. 129.
4. This has been translated into English in the study by David Goldstein, *Hebrew Poems from Spain*, (London, Routledge and Kegan Paul, 1965). See also Imru' al-Qays, *Diwan*, ed. by Muhammad Abu Al-Fadl Ibrahim, (Cairo, Dâr al-Ma'ârif, 1958), p. 353.
5. Ibn Hazm, *al-Akhlâq*, p. 155.

political theory. He no doubt frequently observed his fellows fighting to protect their own positions and to come even closer to the Caliph. He will also have witnessed the constant intriguing among the politicians of his time, especially among the petty kings.

Here Ibn Hazm is touching upon a sensitive part of human nature. Political ambition is a human weakness. Whether the post in question is important or comparatively insignificant, the holder of the post is usually determined to remain in it. Even a post requiring the highest moral standards may tempt its holder to embrace immoral means in order to stay in it.

In every age we see prominent people manipulating the system for the sake of their own ambitions. They cripple society and increase the problems of their nation, preventing worthy individuals from coming forward to benefit society. High position should be open to all. Ibn Hazm is calling for equal opportunity. The posts should go to those who will best serve the nation. If anyone knows that he has the post for life and will never have to defend his position, or be accountable for his successes and failures, publicly and honestly, then he lays himself open to develop psychological illnesses or moral failings, such as megalomania, self-righteousness and arrogance, brushing off any criticism and making many enemies.

As mentioned above Ibn Hazm made a detailed study of the position of the Caliph or head of state. Ibn Hazm's overriding principal aim was political stability. The Caliph is appointed by the people; if he acts against their interests and against their religion he may be dismissed by the people.

Ibn Hazm wrote a whole book on the subject of politics, under the title *In Politics*, but this book has unfortunately not survived, except in fragments quoted in works by other authors. We have evidence that the book was still current in 896 A.H. (1490 AD), since Abu 'Abd Allah Ibn al-Azraq quoted it in his book *Badâi' al-Silk fî Tabâi' al-Mulk*.[1] The same

---

1. Abu 'Abd Allah Ibn al-Azraq, *Badâi' al-Silk fî Tabâi' al-Mulk*, ed. by 'Alî Sâmî al-Nashshâr (Iraq, Kutub al-Turâth, 1978), vol. 2; see also Muhammad Ibrâhîm al-Kittânî, *Sha-dharât min Kitâb al-Siyâsa li Ibn Hazm*, (Morocco, *Majallat Tatwan*, number fifteen, 1960).

author seems to have also made use of Ibn Hazm's book on morality, but neither he nor any of his contemporaries credits any of the ideas to him by name. However, it is clear that the book benefitted several generations, even if they do not acknowledge the fact.

In this chapter an attempt has been made to indicate something of the life of Ibn Hazm, and the historical and personal factors that shaped his thought and attitudes.

His education was unusual, and unusually varied. He moved from the enclosed feminine world of his father's mansion to contact with eminent scholars and learned friends in a sophisticated and respected social setting. Under the pressure of political upheaval and consequent family decline, his experience was broadened to take in personal and stimulating contact with both Christians and Jews, of which he later made use in his writings on comparative religion.

The independence of his mind led him on a restless search for a personally satisfying method of comprehending religious matters, and caused him successively to reject the *Maliki* and *Shafi'i* schools of jurisprudence. He finally adopted the *Zahiriyya* school of thought and became its founding father in its developed form. Persecuted by his countrymen and by both the political and theological authorities during his lifetime, and leading an almost nomadic life, he nevertheless wrote prolifically and earned the admiration of a small circle of pupils and even some of his critics.

The picture is one of a man of enormous intellectual capacity and curiosity with a remarkably wide output of writing over a broad range of subjects. His personal isolation and the climate of hostility and instability in which he lived seems to have been responsible for both his strengths and his weaknesses. His extremism leads him at times into surprising comments; his great strengths are those of unswerving commitment to his own methodology and views in the face of powerful opposition and a rare intellectual integrity which will be diverted by no one.

In this chapter we have dealt with Ibn Hazm's criticism, psychological observations, political views in relation to morality, and concept of history. Our analysis shows that Ibn

Hazm is a moralist in the fullest sense of the word. In all his works, whether secular or religious, he never fails to say something about moral conduct.

CHAPTER II

IBN HAZM'S MORAL THEOLOGY

Definition and Dimension of Morality

The Arabic word *khuluq*, plural *akhlâq*, means "character, natural disposition or innate temper". It is synonymous with *sajiyya* and *tab'*, "the character with which one is created". The Arabic words *khilqa*, *fitra* and *tabi'a* also signify the nature with which a person is born. The word *khuluq* also signifies "custom" or "habit", as being second nature, as when one says "a certain action or behaviour became second nature to him."

The word *khuluq* meaning "morality" is derived from the same root as the word *khalaqa*, "He created or fashioned", and the word *khalq*, "designing or planning" or "an act of measuring or determining the size or proportion of something".

As evidence for this meaning, the philologists quote Zuhayr Ibn Abî Salma's verse in praise of Hirim ibn Sinân:

> You indeed cut truly as you have
> measure it out;
> Others measure but cannot cut it right.[1]

Another related word, *khaluqa*, means "becomes very smooth" or "comes together after separation", like clouds just before rain.

In his dictionary of synonyms in the Qur'an, Muqâtil ibn Sulaymân placed *khuluq* under the rubric *khalaqa*, "He created".[2]

In this context, we should mention that the prophet Muhammad pointed out the relationship of creation and morality when he made the following supplication to God,

---

1. See Abû al-Fadl Jamâl al-Dîn Muhammad ibn Manzûr, *Lisân al-'Arab*, (Beirut, Dâr Beirut (1388 AH; 1968 AD) vol. 10, pp. 80-92; and Edward William Lane, *An Arabic-English Lexicon*, (Beirut, Lebanon, Librairie du Liban, 1968), vol. 2, pp. 799f.
2. *al-Ashbah wa'l Nazâ'ir fî al-Qur'an al-Karîm*, ed. by 'Abd Allah Shihâta, (Cairo, Dâr al-Ma'ârif, n.d.), pp. 61f.

"You have fashioned my body well; please fashion my morality well."[1]

If we look at the whole group of related words we see that morality is God's creation, God's design; morality is created in us when we are created; but there are also moral qualities which we can acquire by education and socialisation.

In the Qur'an the noun *khuluq*, moral bevahiour, does not appear at all in the plural; but it does appear twice in the singular, first in [26:137] "This is indeed a *khuluq*, way of behaving, or a habitude, of the ancients." These words are spoken by the people of the prophet Hûd when he asks them to improve their moral behaviour; they argue that they are keeping to their traditional behaviour, and do not believe that they will suffer eternal torture. So he is wasting his time preaching to them. The second occurrence of *khuluq* in the singular is in Qur'an 68:4: (in praise of the character of the prophet Muhammad - peace be upon him) "Surely thou standest upon a mighty morality [or religion]," as explained by Ibn 'Abbas. Here "morality" and "religion" are synonymous.[2]

We have already referred to the Prophet Muhammad's saying that he was sent to complete the noblest code of morality, and that was through the religion of Islam. The interpreters of the Qur'an comment on the above verse by referring to the following tradition: Once a man asked 'Aisha about the Prophet's conduct. 'Aisha replied "Do you not read the Qur'an?" "Yes," said the man. 'Aisha continued, "The conduct of the Messenger of God is the Qur'an." She meant that his behaviour was in complete accordance with the teachings of the Qur'an. In other words, the Qur'an is a word-picture of Muhammad's conduct, and Muhammad's conduct was the practical implementation of the Qur'an.

There are several books specifically on the merits and

f. Abû Hâmid al-Ghazzali, *Ihyâ' Ulûm al-Din*, (Beirut, Dâr al-Kitâb al-'Arabî, n.d.), vol. 8, pp. 92-96.
2. Ibn Jarîr al-Tabarî, *Jâmi' al-Bayân fî Tafsîr al-Qur'an*, (Beirut, Dâr al-Ma'rifa, 1392 A.H.; 1972 A.D.) vol. 29, pp. 12f; and Ibn Kathîr, *Shamâ'il*, p. 57.

character of the Prophet, known as *al-Shamâ'il al-Nabawiyya*, the prophetic merits and virtues.

From the Qur'an we can build up a complete picture of Islamic morality. The picture of morality provided by the Qur'an is of course not restricted to passages containing the actual word *khuluq*.

In the *hadith* literature, it is said that nothing weighs heavier in the scales on which good and evil will be weighed in the hereafter than the goodness of the moral character.

In the *hadiths*, the word *khuluq* does appear in the plural:

> Those who practise the most acts of morality
> in this life are dearest to me and will be
> stationed nearest to me in the hereafter.[1]

The title of Ibn Hazm's work *al-Akhlâq wa'l Siyar*, in any of its various forms, indicates that its subject is practical morality, and this is also clear from his words in the introduction:

> I have written this book to correct the corrupt
> behaviour of the people, and to heal the sick-
> ness of their souls.[2]

In this book, Ibn Hazm writes about virtues and vices. It is clear from elsewhere in his work that he classified the art of psychological healing as a branch of logic, in fact of philosophy.[3]

In the 19th century the modern Muslim scholar Hajjî Khalîfa similarly considered morality as a part of practical philosophy, quoting Ibn Sadr al-Dîn al-Shirwânî's definition, "This is the science of the virtues and the way to acquire

---

1. Ibn Kathîr, *Shamâ'il*, pp. 57ff; also Abû Umar Yûsuf Ibn 'Abd Allah ibn 'Abd al-Barr, *Bahjat al-Majâlis wa Uns al-Mujâlis*, ed. by Muhammad Mursî al-Khulî and 'Abd al-Qadîr al-Qit, (Cairo, al-Dâr al-Misriyya, n.d.) vol. 1, pp. 594-598; and Ibn 'Abd Rabihi, *al-'Iqd al-Farîd*, (Cairo, al-Maktaba al-Tujâriyya, n.d.) vol. 1, pp. 5ff.
2. Ibn Hazm, *al-Akhlâq*, p. 83.
3. Ibn Hazm, *Marâtib al-'Ulûm*, p. 238.

them, of vices and the way to guard against them."[1]

In Ibn Hazm's book *al-Akhlâq wa'l Siyar* there is no specific definition of morality; this is because his aim was not to write an academic treatise on morality but rather to give the fruits of his long experience and years of observation, conversation and reading. However, it is possible to construct his view of morality from his utterances in his various works.

In the *Ring of the Dove*, he makes the following statement:

> It was not my intention in this essay to discourse upon the human character in general, and the inborn and acquired qualities of man, and how innate characteristics may be increased by cultivation, and acquired attributes disappear for want of natural aptitude; [otherwise] I would have added here the observations necessary to be set down [on] such a subject. But it was my purpose to speak only upon this matter of love.[2]

It is clear from the above quotation that morality is partly inborn, partly acquired. Morality can be increased and strengthened by training and education. But acquired morality is in constant danger of slipping because it is not a part of one's nature. This reminds us of Dhî al-Isba''s verse,

> Each and every man will
> one day revert to his natural quality,
> Though he might for a time have adopted
> a way of behaving that is alien to his
> character.[3]

In *al-Akhlâq wa'l Siyar*, Ibn Hazm says moreover:

---

1. *Kashf al zunûn*, (Tehran, al-Maktaba al-Islamiyya, 1397) vol. 2, p. 1862; see also Carra De Vaux, "Akhlak", in M.Th. Houtsma et al (ed.), *The Encyclopaedia of Islam*, first edition, (Leiden, E. J. Brill/London, Luzac and Co., 1927) vol. 1, p. 231.
2. Ibn Hazm, *Tawq al-Hamâma*, Arberry's translation, p. 152.
3. Ibn Qutayba, *'Uyûn*, vol. 2, p. 5; and Ibn 'Abd Rabihi, *al-'Iqd al-Farîd*, vol. 3, p. 3.

If you study the laws that regulate human nature and the development of different characters according to the mixture of elements rooted in their souls, you will surely become convinced that you have no merit from your own virtues, that they are only gifts from the Almighty, which, if He granted them to another, would have made him just like you, and you will realize that, left to your own devices, you would collapse and die. You should replace the pride that you take in your virtues with acts of grace towards the one who gave them to you and with the fear of losing them, for even the most admirable characters can be altered by illness, poverty, fear, anger or the decrepitude of old age. Show compassion towards those who lack the gifts that you have received....[1]

If a man is dominated by a natural passion, then, however firm and sensible he is, in other ways, he can be overcome if you attack this weak point.[2]

Following the same line of approach Ibn Hazm throws some more light on the psychology and thinking of people bad by nature, "I have seen vile creatures imagine in their vile souls that everybody was like themselves; they would never believe that it was possible, in one way or another, not to have their faults. There is no character more corrupt, there is none more remote from being virtuous and good. Anyone who is in this state, cannot hope to be cured at all."[3]

---

1. Ibn Hazm, *al-Akhlâq*, p. 209; see also Ibn Hazm, *al-Fisal*, vol. 3, pp. 33ff.
2. Ibn Hazm, *al-Akhlâq*, p. 236.
3. *al-Akhlâq*, p.228; see also Ibn Qutayba, *'Uyûn*, vol. 2, p. 5; 'Abd Al-Rahmân Badawî, *Dirâsat wa Nusûs fî'l Falsafa wa'l 'Alum 'Ind al-'Arab*, (Beirut, al-Mu'asasa al-'Arabiyya lil Dirâsat, 1981), pp. 41f, 48-50; *Rasâ'il Ikhwân al-Safa wa Khilan al-Wafâ*, (Beirut, Dâr Beirut, 1376 A.H.; 1957 AD), vol. 2, pp. 312f; and al-Ghazzali, *Ihyâ*, vol. 8, pp. 100f.

Within the same context Ibn Hazm expresses his sympathetic feelings towards those people who have a natural tendency towards a vice: "We should not criticise someone who has a natural tendency towards a vice - even if it were the worst possible fault, the greatest of vices - as long as he does not let it appear in anything he says or does." In Ibn Hazm's view, such a person "would almost deserve more commendation than someone who naturally inclines towards virtue, for it takes a strong and virtuous mind to control a corrupt natural inclination."[1]

Moreover, Ibn Hazm says that "a man who seeks virtues is like the angels; whereas a man who seeks vices resembles Satan. Man has two sides to his nature; he has the capacity for sin and also for obedience to God." In Ibn Hazm's view, the difference between virtue and vice is "the readiness of the soul to do good things, and to feel happy about it, and the reluctance of the soul to do the same."[2]

A happy man is one who inclines by nature towards the good and the virtuous. An unhappy one runs away from the good and the virtuous.[3] The author of *al-Akhlâq wa'l Siyar* believes that the environment affects a person's morality and his natural tendencies. It can help him to do good or to do bad. The good person is one who, when required to go the right way, is able to do so. The bad person is one who, when commanded to do good, always tries to avoid doing so.

There is no difference between men and women in this respect. Ibn Hazm disagreed with those who say that the male sex is more capable of self-discipline. He believes that male and female are tempted equally and resist or succumb to the same extent.[4]

Ibn Hazm is a moralist in the fullest sense of the word. In all his works, whether secular or religious, he never fails to say something about moral conduct.

We have gathered together maxims and parts of his ethical code that are scattered throughout Ibn Hazm's works with the aim of presenting a coherent picture of his moral philoso-

---

1. *al-Akhlâq*, p. 230.
2. Ibid, p. 96.
3. Ibid; see also Ibn Hazm, *al-Fisal*, vol. 3, pp. 33ff.
4. Ibn Hazm, *Tawq*, p. 164.

phy and wisdom. The scattered material is vast and well worth collecting. It forms a valuable complement to the book here translated, throwing extra light on the same subjects.

In his early book *The Ring of the Dove*, there are many moralizing and religious maxims as shall be seen later.

For example, he speaks of the ugliness of sin, the beauty of truth, honesty and faithfulness; he makes occasional mention of other virtues and vices.[1] As R. Arnaldez points out, "The use of more personal examples and of direct observation lends it progressively more depth and psychological truth, while at the same time a hint of pessimism and of bitterness becomes more apparent."[2]

Arnaldez notes the link between Ibn Hazm as a psychologist and as a moralist, observing Ibn Hazm's remarks on apparent resignation, also some remarks on the apparent and the hidden meaning in the words of lovers, and remarks on the dialectic of consolation. Arnaldez focuses on Ibn Hazm's analysis of anxiety, saying that "all of Ibn Hazm's psychology and moral science concentrates on action, but an action purged of any internal motive and entirely determined by the thought of God."[3]

The Inborn Qualities in Human Character

In the introduction to his book *al-Ihkâm fî Usûl al-Ahkâm*, Ibn Hazm gives first place to the subject of virtue, saying that when God created the soul He endowed it with many capabilities such as a sense of justice which enables it to strive for fairness and truth. The Qur'an states that Allah commands us to be true and good:

> Verily, Allah commands justice and the doing of good [in a way that is beyond what is just a mere duty] and giving support and charity to kith and kin, and forbids indecency, dishonour and insolence and oppression, admonish-

---

1. See *Tawq*, e.g. pp. 85ff and 61ff.
2. "Ibn Hazm", the *Encyclopaedia of Islam*, new edition, vol. 3, p. 793.
3. Ibid.

ing you, so that haply you will remember.
[16:90]

> O believers, stand out firmly for justice, wit-
> nesses for God, even though it be against
> yourselves, or your parents and kith and kin,
> whether the person be rich or poor; God
> stands nearer to them both than you [and
> thus can protect them]. Then follow not your
> whim, lest you swerve from justice or truth.
> [4:135]

God also created the anger and desire which lead the soul
to injustice and blind it to the right path. In the Qur'an, God
says:

> And some men there are whose saying upon
> the present world pleases thee, and such a
> one calls on God to witness what is in his
> heart, yet he is most stubborn in altercation,
> and when he turns his back, he hastens about
> the earth, to do corruption there and to
> destroy the tillage and the stock; and God
> loves not corruption; and when it is said to
> him, 'Fear God', vainglory seizes him in his
> sin. So Gehenna (hellfire) shall be enough for
> him - how evil a cradling. [2:205-206]

The virtuous is pleased to know how many good things
Allah has given him and the fool is made happy by things
which look attractive; he does not understand that they may
be worthless or even harmful to him in the hereafter.

Another thing which God created in the soul, according
to Ibn Hazm, is its understanding and reasoning which help
it to find the path to virtue, lighting the way through the
darkness of problems, enabling it to discover the one right
answer.

Another thing is ignorance or foolishness which confuses
the mind and hides the right way from it and makes all ways
seem the same, leaving the mind always in doubt. It may

take a person in a direction which is far from the truth and the right. In the Qur'an God says: "*Are they equal - those who know and those who know not?*" [39:9]. That is to say that beimg sound and firm helps man to be just and God-fearing.

Another thing with which the soul is endowed is what the ancients called logic. God endows the soul with a sense of logic to enable it to understand His revelation and the real value of His creation and allows it to rise to that perception so that the soul may shake off the darkness of ignorance and be able to distinguish between truth and falsehood. Again, God says in the Qur'an:

> So give thou good tidings to my servants who give ear to the Word and follow the fairest of it. Those are they whom God has guided; those - they are men possessed of minds. (39:17-18)

Another thing is strength of mind, or intelligence, which enables the intellectual soul to uphold justice and to prefer everything that can be proved by reason and to accept it as a fact, acknowledging it in words and with gestures and basing one's actions upon this insight. God gives this quality, strength of mind, to support the soul in its strivings to choose the right path and to refuse the wrong and to refuse whatever leads it to foolishness and bad desires, including the anger which gives rise to fanaticism and tribal values. It is important to note that Ibn Hazm follow's Aristotle's division of the faculties, i.e. sensation, reason and appetite or desire. In Ibn Hazm's view, anyone who follows the light of the correct mind will succeed and be saved; anyone who misses the path will fail and be damned. God says:

> Surely in that there is a reminder to him who has a heart, or will give ear with a present mind. (50:37)

Ibn Hazm explains that God uses the term *qalb*, heart, to mean the mind, not the heart as an organ. Everybody has a heart but not everybody has the capacity to understand. Here

Ibn Hazm refers to the Qur'an where God uses the word "hearts" as a reference to "minds".

> ... have they hearts to understand with or ears
> to hear with? It is not the eyes that are blind,
> but blind are the hearts within the breasts.
> (22:46)[1]

Obedience to God is the source of all virtues and the means of avoiding all vice. There is no virtue outside obedience to God's commandments and exhortation to such obedience. No vice is worse than disobedience to God and His commandments.[2]

Ibn Hazm goes on to say that God sent prophets to guide their people and finally sent the Prophet Muhammad as the "Seal of the Prophets". This world, he says, does not last for ever; it is a temporary abode for our temptation and trial. It is a bridge towards the everlasting abode. Everything in this world is valueless except knowing Allah's commandments and teaching them to the ignorant and working according to them. Everything which tempts us to evil doing is transient: the things that the lowly souls seek, such as taking pleasure in pretty pictures, or ephemeral things, or attractive voices which die on the wind, or pleasant odours which quickly fade, or delicious foods and drinks which soon turn to waste, or elegant clothes which soon wear out; in other words, everything that engages foolish people who have no knowledge of right and wrong, transient things like gaining money. There is no profit in the possession of money except that it will buy food whereas if it is given to charity it will bring the giver an everlasting abode. A man should rather strive to lead his fellow men out of the confusion of doubt and the darkness of error into the light of truth.

It is reported that the Prophet Muhammad - peace be upon him - said, "Anyone who is used by God to guide one person shall profit more from that action than if he were given the best of cattle. And anyone who imitates a charitable

---

1. Ibn Hazm, *al-Ihkam*, part 1, vol. 1, pp. 5ff.
2. Ibid.

idea or a thing that profits the people in the time of Islam, he shall earn as great a wage as the people who take up his idea, without decreasing their reward." The Prophet Muhammad praised anybody who acquired wisdom and taught it to others.[1]

The Function of Propethood and its Value in Contrast with Philosophy

In his *Risâlât al-Tawqîf 'alâ Shari' al-Najâ,* Ibn Hazm speaks of the prophets and prophethood in connection with ethics and the morality of souls. He states that the prophets who brought revelation from God benefit the people in three ways. The first is in the correction of the morals of the soul, obliging the people to keep the moral code, practising justice, generosity, chastity, truthfulness, courage, patience, meekness and mercy, and avoiding the opposites of these virtues. This teaching is a great benefit which is of vital importance to the people of the world - without morality they cannot survive. The rational mind cannot doubt that the healing of the sicknesses of the soul is more important than the healing of the body. This is because the healing of the body will follow the healing of the soul. The reason is that a healthy regime for the soul requires abstinence from anything which disturbs the body's function and works against man's interests.

A remedy which can heal the soul and the body together is of course superior and preferable to one which can heal only the body. This is evident and tangible.[2] Here Ibn Hazm touches upon a highly important point. He remarks that the soul cannot be healed by any other philosophy than that of the prophets. Only religious ethics provides the saving guidance since obedience to God is a necessary part of healing and is incompatible with obedience to anyone else.

---

1. Ibid, pp. 9ff; see also Abû al-Wafâ' al-Mubashshir Ibn Fâtik, *Mukhtâr al-Hikam wa Mahâsin al-Kalim,* ed. by Abd al-Rahmân Badawî, (Madrid, Matba'at al Ma'had al-Misri lil Dirâsât al-Islâmiyya, 1377 AH; 1958 AD), pp. 1ff.
2. See *al-Radd,* pp.46ff; Ibn Hazm, *al-Fisal,* vol. 1, pp. 55ff; and al-Shahrastani, *al-Milal wa'l Nihal,* in the margin of *al-Fisal,* vol. 5, p. 175.

There is no agreement among secular moralists about which of their many theories is the correct one which should be adopted. People who perceive the power of anger explain everything in terms of this power. Here Ibn Hazm is touching on an important point which was later developed by Nietzsche in his theory of the 'overman'.

The second way in which prophets can benefit the people is by protecting them from transgression and from aggression on the part of those who cannot be corrected by admonition and verbal reminders and who pay no heed to truth, the cultivation of life, protection of the weak and property. Thus the prophets also bring the people security against evil and no one can survive without it. No one can correct his own behaviour without the right guidance of the Prophets.[1] Ibn Hazm repeats that obedience to any other than God has no divine authentication and that 'other' is powerless to help. The people themselves do not know which of many paths to follow. They can hardly agree among themselves without guidance from above. God is the sole authority in Ibn Hazm's opinion, and God exercises His authority through His prophets and through anyone who applies His religion upon earth. It should be made clear that Ibn Hazm does not exclude the obedience of man to man if it is within the moral realm and based on religion. For example, the governor of the state should be obeyed, as should his officials, insofar as they do not violate God's law on earth. Without this obedience no society on earth can exist. Elsewhere Ibn Hazm writes about the state and the structure of government and the role of the ruler, but it is outside the scope of this discussion to go further into this topic.

The third way that the prophets benefit the people is that they help them to have a good life in this world and achieve salvation in the hereafter. Ibn Hazm continues by saying that there is no way at all to have a real knowledge of God the Creator, or to achieve personal salvation, except through the prophets. The various branches of philosophy have never guaranteed salvation. Anyone who claims that philosophy is a means of salvation is mistaken because there is no evidence

---

1. Ibn Hazm, *al-Radd*, pp. 46ff; also Ibn Hazm, *al-Akhlâq*, pp. 96ff.

to prove it. The philosophers themselves are at variance on this matter. There is no single point of agreement among them. The wise man should seek the reality of things; otherwise he is wasting his time in his reading and observations about a matter that will bring him no benefit.[1]

Ibn Hazm seems here to criticize Abû Bakr Muhammad Ibn Zakariyya al-Râzî (died 313 AH, 860 AD), the most eminent medieval physician, or perhaps the Ikhwân al-Safâ' (4th - 5th centuries AH, 10th - 11th centuries AD).

Al-Râzî argued about the validity of prophethood and prophets. His ideas were directly challenged and criticized by the Isma'ili scholar Abû Hâtim al-Râzî (died 322 AH, 933 AD).

Abû Bakr al-Râzî had said "Why did God need to favour someone by designating him prophet and a guide for others? Why do you say that the Most Wise and All-Merciful selected some, so that his people will fight among themselves and bring ruin upon the earth? Would it not be better if the Most Wise and All-Merciful had inspired all his people to refrain from wrong and to earn benefits in the Hereafter? This would prevent contention and dissension and there would be no more differences of opinion between them. This would be better for them than to have prophets and imams and leaders and to feel fanatical loyalty to their own religion. This has caused many deaths, fanaticism and refusal to follow a certain leader."[2]

Abû Hâtim ar-Razi replied, "God is wise and merciful. We see everywhere that some people are leaders and some are led. Some are teachers, some are students. This is natural and can be found in all religions, all nations, in tradition and philosophy. People cannot live independent of each other. Teachers and priests are necessary. Only obstinate and misleading hypocrites would deny this."[3]

He says to his critic "Do you think you know something that others do not? You have your knowledge from your teachers. If you think that others can learn as much as you,

1. Ibn Hazm, *al-Radd*, pp. 47f.
2. 'Abd Al-Rahmân Badawî, (editor), *Rasâ'il Falsafiyya*, (Beirut, Dâr al-Afaq al-Jadîda, n.d.), pp. 295ff.
3. Ibid.

just look around you at the great variation in capability and nature. People are in dire need of prophets. Prophets bring peace and unity. They do not try to profit materially from their own actions. We cannot impose upon God our own choice of action. He is free to do whatever He wants. We may not fully understand His great wisdom in managing His creatures.[1]

The Muslim Neoplatonists, the *Ikhwân al-Safa'*, valued philosophy very highly and tried their best to reconcile religion and philosophy; there was great interest in philosophy at the time, and many Greek texts were being translated into Arabic, but they were exposed to criticism because of their attempt.

It is worth noting that Abû Sulaymân al-Sijistani al-Mantiqi (c. 3rd - 4th centuries AH, 9th - 10th AD), who was himself a logician, attacked them for this attempt to reconcile philosophy with religion. He considered that philosophy is man-made whereas the divine law is revealed by God. Philosophy poses questions, religion is fixed. The prophet was sent to the philosopher, but the philosopher cannot preach to the prophet.[2]

It should be noted that Ibn Hazm believed that God is the source of all knowledge, language and morality. He taught the first man and showed him how to express his knowledge and how to communicate with others and how to behave. The first man passed the skills down to those that followed.[3]

Elsewhere in his works, he discusses morality and good conduct. Time and again he repeats his belief that the Prophet Muhammad excelled in morality. In his character Ibn Hazm finds all the qualities and codes of moral behaviour. In this respect Ibn Hazm is in agreement with all

---

1. Ibid.
2. Abû Hayyân al-Tawhîdî, *al-Imta' wa'l Mu'anasa*, ed. by Ahmad Amîn and Ahmad al-Zîn, (Beirut, Dâr Maktabat al-Hayâ, n.d.) vol. 2, pp. 18f.
3. See Qur'an 2:31-33; also Ibn Hazm, *al-Ihkâm*, part 1, vol. 1, pp. 1ff; Muhyi al-Din Ibn al-'Arabî, *al-Futûhât al-Makiyya*, (Beirut, Dâr Sâdir, n.d.), vol. 1, p. 32; and Paul Nwyia (ed.), Nusûs Sûfiyya Ghayr Manshûra, *Tafsîr Ibn 'Atâ'*, (Beirut, Dâr al-Mashriq, 1973) p. 37.
4. See Ibn Hazm, *Jawâmi'*, pp. 33f; also Ibn Rabban al-Tabarî, *al-Dîn wa'l-Dawla*, ed. by 'Adel Nuwihad, (Beirut, Dâr al-Afâq al-Jadîda, 1979), pp. 57ff.

Muslim scholars. In his biography of Muhammad, Ibn Hazm talked in detail about the Prophet's character, way of life, actions and so on. He considers Muhammad's moral character as one of his miracles.[4]

Like Ibn Hazm after him, Ibrahim ibn al-Bayhaqî (295 - 320 AH, 908 - 932 AD) wrote a lengthy section about the excellence of the Prophet as a eulogising prologue to his book. In this section he enumerates Muhammad's moral qualities and miracles and compares them with those of other prophets of God: his generosity, meekness, humility etc. He took an example from the humble life that the prophet lived, to the extent that when he died his armour was in pawn to a Jew in order that he might buy food for his family. He never built a house or a mansion. He had only two items of clothing and one ring. He sat on the floor to eat, mixing with the poor and needy, going on foot as a humble man in the street and in the market, used his arm as his pillow, and he always called people who thought he had wronged them to come forward and do the same to him. He never accepted charity, but he would accept gifts, whatever their value. He gave gifts in exchange with even greater generosity. He never ate alone. He never treated his servant badly. He would accept anyone's invitation whatever his social status. When he conquered Mecca, his opponents gathered round him. Among them were the slayers of his friends, and relatives who had persecuted and insulted him, but he took no revenge. Instead, he told them that they were free to go. "I say to you what my brother Joseph said to his brothers: 'Go back without blame. God is merciful to you.'"[1]

Muhammad spent most of his time in silence. He did not speak unless he had something worth saying. He commanded his followers to speak only good or to keep silent. He used to speak to people on their own level, whatever their intellectual abilities. Once a man came to him and asked his advice about the dower that he was giving his wife. He used terms that seemed strange to Muhammad's companion Abû Bakr.

1. *al-Mahâsin wa'l Masâwi'*, (Beirut, Dâr Sâdir, 1390 AH; 1970 AD), pp. 1ff; also Ibn al-'Arabî, *Fusûs al-Hikam*, ed. by Abû al-'Ila 'Afifi, (Beirut, Dâr al-Kitâb al-'Arabî, n.d.), pp. 214ff; and Ibn al-Arabî, *al-Futûhât*, vol. 1, pp. 1ff.

Abû Bakr asked the Prophet, "O Prophet, upon my father and mother, you were born and raised among us, but we have travelled here and there whereas you did not," meaning that he had had no opportunity of picking up different Arabic dialects. "We notice that you understand words that we do not." The Prophet told him that Almighty God had taught him and given him perfect knowledge and wisdom and morality. "This man spoke to me in his own way and I answered him accordingly. He asked me whether a man may delay payment of his wife's dower. I told him that he may if he has no money at all."

Bearing this in mind we may sum up by saying that Ibn Hazm believes that man is God's creation and can tell good from bad. God equipped the human soul with the ability and the inclination to seek goodness and virtue. Moreover God assists and guides the soul in its search for the right path, helping it to distinguish between good and evil, truth and falsehood, the beneficial and the harmful. Ibn Hazm sees man as an intellectual and moral being honoured by God. He believes that God commanded people to use their capabilities of doing good to save themselves in this world and the next. When a man suffers a sickness in his soul, God has shown him the way to a cure. Allah is always ready to forgive. Ibn Hazm believes in the possibility of correcting behaviour and the healing of moral deficiency - this can be achieved by obedience to God and by acting according to His commandments, by exercising self-discipline and seeking real knowledge. The correction and reformation of souls are not impossible. This should be emphasized. It is possible and it is vitally important to attempt it. God is the source of goodness and guidance. The Prophets and the revelation provide us with the means of morality and good conduct. Morality cannot be separated from religion. Philosophy alone cannot in any way serve as a substitute for religious morality. Religious morality has more than one aim; it prepares a man to lead a happy life in this world and a good life in the hereafter.

Vices and the Cardinal Sins

Another important essay written by Ibn Hazm is about religious and moral duties and the diagnosis of the various sicknesses of the soul and how to treat them. This essay contains answers to questions sent to Ibn Hazm by some of his followers who sought advice about the correct way to act in various situations. For example, he was asked what a sinner must do to satisfy God and win His forgiveness. Ibn Hazm's answer was to avoid the cardinal sins, as advised in the Qur'an. In order to explain what a cardinal sin is, and which they are, he referred to the *hadith* of the Prophet Muhammad in which he says, "Avoid the seven capital sins. The seven are polytheism, or the association of another being with God, magic, killing anyone, devouring the possessions of an orphan, practising usury, fleeing from the dangers of war when it is necessary to defend oneself, or spreading malicious gossip about an innocent, devout woman." Muslim scholars disagree about the number of cardinal sins. Ibn Hazm referred to Ibn 'Abbas who stretched them to include seventy. Ibn Hazm agrees that they are more than seven in number and may be stretched to as many as seventy. He says that the above-mentioned *hadith* does not contain anything to say that these seven are exclusive, i.e. that there cannot be any other cardinal sins.[2] Others can be added to the list if they are genuinely sins. Ibn Hazm would add: the utterance of falsehoods or false witness, unkindness to one's parents, telling lies about the Prophet Muhammad, and exposing one's parents to other people's insults. The Prophet also warned strongly against disbelief, against ingratitude towards God the sustainer or any other benefactors, and against yelling and wailing and tearing one's clothes and cutting off one's hair at funerals. Backbiting is also included among the sins; and to neglect to wash after urinating; to be unkind to one's mother's family; to torture animals, or to kill them except when necessary for food; to take pride in one's dress and strut proudly; to deprive a thirsty person of water; to steal

---

1. Ibn Hazm, *al-Radd*, pp. 46f.
2. Ibid.

anything. It is also counted as a sin if one supports a ruler out
of self-interest.

A leader who misleads his people is also committing a
sin. Moreover, the Qur'an also warns against fornication and
adultery, spreading corruption and terror on earth, house-
breaking, assault and robbery.[1]

Ibn Hazm says that he has spent many years thinking
about cardinal sins, their nature and their number. He finally
came to the conclusion that anything that God warns is pun-
ishable with hellfire is a cardinal sin. A man's good deeds
and bad deeds will be weighed and measured, as is stated
again and again in the Holy Qur'an. As long as the good
deeds outweigh the bad deeds by however small a margin, he
shall escape hellfire. For example, it is stated by the Prophet
Muhammad that a prostitute was accepted by God and
entered heaven because she gave water to a thirsty dog.
Another man picked up a branch of a thornbush from a path
and was saved.[2]

Islam is always calling for good deeds and discouraging
bad deeds. The Prophet Muhammad said that envy is permitted in two cases only: in the case of a man to whom God has
given wisdom who teaches it to others; and in the case of a
man who is wealthy and is guided by God to spend it in
charitable ways.[3] Anything that a Muslim does to benefit others, even animals and birds, will be rewarded by God. Charitable and moral activities also include non-material actions
such as glorifying God, putting one's hope in Him, and
expressing love and fear of Him. Such actions are greatly
beneficial to the healing of the soul and the improvement of
one's morals. It also helps to cement the relationship between
God and man and enlightens the mind and soul of men. Each
person shall be rewarded according to his deeds alone. This
belief in the accountability of deeds (and words) encourages
us to do good and avoid mischief and to attempt to return to
our original innocence, or *fitra*. This belief demonstrates the

1. Ibn Hazm, *al-Radd*, p. 46f.
2. See Ibn Hazm, *Risâlat al-Talkhîs li wujûh al-Takhlîs*, in *al-Radd 'Alâ Ibn al-Nighrîla*, pp. 141f; also al-Tabarî, *Jâmi'*, vol. 8, p. 238 and 254, and Muslim, *Sahih*, Chapter on Peace, no. 154.
3.An-Nawawi, *Riyad as-Salihin*, p. 485.

justice of God and also His mercy. Again, this in itself gives us a model for our behaviour in judging others and showing mercy and even helps us to understand our existence and the purpose of our lives.[1]

The fact that our good deeds are recorded by God and recompensed in due measure does not mean that God is severe and terrible. His wrath is tempered with mercy. Ibn Hazm enumerates five favours that God gives to His people. First, God forgives all minor sins as long as cardinal sins are avoided. Secondly, all cardinal sins would be forgiven, however numerous, if they are followed by sincere repentance. This is generally agreed among Muslim scholars. Thirdly, in the case of someone who has committed cardinal sins persistently and deliberately until the day he dies, God will weigh them against his good deeds, and if the latter are sufficient he will enter Paradise. Fourthly, as an act of mercy, God records each sin as a single act but multiplies the good actions as much as tenfold and perhaps more to whomsoever He wills. Fifthly, God puts the sinner into hellfire first, and then once he is purified takes him to Paradise through intercession to stay there for ever. This is an act of grace on God's part.[2] If we look at this in the light of other statements made by Ibn Hazm about God's mercy, we will be astonished at Arnaldez' view that Ibn Hazm was a misanthropist.[3] The best behaviour for a Muslim is threefold: to learn and to pass on what one has learnt; to do full justice to people under your control; and to strive in Allah's way. This is, of course, in addition to the performance of religious duties and the avoidance of sin. A Muslim is not required to spend all his time in worship and religious activities; he may work for his living and follow his own interests as well. Islam forbids complete absorption in religious activities and withdrawal from the world. The latter is harmful rather than beneficial. Moderation is the central tenet of Islamic teaching. Excessive time spent in worship may open the door for Satan to whisper to a man that he is

---

1. Ibn Hazm, *Risâlat al-Talkhîs*, p. 144.
2. Ibn Hazm, *Risâlat al-Talkhîs*, p. 144; see also Ibn Abî Tâlib al-Makkî, *Qût al-Qulûb*, vol. 1, pp. 217ff.
3. R. Arnaldez, "Ibn Hazm," *The Encyclopaedia of Islam*, vol. 3, p. 792.

more pious than Muhammad himself. This would mislead
and destroy the man. In Ibn Hazm's view the Muslim should
know how much worship the Prophet Muhammad used to
offer and not try to outdo this amount in any way. Malik was
asked about a man who put on his *ihram*, his white ceremoni-
al robes, before he reached the correct place to do so. Malik
showed disapproval of this action, saying that he might think
that he was doing something better than Muhammad himself
did and this might ruin him.[1]

Ibn Hazm is emphatic that a Muslim should do as much
good as he can. He should visit his sick neighbours, attend
their funerals, smile at people and show a cheerful face.
Every good act should arise from good intentions and be
done deliberately.[2] Intention is very important in Islam. We
do not do good in order to show off or to win praise. Ibn
Hazm says that anyone who misses his prayers because he is
busy enjoying himself is better than someone who prays
merely for ostentation. The latter is worse than the first
because his prayers are centred on himself, not on God. His
prayers bring him no benefit; he tires himself to no purpose.
Ibn Hazm is well supported in this belief by the Qur'an and
the *Sunna* tradition.[3]

Friendship

Ibn Hazm in many places speaks of friendship. He
approved of friendship between Muslims, Christians and
Jews. All can interrelate and cooperate. He says that one may
trust any religious person, even from a different religion, and
may mistrust a Muslim on occasion. But he reminds us that
such a friendship should not bring harm or oppression to
anyone. We should not praise anyone for a quality which he
does not possess or for doing anything which is not permitted by his religion. A friend should give good advice when-

1. Ibn Hazm, *Risâlat al-Talkhîs*, p .157.
2. Ibn Hazm, *Risâlat al-Talkhîs*, p. 159.
3. al-Makkî, *Qût*, vol. 2, pp. 102ff; Ibn 'Abd al-Barr, *Bakjat al-Majâlis*, vol. 2,
pp. 205f; and Ibn 'Atâ', *Tafsîr*, in *Nusûs Sûfiyya*, p. 108.

ever he is able to.[1]

Promoting the Good and Condemning the Bad

This brings us to the point where we must give a brief account of promoting the good and condemning the bad. This is an important principle in Islam. By promoting the good and condemning the bad we are able to correct our individual behaviour and that of the nation as a whole. It is related to the idea of religious and social freedom. Without expressing our opinions we are like dumb animals led to food and water only according to their master's will. We cannot see our own faults and we need someone else to tell us about them. One man is not capable of seeing everything and doing everything. He should not hesitate to ask advice of others. People should not take criticism personally. Islam gives everyone the right - if they are capable of rational decisions - to play their part in the reform and management of their society. According to Islam, people are not lumps of stone or dumb animals who can live without awareness. To treat them as if they were will ruin any society. Anyone who criticizes and calls for reform and correction is not necessarily perfect himself. If we required perfection of any counsellor we should have to wait forever. In Islam it is sufficient that a man is not committing a sin publicly.

It is reported that Malik Ibn Anas was once asked about something. After he had answered a man said, "O Malik, you do not behave like this yourself." He replied to his critic saying,"O son of my brother, do not copy bad behaviour."[2] Then Ibn Hazm refers to al-Khalîl Ibn Ahmad who said, "Do what

---

1. Ibn Hazm, *al-Akhlâq*, p. 120; also Ibn Hazm, *al-Talkhîs*, p. 174.
2. Ibn Hazm, *al-Akhlâq*, p.258; see also Ahmad Ibn 'Abd al-Rahmân Ibn Qudâma al-Maqdisî, *Mukhtasar Minhâj al-Qâsidîn*, ed. by Shu'ayb al-Arna'ût and Abd al-Qadîr al-Arna'ût, (Damascus, 1398 AH), pp. 123-130.

It is worth mentioning that Sahl Ibn 'Abd Allah al-Tustarî (203 AH; 818 AD) holds that promoting the good and condemning the bad should not be undertaken when the society is dominated by corruption and injustice, see *al-Mu'ârada wa'l Radd 'Alâ Ahl al-Firâq wa Ahl al-Da'âwa fî'l Ahwal*, ed. by Muhammad Kamâl Ja'far, (Cairo, Dâr al-Insân, 1400 AH; 1980 AD), p. 110.

I say and not what I do myself, then you will profit from my experience; learn from my teaching and benefit from it, then my misbehaviour will not cause you harm."[1] Both Malik ibn Anas and al-Khalîl Ibn Ahmad were ascetic and highly moral persons.

Ibn Hazm's moral poetry

Poetry is highly regarded among Arab people. It is the basis of all Arab culture and the record of all their annals. The pre-Islamic Arab people valued their poetry highly. They selected ten poems from all their heritage, wrote them on a scroll and hung them inside the Ka'ba in Makka. This pre-Islamic poetry contained a mass of wisdom in the form of maxims.

In the Qur'an, poetry is always taken as the antithesis of the Qur'an. Muhammad is pictured not as a poet but as a receiver of the Qur'an.[2] Muhammad says about poetry:

Some poetry is wisdom,
Some rhetoric is magic.

The Prophet said that Abû al-'Alâ'' al Hadramî came to him and read out the following verses:

Greet your enemies;
    capture their hearts.
Greet them as you would your family
    and friends. Shoes can be mended.
If someone gossips and spoils your
    friendships you should nobly forgive them
Even if they whisper in front of you,
    you should not cast them out.
It might be better not to know
    what they are saying.

---

1. See Ibn Hazm, *al-Akhlâq*, pp. 258ff; also Ibn Zakariyya ar-Râzî, *as-Sira al-Falsafiyya*, in Badawî, *Rasa'il Falsafiyya*, p. 111.
2. See e.g. Qur'an 36:69; 52:30; 69:41.

> It gives you a chance to pretend
> that they have not said it.[1]

Ibn Qutayba describes poetry in the following terms:

> Poetry is the treasury of the knowledge of the
> Arabs. It is the record of their wisdom and
> the annals of their history and the store of
> their actions and days. It is the great wall
> which surrounds their tradition and her-
> itage...

Ibn 'Abbâs described the following verse as the word of a
prophet:

> Days to come shall reveal to you things that
> you did not know, and news shall reach you
> by means of a man that you did not expect to
> bring it.[2]

There are countless Arabic verses about wisdom and morality and good behaviour. Morality is a central theme in Arabic
poetry. There are many Arab poets famous for their verses
about morality. Among them Ibn Hazm counted the following: Hasan Ibn Thâbit (d.54 AH; 673 AD), Ka'b Ibn Mâlik
(d.50 AH; 670 AD), 'Abd Allah Ibn Rawâha and Sâlih Ibn
'Abd al-Quddûs (d.167 AH; 783 AD).[3] There is a wealth of
wisdom in Arabic literature, particularly in the works by
Sufis, Muslim ascetics.

Ibn Hazm is therefore not unique in this aspect. He followed a well-trodden way, but nevertheless the best of his
poetry is that which bears on morality.

Ibn Hazm's poetry has recently come under the focus of
researchers and scholars. He was a poet no less than he was a

---

1. Ibn Qutayba, *'Uyûn al-Akhbâr*, vol. 2, p. 18.
2. Ibid, and p. 185; see also 'Amr Ibn Bahr al-Jâhiz, *al-Bayân wa'l Tabîn*, ed. by
'Abd al-Salâm Hârûn, (Cairo, Lajnat al-Ta'lif, 1369 A.H.), vol. 1, pp .6ff; and
'Abd al-Karîm al-Nahshalî al-Qirawanîi, *al-Mumti' fî 'Ilm al-Shi'r*, ed. by M.
al-Ka'bi, (Libya and Tunis, 1398 A.H.; 1978 A.D.), pp. 44ff.
3. Ibn Hazm, *Marâtib al-'Ulûm*, pp. 95 and 222.

thinker. The poetry he wrote "stretches from A to Z" in the phrase used by his remarkable student al-Humaydî.[1] Most of the poems still available to us are contained in *The Ring of the Dove*. In his anthology of Andalusian poetry, A. R. Nykl devoted a large section to Ibn Hazm's work. Most of Ibn Hazm's stanzas are on the subject of morality and ethics. It is very clear that the poet is an Imam and moralist.[2]

Ibn Hazm is a poet by nature and by reason of his upbringing. He lived in a country which was renowned for its beauty. He was surrounded by slave-girls, singers, poets. No wonder that he became a great poet! We may only wonder that he could also be a tough debater and serious jurist etc. In his early and formative years he already displayed a poetic sensitivity. We know that he attended a meeting at which an eminent poet was reciting before the prime minister. Ibn Hazm's face betrayed his excitement, the poet noticed his young admirer and wrote out the poem for him, as has already been mentioned.[3]

The daughter of al-Mansûr the Chamberlain, Danâ, suggested some themes to him which she wanted put into verse so that she could sing it.[4] When he was still young and attending classes of poetry in the mosque, he read the long poem by the pre-Islamic Arab poet, Tarafa Ibn al 'Abd, and created a clever variation, supplying a new first half for each line, but preserving the original endings.[5] This is an example of his creativity and of his mastery of classical Arabic.

Ibn Hazm wrote on the subject of poetry, giving his own theories and opinions. His criticism of poetry written before his time shows a wide knowledge of Arabic poetry. For example, he refers to the man of letters and leading critic Qudâmah ibn Ja'far (died 337 AH; 948 AD) and the critic Abû 'Alî al-Hâtimî (died 388 AH; 998 AD).[6] In his view, as he states very clearly, all writing contains some element of truth

1. *Judhwa*, pp. 309f.
2. *Mukhtârât min al-Shi'r al-Andalusi*, (Beirut, Dâr al-'Ilm lil Malain, 1949) pp. 48-59.
3. See above, p. 23.
4. Ibn Hazm, *Tawq*, p. 150.
5. Ibid, pp. 100f.
6. Ibn Hazm, *al-Taqrib*, pp. 204 and 207.

except that of scandalmongers and poets. Poetry requires three things: first, craftsmanship, then natural ability, and thirdly a certain brilliance. Poetry heightens reality. Ibn Hazm recommends that moral and wise poetry should be learnt by heart and other poetry should be avoided and forgotten.[1]

It should be noted that in his book on morality he wrote only two short stanzas, mere verses rather than poetry, being didactic in intention.[2] Here we will give some examples of his verses about wisdom and good conduct from his book on love and lovers. We shall not stop to analyse them, only giving such explanation as may be necessary to understand them. The first stanza we choose to cite here is an admonition against indulging in passion. The second is about obedience to God and the necessity of doing His will in order to win a place in Paradise. The third is about acceptance of God's will. We must however remember that the texts have not come through to us in their original form - scribes have made mistakes in copying, lines have perhaps been lost.

[1]   I say to my soul, "Crystal-clear, not at all obscure.
     The fact is that all people are born to die,
          Being the sons of others who were born to die. Keep yourself well away from anything that may disgrace you;
          Refuse all lusts; lust is the key that opens the gate to disaster.
     I have observed that lust is easy and sweet at the beginning but bitter at the end and hard to negotiate.
          No matter what the pleasure, they are all followed by death, even if a man lived twice as long as Noah, the son of Lamech.
          Do not be tempted by the attractions of this world which will only last for a short time;
          Death always hovering near us, warning us that this world will pass away.
          It is not possible to rise above the attractions of this world unless you start by being greatly attached to it and

---

1. Ibn Hazm, *al-Taqrîb*; also Chejne, *Ibn Hazm*, pp.174f.
2. Ibn Hazm, *Al-Akhlâq*, pp.239f.

have many possessions.

Many have already attempted to rise above the world but their minds are still firmly fixed on it.

A man who renounces hopes and pride in an empty world which has been sucked dry

Is not like one who leaves it when it is like a milch cow with heavy udders.

A man who remembers the things that he shall receive in the world to come, desiring them with a lover's passion and a holy mind,

Is most worthy in Paradise where he shall be furnished with a footstool and canopy.

Anyone who has a certain knowledge of his own desires will see that everything in other people's hands is mean and insignificant.

Anyone who has a sure knowledge of God would never disobey His commandments even if he were given all the kingdoms of the world.

The best of all ways in life is the way of piety and asceticism and the person who chooses this way is wise and the best of people.

But anyone who misses this path will find himself always in trouble

And have no enjoyment from his life, since he has not obeyed the commandment to be pious.

Paradise is for those who march towards it light in spirit and virtuous in character.

They are purged of the soul's grudges and have been granted the privilege of feeling as powerful as kings and as carefree as beggars.

They lived as they wished, and they died as they desired,

And they won a lasting abode which is spacious and blessed.

They disobeyed the call of their bodies in every aspect of pleasure, lit by their spirit which dispelled the darkness of strong lusts.

Were it not for their mortal bodies one might think they were living the life of angels.

O God, grant them the best position and increase

their goodness;
Shower them with mercy wherever they are, and bless them.
If people thought deeply about the reason for their creation, nobody alive would laugh."[1]

[2]   The heart refrained from amusement and pleasure,
        It abstained in its appetite for love and liquor,
        It did not desire to drink wine, nor to hunt gazelle.
        The time had come for the heart to awaken and cast away the covering veils of darkness;
        Its attention was drawn away from all that it usually admired from fear of the day when God will reveal all secrets.
        O soul! Work hard, gird your loins,
        Abandon the empty quest of lust which exhausts you.
        Hasten towards salvation and work to be delivered from passion's anxiety and eternal punishment.
        It is possible that I may be victorious and escape from its flames and hardship.
        You trifler! Time is rushing past,
        Are you not afraid of the pain of destruction?
        After all the admonishments, it should be enough for you just to see
        The amazing invention of Time and what it does to people.
        Abandon the place that provides no reliable pleasures.
        Do not worry about gaining money which is only bringing ridicule upon you; in this world
        No one is so sure-footed that he never slips;
        The world is taken from under his feet and he is left in his misery.
        Anyone who knows God in the real sense will refrain from disobeying Him,
        And the fear of God will be deeply seated in his heart.
        The transitory world is not like the everlasting one,

---

1. Ibn Hazm, *Tawq*, pp. 182f.

And true piety is not like an assumed garment.

A pious man is not like the impious.

True words are different from lies.

Even if we feel secure from God's punishment,

And have no fear of His anger, or of the hellfire which He created

For wrongdoers who tell lies and amass sins,

Obedience to God should still be incumbent on us and help us to beat back the temptations of lust.

We have seen how the world treats its own.

It is like fire making ashes.

How many of those who wear out their bodies in the service of God

And found their pleasure in hardship and trouble such as no one would wish upon himself.

A man working hard to snatch the rosebuds of this world is suddenly snatched by death and loses everything.

How many who achieved their desires, captured good things they longed for,

Then found themselves facing what they always feared.

A man striving his hardest after his desires may in fact be chasing his own ruin.

Sometimes when we see someone at the peak of society, the next moment we see him brought low,

Having lost all his position and ranking,

Like a field of strong wheat, ready for harvesting, suddenly trampled underfoot.

How many there are who nearly kill themselves from longing and lusting after some rapidly disappearing object.

Is this not a wonderful word of warning to the wise, confirming the merit of their way of life?

Hellfire awaits the wrongdoer if he turns aside from the right path.

In the day of final reckoning, Allah will expose him and reveal all his secrets.

As for those whom God has favoured with unending mercy and ever increasing bounties,

But from ignorance they have misused God's gifts in ways that are condemned by the holy books,
Do they not deserve God's punishment on the Day of Resurrection,
To be cast into His wrath and fire?
Give thanks to the Lord God whose gentle might works in us as near as the jugular vein,
Who has sustained all the people who have ever lived in this world, whether Arabs or not,
And praise be to Allah for the favours He bestowed on us, Who is the master of time and its vicissitudes.
He subjected to us earth and heaven and whatever is in the air, the water and stars.
Listen (to Allah) and leave the sinner in his sin, for each of us must carry his own load.[1]

[3]   This mortal world that gives us such lovely things always takes them back again.
We flourish in our prime, then wither and decay.
Can a prudent man wish for anything so shortlived
And always followed by death?
How can eyes enjoy one hour of sleep
When they have observed the transience of everything?
How can the soul settle in a place known to be transitory?
How can it find time on earth to think when it does not know where it will be after death?
How can it feel secure in a stronghold which can be overthrown?
One hour of pleasure leads the ill doer to the eternal fire;
The soul is constantly goaded towards a destination
It gave no thought to. The soul was created for one purpose and yearns after a different one;
It does not know where its true happiness lies,
And chases after the wrong goal. It rushes towards something that will eventually torture it,

---

1. Ibn Hazm, *Tawq*, pp. 189-191.

And has no thought for God's punishment.
It neglects her obligations towards God;
It busies itself with trifling things.
An arrogant ruler goes too far in oppressing his people,
Blind to the fate that awaits his soul, happily working towards its ruin,
Turned away from all that would bring true success.
His soul turns away from God's guidance and chases the elusive pleasures of this world.
Wake up, arrogant people, and hasten back to God!
God has an abode full of unending fire. Do not choose transitory things and lose something that lasts forever.
A man chooses and thereby reveals the strength of his intellect[1]...

The poem continues at some length in this vein. We have translated the meaning as literally as we could, and are well aware that the power of the original is lost in translation. A comparison with Arberry's version[2] show that he has had to take considerable freedoms for the sake of the rhyme. We feel that our version is closer to the meaning and imagery of the original, but Arberry's version is useful in its own way.

Virtue and Vices in *al-Akhlâq wa'l Siyar*

In his slim volume *al-Akhlâq wa'l Siyar*, Ibn Hazm covers most aspects of moral values. He believes that Allah is the source of moral values, not man, whether as an individual or as society. Allah is the creator of mankind and the whole universe and thus He knows best what is good and what is evil

---

1 Ibn Hazm, *Tawq*, pp. 191-194.
2. Ibn Hazm, *Tawq al-Hamâma*, translated into English by A. J. Arberry, under the title *The Ring of the Dove*, (England, Burleigh Press, 1953).
3. See Ibn Hazm, *al-Fisal*, vol. 3, pp. 18ff.
4. See Abû al-Hasan al-Ash'ari, *al-Ibâna An Usûl al-Diyâna*, ed. by Fawqiyya Husayn Muhammad, (Cairo, Dâr al-Ansâr, 1397AH; 1977 AD), vol. 2, pp. 225ff.

Ibn Hazm's Moral Theology 85

for man. It is God alone who lays down the law about what is permitted and what is prohibited *halal* and *haram*, about what is true and false, what is right and wrong.[3] This is the attitude taken by the Sunnites and Ash'arites in Islam,[4] and it is also the attitude of the Christians and the Jews. In recent times Descartes held the same view, expressing it in phrases close to Ibn Hazm's own.[1]

It should be noted that God created things in a way that accords with His commandments and with the human mind. For example, God tells us that fire burns and we should not touch it, and our mind understands and accepts this. God always commands what is good for us, and we understand that this is so. When He speaks of good and evil, we know very well what He means.

Following the same context, masters cannot set up values for themselves that differ from those of their servants, nor can servants set up values for themselves that differ from those of their masters, because moral values are fixed and laid down by God. Man either follows them or he does not. The criterion by which we classify people is their piety and moral commitment, not their wealth or position.[2] People differ not by their moral values but by manners and changing fashions which alter only their outward side. The master may become a servant and have to act accordingly; the servant may become master or even king, not metaphorically but in real terms.[3] The prophets of God came to free the people from the bonds of poverty, humility and ignorance.

Ibn Hazm speaks about the different kinds of virtue. The first kind is religious virtue, meaning the performance of religious duties and obedience to God's commandments. Secondly, there are the intellectual virtues concerned with intellectual abilities such as wisdom and good judgment.[4] Finally, Ibn Hazm comes to the moral virtues such as courage, prudence, justice, chastity and faithfulness. It is clear that he believes that virtue has many faces but stems from one main

---

1. See 'Abd Al-Rahmân Badawî, *al-Akhlâq al-Nazariyya*, (Kuwait, Wakâlit al-Matbû'ât, 1975), pp. 94f.
2. See Qur'an 49:13.
3. See Ibn Hazm, *al-Akhaq*, p. 223.
4. Ibid.

virtue, which in his view is disciplining one's soul to be obedient to God's command. It has already been said that Ibn Hazm followed Aristotle in his definition of virtue. Virtue is a medium course between two vices. For example, courage is the medium course between fear and rashness. It helps the fighter to stand in the face of danger, not to run away but also not to throw himself into the line of fire.[1] Aristotle's theory of the middle course is not applicable to evil matters, such as theft, murder, envy, treason etc., since these things are evil in themselves and should be absolutely shunned. Aristotle explains elsewhere the meaning of the middle course, saying that it is the midpoint between extreme and shortfall. For example, generosity is the moderate action, extravagance and miserliness are the evil extremes.[2]

Ibn Hazm used Aristotelian terms in his writings about morality but the concept of the middle course was not created by Aristotle but was current long before his time among the Greek poets.[3] It should be noted that Islam places a high value on the moderate way; it is called "the moderate religion" and its people "the middle nation".[4]

Ibn Hazm lays emphasis on the intention in both one's words and one's deeds. Intention is an important matter in Muslim morality. (Works are judged by intention, etc.)[5] Outward appearances, hypocrisy, social manners and etiquette are valueless without a foundation of good intentions.

While Ibn Hazm believed in divine destiny, *Qadâ'* and *Qadar*, he also believed that virtues can be taught and acquired through practice. Man has the ability to diagnose the sickness of his soul and seek the remedy. Vices can also be transmitted by example.[6] Ibn Hazm is in line with all

---

1. Ibid.
2. See Aristotle, *The Nicomachean Ethics*, translated by J. E. C. Welldon, (London, Macmillan and Co., 1892), pp. 47f; also Abû al-Walîd Ibn Rushd, *Talkhîs al-Khatâba*, ed. by Muhammad Sâlim Sâlim, (Cairo, al-Majlis al-A'lâ lil Shi'ûn al-Islâmiyya, 1387 A.H.; 1967 A.D.), p. 298.
3. Badawî, *al-Akhlâq al-'Amalilyya*, p. 147.
4. See Qur'an 2:143.
5. See al-Makki, *Qût*, vol. 2, pp. 158.
6. Ibn Hazm, *al-Akhlâq*, p. 200.

moralists in this belief.[1] He values virtues and ethical principles, and calls for goodness and good behaviour. He stresses
the virtue of truthfulness which should imbue all our life and
our activities. We should be truthful in what we say, what we
do and what we think, truthful with others and with ourselves. The scholar and scientist should be truthful in his
researches and honest in revealing what he knows.[2]

The vice of Telling Lies

Telling lies is the thing that Ibn Hazm most abhors. It is
the source of disbelief in God Himself. It is the fountainhead
of other vices and sicknesses.[3] Here Ibn Hazm does not tell
us specifically about the cause of lying and the purpose of
the liar. However, his phrase "the liar's psyche is valueless"
may reflect the liar's impulses and imply that his lying is an
attempt to dispel the humiliation of his self, a fruitless
attempt to build up his own ego. The liar believes that by
telling lies he may justify his own existence and bring benefit
to his soul.[4]

The Qur'an mentions some matters related to the telling
of lies such as arrogance, confusion, embellishment of the
truth, perjury and false oaths, gossiping, backbiting, sowing
dissension. The liar is psychologically weak and tries to
appear otherwise. The liar cannot change the true facts, he
can only confuse people about them and try to prevent them
from obtaining them. The Qur'an compares the effect of
telling lies with a layer of tar covering the heart and the

---

1. See Ibn Qutayba, *'Uyûn*, vol. 2, pp. 1ff; al-Ghazzâlî, *Ihyâ*, vol. 8, pp. 98ff;
see also R. Levy, *The Social Structure of Islam*, (Cambridge, Cambridge University Press, 1969), p. 217; and al-Kashani, *al-Haqâ'iq Fî Mahâsin al-Akhlâq*,
ed. by Ibrâhîm al-Mabanjî, (Beirut, Dâr al-Kitâb al-'Arabî, 1399 A.H.; 1979
A.D.) pp .56ff.
2. See Ibn Hazm, *al-Akhlâq*, pp. 188f; Ibn Hazm, *Tawq*, pp. 85f; and Ibn Hazm,
Marâtib al-'Ulûm, pp. 233 and 239.
3. Ibn Hazm, *al-Akhlâq*, p. 188; and Ibn Hazm, *Tawq*, p. 86.
4. Ibn Hazm, *al-Akhlâq*, p. 188; see also Abû Bakr al-Râzî, *Kitâb al-Tîbb al
Rûhânî* in Badawî, *Rasâ'il Falsafiyya*, pp. 56-59; and Kai Ka'us Ibn Iskandar,
A Mirror for Princes (The Qabus Nama), translated from the Persian by R.
Levy, (London, The Cresset Press, 1951), p. 35.

mind,[1] and in the *Hadith* the telling of a lie starts like one
drop of black ink which then spreads and grows until it covers everything. Thus a liar deserves eternal punishment.[2]

Telling lies is a sickness which has no medicine. It leads
to all vices and inhibits all virtues. The Prophet Muhammad,
peace be upon him, commands us not to talk too much
because it can lead to nonsense and lying. The sharpest
weapon held by a liar is his tongue. Islam does not value
empty words that are not backed up by works.

> O you who believe, why do you say what you
> do not do. It is a great sin in the eyes of Allah
> that you do not do what you say. (Qur'an
> 61:3)

> And do not say, as to what your tongues false-
> ly describe, 'This is lawful, and this is forbid-
> den', so that you may forge against God false-
> hood; surely those who forge against God
> falsehood shall not prosper. (Qur'an 16:116)

About the hypocrites God says that they say

> ...with their mouths that which never was in
> their hearts; and God knows very well the
> things they hide. (Qur'an 3:167)

> When the hypocrites come to thee they say,
> 'We bear witness that thou art indeed the
> Messenger of God.' And God knows that thou
> art indeed His Messenger, and God bears wit-
> ness that the hypocrites are truly liars ...
> When thou seest them, their bodies please
> thee; but when they speak, thou listenest to
> their speech, and it is as they were propped-
> up timbers. (Qur'an 63:1-3)

---

1. See Qur'an e.g. 2:8-20, 204-206; 3:78; 47:30; 63:1-5; 66:116; 83:14.
2. See Abû al-Fidâ' Ibn Kathîr, *Mukhtasar Tafsîr*, ed. by Muhammad 'Alî al-
Sâbunî, (Beirut, Dâr al-Qur'an al-Karîm, 1402 A.H.; 1981 A.D.), vol. 3, p. 615.

Talking too much may make a man feel that he has achieved something and has no need to act.

The Remedy for Vices

Like all moralists, Ibn Hazm prescribes the method of getting rid of all our vices and diseases. The best and most effective way is to do the opposite of each vice and sickness and to persevere until the opposite becomes habitual. The medicine for arrogance is to humble oneself, to suppress one's pride, to force it to obey you and to go the right way, to consider those who behave better than you, so that you may feel humble.[1] Ibn Hazm makes an impassioned plea for the retention of "promoting the good and condemning the bad". Through this we can purify ourselves and our society of all kinds of diseases. He warns against the abandoning of this institution. Someone may say, "I am not perfect myself so I cannot advise anyone about morality." Ibn Hazm sees this as a dangerous and misleading notion. Satan would be happy if everyone thought like this, since nobody is perfect, nobody is without blemish, and that would leave nobody to preach and society would collapse into vice.[2] We may compare it with a society suffering from the plague. Physicians suffer along with their patients but they continue to attempt to treat them. In fact, Islam does not compromise on the principle of "promoting the good condemning the bad", because it is important to correct ourselves and others, without criticizing them unkindly. No one can change without advice and encouragement. Without any criticism they would persevere in wrongdoing and entice others to follow their bad example. Criticism should be wise and well-intentioned.

Ibn Hazm writes also about envy and grudging. This is a sickness of the soul which disturbs the life of an individual

---

1. See Ibn Hazm, *al-Akhlâq*, p. 188; also Badawî, *Rasâ'il Falsafiyya*, pp. 114, 145, 231; and al-Maqdisî, *Mukhtasar Minhâj*, pp.151ff.1. See Ibn Hazm, *al-Akhlâq*, p.188; also Badawî, *Rasâ'il Falsafiyya*, pp. 114, 145, 231; and al-Maqdisî, *Mukhtasar Minhâj*, pp. 151ff.
2. Ibn Hazm, *al-Akhlâq*, pp. 86ff and 113ff; also al-Râzî, *al-Tîbb al-Rûhânî*, pp. 56-59; and al-Mubashshir Ibn Fâtik, *Mukhtâr al-Hikam*, p. 198.

and society as a whole. It is like an epidemic of the plague. When a society suffers from this psychological disease its foundations are shaken, the people are divided, and the well-being of the whole nation is affected. Envy, as defined by Ibn al-Haytham, is the pain felt when you see that another person has something good or good moral qualities, and you do your utmost to destroy his possessions or his qualities.[1]

It is said that envy was the first sin committed in heaven when Satan envied Adam. It was the first sin committed on earth when Cain envied Abel and killed him.

Yahyâ Ibn Khâlid says that an envious person is a mean enemy who cannot fulfil his wicked desire except by wishing harm on others. Al-Ahnaf ibn Qays says that a bored person has no friends, a liar never keeps his word, an envious person can never relax, the miser has no nobility, and the corrupt person has no dignity.[2]

Here Ibn Hazm says:

> Ruthlessness arises from covetousness, and covetousness arises from envy. Envy arises from desire, and desire arises from injustice, greed and ignorance.[3]

Having analysed the different kinds of love and the motive of lovers, Ibn Hazm talks at length about covetousness and desire, saying:

> It is the cause of all kinds of cares, even those which concern one's fortune and social position. Thus it may be observed that a man who sees the death of his neighbour or of his maternal uncle, his friend, his cousin, his great-uncle, his nephew, his maternal grandfather or his grandson, having no claim on

---

1. See Badawî, *Dirâsât wa Nusûs fi'l Falsafa*, p.106; also Ibn Rushd, *Talkhîs al-Khatâba*, pp .391f.
2. Ibn Qutayba, *'Uyûn*, vol. 2, p. 10.
3. *al-Akhlâq*, pp. 172f; also Ibn Abî al-Hadîd, *Sharh Nahj al-Balagha*, ed. by Muhammad Abû al-Fadl Ibrâhîm, (Cairo, al-Halabi, 1387 AH; 1967 AD) vol. 11, pp. 198ff.

their property, does not fret because it has
escaped him, however large and considerable
their fortunes might be, because he had no
expectation of them. But as soon as a distant
member of his father's family dies, or one of
his remotest clients, he begins to covet their
belongings. And with the coveting comes
crowding in anxiety, regret, anger and great
sorrow if some tiny part of their fortune
escapes him. It is the same with one's position
in society: a man who belongs to the lowest
social class does not fret if he is not consulted
when someone else is given charge of the
affairs of the land. He does not fret if someone else is promoted or demoted. But as soon
as he begins to feel an ambition to better himself, it provokes so much worry, anxiety and
anger that it could make him lose his soul, his
world and his position in the hereafter. Thus
covetousness is the cause of all humiliation
and every kind of anxiety. It is a wicked and
despicable kind of behaviour. The opposite of
covetousness is disinterest. This is a virtuous
quality which combines courage, generosity,
justice and intelligence.[1]

Ibn Hazm goes on to say:

Greed is a kind of covetousness which would
like to possess everything; it is insatiable and
ever increasing in its demands. If there were
no such thing as covetousness, nobody would
ever humiliate anybody else. Abû Bakr Ibn al-
Fayyâd has told me that 'Uthmân Ibn
Muhâmis [died 356 AH, 966 AD] inscribed
upon the door of his house in Ecija [in Seville]
'Uthmân covets nothing'.[2]

1. *al-Akhlâq*, p. 172.
2. Ibid, p. 173.

Ibn Hazm moreover makes the following remarks about the psychology of the envious:

> Something peculiar about envy is when you hear a jealous person say, when someone has done original work in some branch of science, 'What a silly person! Nobody has ever put forward that hypothesis before and nobody has ever believed that.' But if the same person hears someone expound an idea which is not new, he exclaims, 'What a silly person! This is not a new idea!' This sort of person is harmful because he is bent on obstructing the path of knowledge and turning people away from it in order to increase the number of his own sort, the ignorant.[1]

Ibn Hazm himself, like all great scholars in history, suffered from envy and thus was subjected to many accusations and severe attacks; his biographer and rival Ibn Hayyân was quite aware of this fact.[2]

Within the same context it is interesting to refer to al-Jâhiz who was greatly affected by and concerned about envy. Al-Jâhiz attacked envy and particularly criticized people who claimed to be scholars without justification. They mimicked the gestures, attitudes, tones and costume of real scholars, hoping to be taken for them. These false scholars won the hearts of a credulous public and ignorant rulers. The enemies of the real scholars use the pseudo-scholars as a means of attacking them. The false scholars attack the real ones bitterly and incite others to join in the attack, taking their strength from the ignorance of the public and the king's desire not to have to change his ways.[3]

Again, the false scholars like to occupy high positions and to have power over the people. The love of power always

1. Ibid, p. 228.
2. Yaqût, *Irshâd*, vol. 12, pp. 1237ff; Ibn Hazm, *Risâla fî Fadl al-Andalus* in al-Maqqâriî, *Nafh*, vol. 2, pp. 166ff.
3. See Abû 'Uthmân 'Amru Ibn Bahr al-Jâhiz, *Majmu'at Rasâ'il*, (Beirut, Dâr al-Nahda al-Hadîtha, 1972), pp. 9-18.

brings ruin, at every time and in every society. No one is safe from this human inclination.

Al-Jâhiz himself suffered from envy, to the extent that he would sometimes publish his books anonymously so that he could have a fairer hearing.[1]

In the view of al-Jâhiz, dislike may pass away but envy never. You can share your possessions and thereby win your enemies over as friends, but the envious would only be content with all your possessions. Every religion attacks envy and calls on people to avoid being envious. The envious man can be recognized by his facial expression, particularly his eyes when they see the object of his envy.[2]

In order to have a full picture of the nature and effect of envy and also to understand Ibn Hazm's analysis in the context of his ancestors, reference should be made to Abû Bakr Muhammad Ibn Zakariyya al-Râzî (died 313 AH, 925 AD) who says about envy that it is one of the most pernicious diseases of the soul, arising from miserliness and covetousness. It is a characteristic of the most evil person, one who by his nature takes pleasure in doing harm to others and is annoyed by their good fortune, even if they do him no harm.[3]

Al-Râzî sees that envy is worse than miserliness. The miser merely does not give anything away from his own possessions, but the envious does not like anyone to have anything good, from himself or anyone else, and this is a psychological disease which is greatly harmful.[4]

The envious person is sad when someone has good fortune. In this he is different from an enemy who dislikes a person, having a reason to dislike him which may be cleared up so that he becomes a friend. But the envious person cannot be reconciled. We have touched on this point elsewhere. An envious person deserves the curse and wrath of God and His people. This is because he is criticising God's wisdom in granting good fortune to others. The people, too, hate him

---

1. Ibid; see also al-Makkî, *Qût*, vol. 1, pp. 139ff and 164ff; Ibn 'Abd al-Barr, *Bahjat*, vol. 1, pp.460ff; and *al-Kâshânî, al-Haqâ'iq*, pp. 76ff.
2. al-Jâhiz, *Risâlat al-'Adâwa wa'l Hasad*, in *Majmu'ât Rasâ'il*, pp.364f; also Ibn al-'Arabî, *al-Futûhât*, vol. 2, pp. 195f.
3. See *al-Tîbb al-Rûhânî*, pp. 48-54.
4. Ibid.

because he does them harm. He was not harmed by the one
he envied; he was not deprived.

The cure for envy is to imagine that the object of one's
envy lies far away, perhaps in China or India, and is of no
concern to oneself.

Envy occurs frequently between neighbours, acquaintances and relations. We find that when a new ruler comes
from outside, the people feel no envy, but they do if one rises
to power from their own number. The reason is the people's
self-interest and egotism and desire to rank higher than the
others in achieving power or other things. When they see
someone rise to power who was like themselves the day
before, they become sorrowful and are dissatisfied with him
as a ruler, however well he treats them. They strive constantly
to unseat him from the position that they wanted for themselves. However, if a stranger comes whose history is
unknown to them, they do not have these feelings towards
him. The envious person does not behave fairly towards the
object of his envy because the latter does not hinder him in
any way. The good fortune which fell to the envied person
was not deserved by the envious one and would not have
fallen to his lot.

In fact, the envious are often lazy and have not made the
effort to achieve the heights that they now see another take
into possession. There is no pleasure in envy except maybe a
very slight pleasure. It harms soul and body; it occupies the
soul when it could have been engaged in fruitful contemplation; it brings no profit to the body, only sadness, sorrow,
anxiety, insomnia and grudging anger. It takes away one's
appetite, one's complexion grows pale, one's features become
ugly, one's mood becomes sour.

The Way How to Cure Envy

To get rid of envy, the envious person should remember
that what he imagined about the object of his envy and the
life he leads and the pleasures he enjoys are probably distort-
ed. Man desires things always and thinks that those who
have them are happy, riding the crest of pleasure's wave.

When he does achieve it, however, he is only happy for a moment before he thinks of the next thing to covet. The position which he longed for yesterday no longer seems worth wanting. The same happens when he achieves the next higher position; he is never happy, since he spends all his time planning his next ascent.

It is wrong to think that those who enjoy wealth and pleasure are commensurately happy. Those who have everything in the world lose the ability to enjoy them. They are too familiar with the pleasures. The good things in their hands which other people desire become the things that they regard as day-to-day essentials. The pleasure that they take is no greater than anyone takes in what he has. This is because they are always belittling what they have and longing for more; they are always tense and ambitious and have less relaxation than those below them.

If a thoughtful man remembers all this, and does not chase after every whim, he will know that happiness and relaxation is within his grasp; he only has to be happy with what he already has. Sufficient is enough.[1]

It is useful to add some points in the context of the cure for envy. A prosperous person who attracts envy should not encourage the development of envy by spending extravagantly. He should be moderate in his life-style. He should not be arrogant towards the people; he should try to soften their hearts so that they feel no grudge or envy. He should be charitable towards the needy and give alms from his wealth. This will safeguard him against envy and give him the strength to withstand misfortune. He should pray, invoking God's name and seeking His assistance and protection. There are certain formulae of supplication in the Qur'an and *hadiths* which are designed to protect belongings. If he is a great scholar he should not boast of the fact; he should be humble, and cultivate the goodwill of his fellow-scholars. Envy between scholars is proverbial.

If someone is beautiful or handsome, he or she should not boast of it, but always give thanks to God for it and seek His protection.

---

1. See *al-Ṭibb al-Rūhānî*, pp. 48-54.

In this context it is worth noting that the word *hasad* expressing envy also signifies the evil eye, *al-'Ayn*. The belief in its bad effect is primeval and universal. The word "eye" in this sense has its equivalent in every written language, living or dead. According to Bacon, the belief in the power of working evil by a glance upon any object is common in all countries and societies. In the Muslim tradition, envy and the evil eye are synonymous. The Prophet Muhammad says that the evil eye can put a camel in the cooking-pot and a boy into the grave. The evil eye can make the animal sicken and die, can put a blight on a crop, make a cow lose her milk, make an accident happen, all because an object has been spitefully and malignantly looked at by someone.

This belief is still current among the Muslims, Jews and Hindus and in some parts of Europe and America. To the Muslims it is a matter of fact, and envy or the evil eye is also connected with black magic. The Qur'an forbids the learning of magic and provides the means of protection against it.

There are certain Qur'anic verses and *suras* and prophetic prayers which can be read to diffuse the effect of magic or the evil eye upon a sufferer.

Freedom

Religions may seem to infringe our liberty by imposing duties and restraints upon us. However, the fact is that religions protect our freedom by the institution of justice and also release us from the captivity of fear, superstition and ancestral traditions. Islam specifically came to liberate man from being a slave to stones and to humans who had been set up in authority by other mere humans. Islam established freedom in a broad sense and in a narrow, precise sense. Religious duties and the system of punishment in Islam all serve to protect the individual's freedom, rather than be a bondage on him.

It should be pointed out that Islam does not forbid slavery, but we must remember that neither does it encourage slavery. It rather discourages it and tries by all possible means to eradicate the practice. When Islam came, slavery was a universal institution. It was one of the pillars of society at the time.[1] Islam does not try to disrupt society. Islam does not forbid something that may be an essential part of a distant society which may yet embrace Islam.

Islam acknowledges the full humanity of slaves, treats them as men, commands the master to regard them as his brothers in religion. The slave can reach Paradise through his works and deeds. Among Muslims, slaves and slave-girls rose high in politics, literature and even administration. Ibn Hazm spoke of his slave-girls with admiration and respect. When you read his writings about them you find no hint of disparagement.

The Qur'an speaks of freedom, but the word *hurriyya* ("freedom"), as such, does not occur in the Qur'an or the *hadith* or in Ibn Hazm's book. In the Qur'an we find mentions of free man, free woman, oppression - it attacks oppression in the strongest terms, saying that people should be free, even to the extent of choosing their own religion.[2] Man has the freedom of arguing, even against God Himself in the hereafter,[3] even against the Caliph or head of state.[4] He can object and fear no torture or imprisonment.

The Qur'an also speaks of prison in the context of Joseph in Egypt; speaks of legal punishments, corporal and verbal; of exile and evacuation. In this context, Franz Rosenthal refers to the Qur'anic verse (12:32ff) about Joseph and assumes that the word used for prison was a later insertion. This cannot be the case. At the time of Ibn Hazm and before, there were various prisons for various kinds of criminals. Abû Qâsim ibn Ridwân refers to Ibn Hazm who says that respectable offenders should be housed separately from dangerous criminals, and women should also have a separate prison. Ideally, the prisons for respectable female offenders should also be separate from those for women charged with infamous crimes. He was giving consideration to the psychology of the prisoners; their social class would make a differ-

1. See M. al-Shak'a, *Islâm bilâ Madhâbib*, pp. 70ff.
2. See Qur'an e.g. 2:256; 10:99; 24:33.
3. See Qur'an 4:109; 16:111; 22:8.
4. See Qur'an, 58:1; also Ibn Abî al-Hadîd, *Sharh Nahj al-Balâgha*, vol. 12, p. 29.

ence to the effect prison would have on them.[1]

Ibn Hazm speaks of freedom but in its moral sense. He speaks elsewhere of predestination. He says that people have often misunderstood the common words *qadâ'* and *qadar* and confused them. They have wrongly understood them to mean bondage. Ibn Hazm explains that in the Qur'an *qadâ'* means "he commanded" and also "he told or reported" and also "he wishes". *Qadar* in Arabic means to arrange or classify, to mould to a certain shape, for example in the Qur'an it says, "God has created the earth and arranged the substances in it."[2] Ibn Hazm says that *qadar* means that God arranges everything and gives order to everything and passes judgment on its correct value and nature. According to him, God decides everything and establishes it in a way that cannot be changed. God has a book showing He is merciful and just; He never asks people to do anything beyond their capabilities. Anyone who claims that they can do anything beyond God's design or will is a transgressor. We should believe in the absolute justice of God in all aspects of our life. The things that seem to be unjust are not so; it is our understanding that is limited. God's justice and goodness are manifest in everything but more clearly sometimes than others. There is no defect in God's creation. We believe that everything comes from God though we should feel responsible for our own faults. We should not blame God for our failures and resultant misfortunes.[3] God also laid down that good comes of good deeds, bad of bad deeds. If we fail to do a good deed, we are doing evil, and if we do a bad deed, we have let slip the chance to do good. Even omission counts as an action. Everything shall be weighed by God and we shall be rewarded or punished accordingly. No reward comes without work just as fruit cannot be enjoyed without effort. Ibn Hazm therefore urges us to work, and God guarantees to provide guidance and assistance if we are sincere in our efforts.

He noticed that some people act badly and try to justify it by saying it was God's will, predestined, but when they are

---

1. See F. Rosenthal, *The Muslim Concept of Freedom*, pp. 58f and 75.
2. See Qur'an 10:41.
3. Ibn Hazm, *al-Fisal*, vol. 3, pp. 39f.

commanded to do good they are lazy and avoid it. This makes it seem that predestination encourages only bad deeds.[1]

There is an obvious problem here, and Ibn Hazm faces up to it. If God creates everything, how can man be responsible for his own sins, which are part of creation? In Ibn Hazm's view, when a man desires to act wrongly and to use his God-given body or property for bad purposes, that is his choice, his fault, and he must reap the consequences. Here Ibn Hazm is employing the theory of *kasb* ", acquisition, gaining, deserving".[2]

When God created people, He determined the span of their years, and this cannot be changed. He determined the span of each individual life and advises against harmful things which might shorten it. Ibn Hazm refers to some verses of the Qur'an which seem paradoxical, seeing no contradiction with what God said about predestination and the freedom of man.

In his book *The Philosophy of the Kalam*, Wolfson, without attempting to consider the whole passage and the wider dimensions of this problem, assumes that the Qur'an is contradictory here. What has horrified me personally is his translation of the Qur'anic verse[3]

> His is the kingdom of the heavens and the earth; He maketh alive and killeth.

It should be translated more precisely

> "He gives life and He makes to die."

God's decision is unchangeable.

Ibn Hazm states that God gives man ability and will. If a

---

1. Ibn Hazm, *al-Fisal*, vol. 3, pp. 41-72; see also Ibrâhîm Ibn Muhammad al-Bayhaqî, *al-Mahâsin wa'l Masâwi'*, pp. 286ff.
2. Ibid; also Abû al-Hasan al-Ash'arî, *al-Ibâna* , vol. 2, pp. 23f and 271; and Abû Hâmid al-Ghazzâlî, *Ihyâ'*, vol. 9, pp.205ff.
3. Harry Auslryn Wolfson, *The Philosophy of the Kalam*, (U.S.A., Harvard University Press, 1976), p. 600.

man wills to do something and has the ability to do it and he does it, then he is responsible for his action. It is enough here to say that capability is matched by personal responsibility. In his view, God creates the capability of each individual and His guidance enables us to do good. Some are good by nature and others bad by nature. No one can change his nature.[1]

In *al-Fisal*, Ibn Hazm reviewed the theories of Muslim theologians about predestination but we need not say more about this here. It is enough to say that everything is in the hands of God and man is a free and responsible being.

---

3. Ibn Hazm, *al-Fisal*, vol. 3, pp.41-72.

CHAPTER III

AL-AKHLAQ WA'L-SIYAR: A TEXTUAL STUDY

Title, Date, Circulation

The author provides a short introduction from which we may gain certain pieces of information which are worth emphasizing. First, Ibn Hazm's own term for his work is "book" not "essay". Despite this, many historians and most of the manuscript scribes refer to it as an "essay". Secondly, Ibn Hazm makes it clear that this book is the result of a lifetime of traumatic experience and the resultant wisdom. He tells us that he prefers to spend his time setting down his experiences, rather than devoting himself to any common pastime or pleasure. His purpose in writing is to bring benefit to others rather than to reap any reward for himself, except for such reward as may come from God. His wish is to help his fellows to correct their corrupt morality and to heal the sickness of their souls.

Nowhere in the book is a specific date given for its composition. We must bear in mind the author's statement that he has spent most of his lifetime recording his experiences. The book as it stands must have been written towards the end of his life, and gathers together the accumulated wisdom of this eventful life. There is no reference at all to Ibn Hazm's al-Akhlâq in any of his other works. However we may be fairly confident that Ibn Hazm began to plan this book very much earlier, as soon as he had completed The Ring of the Dove. The latter book faithfully mirrors the society of his time, with special reference to the behaviour of lovers, and contains passages on the subject of morality and psychology. There is a clear natural relationship between this book of his youth and the book of his mature years.

In this book, Ibn Hazm also describes the decay and corruption of contemporary morality, and offers remedies based on psychology and ethics. We may venture to say that the book of his mature years is a supplement to the earlier work. Al-Akhlâq, "morality" also describes "the sickness of souls and the sad state of morality" and offers remedies. This was at a time when contemporary society wallowed in uncontrolled pleasure, and there was a spate of feuds, disputes and murders. If we may say that *The Ring of the Dove* paints a picture of society as it was, warts and all, we may say that Ibn Hazm's book *On Morality* is a call for reform and correction, both in the individual and in society as a whole.

Unless we know that we are sick and the nature of our sickness, we cannot do anything about it. Unless we are told the means of healing we cannot become better. And above all, unless we have the will to change ourselves, nothing can be done. This is precisely what God says in the Holy Qur'an: God never changes a person's situation unless that person changes within himself. (Qur'an 13:11)

It seems to us that Ibn Hazm's book was not known to his students in the complete form that we have it. We say this because not one of his intimate students referred to it. The first reference is in Ibn Bassâm (died 542 AH, 1147 AD). The latter had his information from a lost book written by a contemporary of Ibn Hazm, Ibn Hayyân. The title appears in the source as *"Akhlâq al nafs"*.[1] This form of the title is unique, although it agrees substantially with the other versions of the title that we have. The first Syrian historian to refer to this book is Yâqût (died 626 AH, 1228 AD) and he takes the title from Ibn Bassâm in the same form, *Akhlâq al-nafs*.[2] It is not clear whether Yâqût actually read the book or only quoted the title. If he read the book, it must have already been in circulation in the eastern part of the Muslim world at this time. Later, Al-Dhahabî (died 748 AH, 1347 AD) also refers to Ibn Hazm's book, but his description of it is somewhat confusing. He states that the book was in two volumes,[3] and this would seem to indicate that al-Dhahabî read the actual work, whereas in fact all the manuscripts have it as a single volume. The book is not of such a length as to require division into two volumes. There is the possibility that a second volume has been completely lost, or at least some part of it, as is the case

---

1. *al-Dhakhîra*, part 1, vol. 1, pp. 171ff.
2. *Irshâd*, vol. 12, p. 252.
3. See *Siyar*, p. 35.

with his book *The Ring of the Dove*. The title as it appears in Al-Dhahabî is different from the one mentioned above, and is closer to the title on the manuscripts: *Al Siyar wa'l Akhlâq*,[1] and it is clear that Al-Dhahabî was not copying Ibn Bassâm's reference to it.

Another historian, Al-Maqqarî (died 1021 AH, 1632 AD), made mention of the book, but in the exact form used by Ibn Bassâm.[2] Clearly, this line of references goes back unbroken to the first mention in the lost book of Ibn Hayyân. None of Ibn Hazm's other biographers or any other historian mentioned the book at all. The reason is obvious. It was written so late in his life that it was not available to the public - or even to his students - during his lifetime.

Manuscripts and Editions

It is not our aim here to give a full, detailed description of the various manuscripts. Our purpose is to provide a translation, not an edition. However it is useful to give a brief account of the surviving manuscripts.

Ibn Hazm's book was discovered among other works by him in Shahîd 'Alî's library in Turkey, no. 2704. The title given in this manuscript is *Risâla Fî Mudâwât al-Nufûs*. It was published by Ihsân 'Abbâs under the title *Risâla fî Mudâwât al-Nufûs wa Tahdhîb al-Akhlâq wa'l-zuhd fî'l-Radhâ'il* (Cairo, 1954). There is another manuscript which was discovered by UNESCO in 1963, dated in the 5th Century AH, i.e. shortly after Ibn Hazm's death, which makes it the oldest one available to us. This manuscript was used by Nada Tomiche in editing the text when she translated it into French.

The first edition of Ibn Hazm's book to be published in a printed form appeared in Cairo in 1395 AH (1908 AD) bearing the title *Al Akhlâq wa'l Siyar*. The publisher was al-Sa'âda. It filled 106 medium-sized pages. The editor was Ahmad 'Umar al-Mahamasânî. This is a good critical edition with only one editorial mistake, noticed by Asín when he translat-

---

1. Ibid.
2. See *Nafh*, vol. 2, p. 79.

ed it into Spanish. The editor wrote a short introduction to the book giving a concise explanation of difficult words and phrases in the text. He borrowed from the manuscript the division of the book into chapters and sections. We are indebted to Al-Mahamasânî for rescuing this great work from oblivion. He also deserves our gratitude for his conscientious editing of the text.

Another edition seems to have appeared soon after; no date is given but al-Tâhir Makkî thinks that 1912 is probable.[1] This time the editor was a librarian and bookseller called Muhammad Effendi Adham. His edition appeared in Cairo, with 78 pages, quarto. This is a poor and confusing edition. The book is given two titles, one on the title-page and one at the head of the text. The first title runs *Falsafat al-Akhlâq al-Musammâh Mudâwât al-Nufûs wa Tahdhîb al-Akhlâq wa'l-Bu'd 'An al-Radhâ'il, The Philosophy of Ethics, entitled the Healing of the Soul, the Purification of Morals and the Cleansing of Vices*. The title agrees with that given by Assitani's manuscript. The second title is *Mudâwât al-Nufûs wa Tahdhîb al-Akhlâq wa'l-Zuhd fî'l-Radhâ'il, The Healing of Souls, the Purification of Souls and the Cleansing of Vices*. It must also be said that this edition is inaccurate, not at all faithful to the original text.

Another edition was published in Alexandria by 'Alî Effendi al-Hattâb. Again, no date is given but it seems to have appeared shortly after the first two. This time, the editor included with it a short work on morality by the modern Egyptian scholar Qâsim Amîn, and wrote a short introduction of his own praising Ibn Hazm and his work. He also displayed great enthusiasm for Qâsim Amîn, ranking him as Ibn Hazm's equal in the field of morality.

The fourth edition was published in Alexandria in 1913 by al-Jamâliyya and also included Qâsim's essay, under the title *Kalimât fî'l Akhlâq, Words on Morality* Ihsân 'Abbâs refers to another edition, which makes it the fifth. This appeared in 1394 AH, 1906 AD.[2] We have not been able to find this edition. Ihsân himself published an edition under the title *Risâla fî Mudâwât al-Nufûs wa Tahdhîb al-Akhlâq etc., The Heal-*

1. See Ibn Hazm, *al-Akhlâq*, editor's introduction, p. 58.
2. See Ihsân 'Abbâs's introduction to Ibn Hazm, *al-Akhlâq*, pp. *ba'* and *Jim*.

ing of Souls, the Purification of Morals, etc.[1] This title agrees with the edition of Muhammad Effendi Adham. Ihsân's edition uses Assitani's manuscript and seems to pay no attention to the previous editions of the book. This has resulted in some serious errors.

Finally, in 1401 AH, 1981 AD, al-Tâhir Makkî produced his critical edition of Ibn Hazm's book with a lengthy introduction about the author and the text.[2] We have found Makkî's introduction very useful, especially his references to Asín. Makkî himself showed great interest in Ibn Hazm and his works. Within the space of a few years he published several works about him; he translated from Spanish Asín's first introductory volume to his translation of *al-Fisal*.[3] The title page of Makkî's edition is *al-Akhlâq wa'l Siyar Fî Mudâwât al-Nufûs*. The editor provides explanatory notes and information about the historical figures mentioned in the book, and shows some concern for the theological, political and juridical issues. There is no indication that Makkî consulted more than one manuscript. It is important to note that he used the UNESCO manuscript discovered in Egypt.

Makkî mentioned that the book had been translated into French by someone more expert in French than Arabic. He gives no examples to support this condemnation, and does not name Nada here. In another place he does name Nada, saying that she had published a French translation with an introduction in 1961 in Lebanon, but he had not been able to obtain a copy.[4] Nada's translation is in fact the one published by UNESCO, and in our opinion it is a good piece of work, though it contains some editorial mistakes [see e.g. pp 131, 187].

This series of editions produced during the present century and the number of articles written on Ibn Hazm and his work show the importance and continuing relevance of this text.

---

1. Ihsân 'Abbâs published this *Risâla* together with some other essays by Ibn Hazm under the title *Rasâ'il Ibn Hazm al-Andalusi, al-Majmû'a al-Ulâ*, (Cairo, al-Khânjjî, Baghdad, al-Muthanna, 1954).
2. (Cairo, Dâr al-Ma'ârif, 1401 AH; 1981 AD).
3. Makkî's introduction to Ibn Hazm's *al-Akhlâq*, pp. 65ff.
4. Ibid, pp. 67ff..

Al-Akhlâq wa'l-Siyar in other languages, translations and editions:

1. Spanish Translation

The first translation of *al-Akhlâq wa'l-Siyar* into a European language was made by Asín Palacios, who translated the book into Spanish and published it in Madrid in 1916 as referred to above. The translation consists of 165 pages, making it a medium sized volume.

The introduction makes up pages 1 to 31. The translation is good in general but there are some points to be noted about it. In some cases he failed to understand Ibn Hazm's idiomatic and highly sophisticated style and eliptical expressions. As an illustration, in Ibn Hazm's words, staring much at a person makes him familiar; such familiarity may "breed contempt". Asín Palacios misunderstood the word *'ayn,* "eye", as being a reference to spying. In his introduction he also explained many of the ideas about ethics by referring overmuch to the Gospels. He omitted Ibn Hazm's statements about virtue on the pretext that they would confuse the reader, would serve no useful purpose, and that they were not well attested.[1]

2. French Translation

Ibn Hazm's *al-Akhlâq wa'l-Siyar* was translated into French by Nada Tomiche and published in Beirut in 1961 under the title *Epître Morale: An Epistle about the Treatment that should be Given to Souls, the Education of Character and the Avoidance of Bad Behaviour.*

The French translation is published together with the Arabic text and is furnished with an introduction and glossary. It is a medium sized volume. The introduction makes up pages I to LV (55 pages). Then the translation follows, from page 55 to page 119 (64 pages). The glossary takes up pages 123 - 142. Then comes the index and bibliography. This

---

1. See Makkî's introduction to *al-Akhlâq,* pp.66f; and N. Rif'at, *Ibn Hazm on Jews and Judaism,* pp. 7f.

brings us to page 174. The Arabic text starts at the other cover and its pages are numbered from 12 to 93.

In her introduction, Tomiche begins with an account of Ibn Hazm's times and the politics of the state in which he lived, the political conflicts and the decline of the Umayyad caliphate and the emergence of the petty kingdoms. She emphasizes Ibn Hazm's enthusiastic support for the principle of monarchy (which he believed belonged by divine right to the Prophet's family, the Qurashites) and his attack on the petty kings.

She moves on to discuss Ibn Hazm as a thinker. She studies his works on law, theology and logic, and explains his literalist theories. Ibn Hazm attempted to systematize the use of the *hadith* in matters of law and debate in order to prevent their arbitrary use which was prevalent among the Shâfi'ites, Hanbalites and Zâhirites.

Under the heading "Ibn Hazm as humanist", Nada Tomiche outlines his knowledge of ancient philosophy. She points out that the works of the Greek philosophers had been translated into Arabic in Baghdad at the time of Hârûn al Rashîd and were certainly available in Andalusia nearly two centuries later. Theorists and moralists prior to Ibn Hazm quoted Greek philosophers in translation, such as Socrates, Aristotle, Plato and Hippocrates. She points out that critics of Ibn Hazm accused him of not understanding Aristotelian logic when he spoke of it. It is self-evident that Ibn Hazm read all the available Greek works and benefited from them. He himself wrote on logic, philosophy and morality. He criticized Galen in his assumption that every language except Greek sounds like the croaking of frogs.

In Ibn Hazm's book on morality which is translated here, there are many clear instances of Aristotelian influence and it is important to note that when it is a question of wisdom or morality Ibn Hazm does not hesitate to quote from the Bible or Greek philosophy. Islam freely accepts any knowledge of ethical discipline and morality no matter what its source.

The French translator puts numbers on the paragraphs of the Arabic text and the equivalent paragraphs in her version. They amount to 349 in all. The Arabic text has a footnote which merely gives the different manuscripts. The translation has more ample footnotes, referring to previous scholarly discussions of the work. She consulted the Spanish translation made by Asín, and when her interpretation differs she explains her reasons.

To give an idea of the nature of her comments on Ibn Hazm's text, on page 84 she comments on the categorization of some branches of knowledge as "minor".

> Ibn Hazm, typically, classes the different branches of knowledge on a scale of values. He himself had written a book called *On the classification of the sciences*, probably influenced by the categories of Aristotle. See above § 35 and note. It is curious to note that, contrary to the Arab concept which placed poetry in first place among the disciplines, Ibn Hazm, perhaps influenced by certain verses of the Qur'an and certain *hadiths*, considers it as a minor science. Asín, *Los Caracteres*, translates *shi'r*, poetry, as *"las siencias modernas"* p.114. It is true that the Arab philosophers adopt the word *sughra* for "minor" (cf. Goichon, *Vocabulaire comparé d'Aristote et d'Ibn Sina*, Paris 1939), but it is difficult to regard poetry as a "modern science" in the eyes of an Arab. In a personal note, M.R. Arnaldez writes to me, 'I believe that Asín is right: a modern science (recent) which does not bring profit.' (There doubtless was ancient poetry, but the poetic art in Spain at the time of Ibn Hazm had a modern character, cf. Peres).

Our translation has been closely checked against the French translation. We have noted divergences; some can be explained from differences in the manuscript used. Some are due to a misunderstanding of the Arabic words. But on the whole the French translation is very faithful to the original and gives a true picture of the work. There are some serious differences between our translation and the French, and these are mentioned between two asterisks when they arise.

3. Ibn Hazm's book has also been edited, with a critical introduction in French, by Eva Riad, Uppsala, 1980. Her interest
began while studying Miskawayh's *Tahdhîb al-Akhlâq*. Need-
ing to draw comparisons with Ibn Hazm's work she found
that there was still much to be studied about it, and proceed-
ed to write her dissertation, which examines all the
manuscripts. She rightly notes the connection between this
work and Ibn Hazm's more famous *The Ring of the Dove*.

Eva Riad says that she has been able to examine all
except two of the many editions of the work which have
appeared in the 20th century (from 1906 onwards). She
describes the different surviving manuscripts in great detail.
Her study runs from page 11 to page 57. She concludes her
examination of the manuscripts by saying that there are certain additions which could be explained in many different
ways. She suggests a stemma but points out that it is not the
only possible one. The extra material in B could have been
added comparatively late. It may have been taken from other
works by Ibn Hazm, or it may be an interpolation by the
scribe or the person who commissioned the manuscript. It is
not unusual for books on morality and wisdom to be given
extra material which is then ascribed to the original author.
This is clear when we hear of sayings attributed to Socrates
or Aristotle.[1]

It is not our purpose here to make a new edition of Ibn
Hazm's book. We shall use Makkî's edition as the latest and
best, although we shall take other versions into account and
make use of them where necessary. Our aim is to give a good
translation and a clear text, faithful to the original, and useful
to the modern reader.

The Contents, Arrangement and Sources of Ibn Hazm's Book

The book consists of twelve sections, plus a short introduction. The titles of the sections are as follows:

---

1. Ibn Hazm Al-Andalusi, *Kitâb Al-Akhlâq wa'l-Siyar*, Introduction, Edition
Critique, Remarques par Eva Riad, (Sweden, Uppsala, 1980), pp. 34ff.

1. The treatment to be given to souls, and the reform of vicious characters.

2. The mind and repose.

3. Knowledge.

4. Morals and behaviour.

5. Friends, close friends and the exchange of advice.

6. The different kinds of love.

7. The different kinds of physical beauty.

8. Practical morality.

9. The treatment of corrupt characters.

10. Curious particularities of the characteristics of the soul.

11. A man's desire to know, what you should tell him and not tell him, and how to be praised and renowned.

12. The way to attend study sessions.

The arrangement of the book within the sections and paragraphs is Ibn Hazm's own. It is not modelled exactly on any of the moralists and collectors of moral sayings who preceded him, although of course he shared their aim of helping people to become more moral. Nor does Ibn Hazm classify his material according to academic criteria. He had no intention of providing an academic discussion and analysis of the nature of morality, or an inward-looking description of his own psychology. His intention was to share with others his own experience and ideas, the moral principles which he had developed, and to encourage others to profit from them.

If Ibn Hazm had wanted to produce an academic work, he would have arranged his material differently: the first section would have been followed by the ninth and tenth, then by the eighth section. Section three would have come after section twelve, which in fact comes last. This arrangement would have provided a logical sequence of ideas and subject matter. There is no need to say more about the contents since we have supplied a translation of the complete work.

Ibn Hazm lived his own life according to his principles; he searched out his own faults and endeavoured to rectify them; he practised what he preached.[1] In the book, he is putting his own self under the microscope, and analysing his own character. While we may admire his readiness to admit to faults, and his attempts to get rid of these faults with divine help, the question arises as to what caused him to subject his own character to such a detailed dissection and analysis. To be sure, he reveals himself as human through and through. But the particular stimulus to undertake the exercise may have been his realization that he had been unusually protected in his youth, first in his father's house and later among friends; then as an adult he found himself the target of criticism and was forced to examine the true state of affairs.

Who was right, his loving, indulgent father, or his critical public? In any case, his personal stocktaking is one more reason for us to warm to Ibn Hazm as a man, as we see him taking a long, cool look at his own strengths and weaknesses. Of course, this lengthy self-defence again reflects his sharp sense of being treated unfairly by society and of deserving more respect and appreciation. Ibn Hazm compiled this book of wise sayings after he had withdrawn from society. It is a self-portrait, very self-conscious, inward looking, but in analysing his own nature he forges links with all mankind. This gives extra force to his book and makes it exceptional in its field.

Here in this book we find that Ibn Hazm occasionally touches upon theological problems, either clearly or by implication, for example the balance on which God will weigh the deeds of His people in the hereafter. Like the Mâlikîs he took the Qur'anic verses in their literal meaning, that there would

---

1. See Ibn Hazm, *al-Akhlâq*, pp. 130ff.

really be a great pair of scales. This may have been because the metaphor of scales and weighing occurs so frequently in the Qur'anic texts referring to the last judgment. God says that He will take account of the smallest atom; nothing can escape His knowledge even if it weighs no more than an atom.[1]

There is another theological problem raised by Ibn Hazm, the possibility of seeing God. It is a matter of controversy among Muslim theologians. They differed in their belief about this. The orthodox believed it to be possible, i.e. that God can be seen. But the Mu'tazilite and other less significant Muslim sects denied the possibility. The latter took evidence from the Qur'an: "Sight cannot reach Him". But the Mujassida believed that God can be seen, both in this world and in the hereafter.[2] Ibn Hazm dealt with this question in detail in *al-Fisal*. He denies that God can be seen with our physical eyes, but contrary to the Mu'tazilite view, holds that it is possible to see Him spiritually since we can know God with our own heart and spirit, and in the hereafter we shall see Him through a power which is different from our present eyesight, a power which He will grant us, which some ancients have called the sixth sense. In this world, God put the ability into our hearts to know Him, and gave Moses the ability to see and hear Him.[3]

He moreover touches upon the question of life in the hereafter and the relationship between the living and the dead. He thinks that there can be intercourse between the living and the dead in dreams and that this can be arranged and promised. He also thinks that life in the hereafter is real and that the departed may forget and be busy in his last abode.[4] But it is clear that the idea of death did not disturb him. Elsewhere he speaks of the question of death and whether there is pain in dying. This is a theological question which has also been discussed by other philosophers. [Ibn Hazm's text

1. See Qur'an, e.g. 21:47; 99:6-8; also Ibn Hazm, *al-Akhlâq*, pp. 117f; Ibn Hazm, *al-Fisal*, vol. 4, pp. 85ff; and al-Ghazzâlî, *Ihyâ*, vol. 1, p. 122.
2. See Ibn Hazm, *al-Akhlâq*, pp. 167f; also Ibn Hazm, *al-Fisal*, vol. 3, pp. 3ff; and al Ash'ari, *al-Ibâna*, vol. 1, pp. 47ff.
3. See Ibn Hazm, *al-Fisal*, vol. 3, pp. 3ff; and al-Makkî, *Qût*, vol. 1, p.m 86.
4. Ibn Hazm, *al-Akhlâq*, p. 122; also Ibn Hazm, *al-Fisal*, vol. 5, pp. 89ff.

p.123, first two lines, could be understood to refer to the soul in its abode after death and before resurrection; or in its abode before it entered the body for the first time. This is made clearer in *al-Fisal* where he deals with the subject *per se*, in proper theological terms.][1]

Al-Akhlâq wa'l-Siyar's Sources:

This is an appropriate moment to examine Ibn Hazm's sources. We should remember that he had read and memorized a huge amount during his life. One of his pupils described his master's knowledge as being as vast as the ocean.[2] He is bound to have drawn upon this store of knowledge in addition to the traumatic experiences of his own life.

As is to be expected, his prime source was the Qur'an, to which he alludes both directly and by implication. We must then add the *Sunna* literature, the Muslim tradition, the literature of the Muslim *Zuhhâd* (ascetics), Greek philosophers, Persian sources and the Old and New Testaments. He refers specifically to 'Alî Ibn Abû Tâlib, al Hasan al Basrî, Abû al Aswad, al-Duáli, Abû al 'Abbâs Muhammad Ibn Subayh Ibn al-Sammâk (died 183 AH, 799 AD) and the celebrated political minister, Abû Zarj Mihr, in the government of Khosrau Noushirwin.[3] Abû Zarj Mihr is often quoted by Muslim moralists and men of letters.

Ibn Hazm's statement concerning the worthlessness of material things reminds us of 'Alî Ibn Abû Tâlib (who is called by Maskawiyh "the philosopher of Islam".) Ibn Abû Tâlib said to 'Ammâr, when he found him deeply sighing, "Oh 'Ammâr, why do you sigh? Do you sigh for the hereafter or for this world? By Allah I swear that this world is not worth sighing for, because its pleasures are of five kinds, food, drink, sexual intercourse, clothes and perfumes. The best of all foods is honey and it comes from a bee, an insect. The best of all drinks is water, and it is the most freely available. The best of all clothing is silk, and it comes from the

---

1. *al-Fisal*, vol. 2, p.106; vol. 4, p.71, vol. 5, p. 88.
2. al-Humaydî, *Judhwa*, pp .309f.
3. See Ibn Hazm, *al-Akhlâq*, pp. 106, 206f, 222 and 258f.

mouth of a worm. And the best of all perfumes is musk, which comes from a rat. And the best experience of sexual intercourse is the union of two urine-making areas."[1]

In his analysis of anxiety and the means of escaping from it, Ibn Hazm explains all man's activities and emotions as stemming from anxiety and the attempts to dispel it.[2] Other philosophers before him had come near to making this central point. For example, Galen, Ahmad Ibn Muhammad Ibn Miskawayh (died 421 AH; 1013 AD), and other moralists call upon us to search our souls for faults and vices in order to cure them.[3] The Arab philosopher, Abû Ya'qûb al-Kindî (died c. 257 AH, 870 AD), wrote an essay on how to dispel sorrow and fear,[4]which is close to Ibn Hazm's approach. We have no direct evidence that Ibn Hazm ever read al-Kindi's epistle on sadness, but there are some internal similarities which suggests the possibility. Each of the two great scholars' works is quite distinct. There is evidence that Ibn Hazm read the philosophical writings of al-Kindî. He criticized the latter's theories of metaphysics, specifically his theories of the first cause and the origin of the world.[5] According to Anwar Chejne, Ibn Hazm derives the most part of his terminology in his book on logic, particularly in *Balâgha* (rhetoric), from al-Kindî.[6]

Ibn Hazm's text states clearly that he has been told that the spleen is the seat of both good and bad temper. He may have come across this idea from reading the works of Ibn Qutayba (died 176 AH; 889 AD) who reported it from Wahb Ibn Munabbih, who in his turn ascribed it to the Torah. God created man from the four elements water, earth, fire and air; wet, dry, hot and cold. God then gave him a mind in his

---

1. See Badawî, *Dirâsât wa Nusûs*, p. 104.

2. Ibn Hazm, *al-Akhlâq*, pp. 87ff.

3. See Abû 'Alî Ahmad Ibn Muhammad Ibn Miskawayh, *Tahdhîb al-Akhlâq*, (Beirut, Dâr Maktabât al-Haya, n.d.), pp. 33ff, 88ff, 110 and 160; [Ibn Miskawayh's book has been translated into English by Constantine Kzrayk under the title *"The Refinement of Character"*, (Beirut, American University, 1966)].

4. Badawî, *Rasâ'il Falsafiyya*, *Risâlât al-Kindî*, pp. 6-36; see also our forthcoming book, *Islamic Morality and Psychology*.

5. See Ibn Hazm, *al-Radd 'Alâ al-Kindî al-Faylasûf*, in *al-Radd 'Ala Ibn al-Nighrîla*, pp. 189-216.

head, covetousness in his kidneys, anger in his liver, determination in his heart, fear and terror in his lungs, emotions, laughter and tears in his spleen, happiness and sadness in his face, and in the human body God made 360 joints.[1]

He shows the influence of Greek philosophy in his definitions of moral and philosophical courage; terms such as virtue, justice etc.[2] There are other similarities relating to ideas and moral discipline. For example he agrees with Aristotle and also with some great early Muslim authorities, that man should not take many friends; but Ibn Hazm colours the idea with his own experience and breathes new life into it. He says that taking many friends is a virtue which has the appearance of a vice.[3] Aristotle says that many friends are neither to be desired nor expected - the fewer, the warmer intimacy. The most celebrated friendships have subsisted between two only. Neither should those chosen for motives of mere pleasure be numerous; for too much seasoning in our diet is pernicious.[4]

Ibn Hazm spoke intensively about knowledge and scholarship within the framework of ethics. This subject had been treated by other Muslim authorities before him, e.g. al-Shâfi'i (died 204 AH, 819 AD) asks the seeker after knowledge not to refrain from listening to his opponent, for he may by listening learn something which he has mistaken or forgotten, or else become more certain in his own beliefs. He also said, "I never entered a debate with anyone at all except that I minded not whether Allah put the truth on my tongue or upon his." He also said, "I never debated with anyone and wished him to fail in presenting his argument."[5]

---

1. See *'Uyûn al-Akhbâr*, vol. 2, p. 62.
2. See Aristotle, *The Nicomachean Ethics*, pp. 36ff, pp. 88ff; also Ibn Miskawayh, *Tahdhîb*, pp.40, 51, 85, 152, 186f; and al-Bayhaqî, *al-Sa'âda wa'l Is'âd*, pp. 57ff.
3. Ibn Hazm, *al-Akhlâq*, p. 149; see also al-Makkî, *Qût*, vol. 2, pp. 214ff; and Ibn Miskawayh, *Tahdhîb*, pp. 147ff.
4. See Aristotle, *The Nicomachean Ethics*, pp. 309ff; also Badawî, *al-Akhlâq al-Nazariyya*, pp. 142ff.
f. Muhammad Ibn Idrîs al-Shâfi'i, *al-Risâla*, (Cairo, al-Halabî, 1403 AH; 1983 AD), p. 222; see also Ibn Abî Hâtim al-Râzî, *Adab al-Shâfi'i wa Manâqibuh*, ed. by 'Abd al-Ghanî 'Abd al-Khâliq, (Syria, Maktabât al-Turâth, 1372 AH; 1953 AD), p. 91.

There is again a striking similarity between Ibn Hazm's statement about the accessibility of knowledge and that of Occlides, who says, "The master of wisdom should not lock it away, because to deprive people of wisdom is like keeping a thirsty man from water when he is in dire need of it. Equally, it should not be given to those who do not seek after it, because this undermines the value of wisdom and makes it cheap. This is like giving salt water to a man who is not thirsty."[1]

On some occasions Ibn Hazm quotes moral and wise sayings from sources other than the Qur'an. For example, he sometimes quotes from the Bible, e.g. Jesus' saying, "A prophet is not without honour save in his own country." He compares this with the life of Muhammad.[2] Ibn Hazm is broadminded enough to see that morality is to be found not only in Islam but can also be learned from other Prophets of God and other wise men, whether Muslim or not. Morality is a treasure which belongs to all humankind. Law is something different from rites; Ibn Hazm can follow only the rites of Islam.

It is possible to draw some comparisons between Ibn Hazm and other earlier authorities on morality, but he remains distinct and exceptional in his approach and achievement. In the final analysis, all moral teaching has a common basis.

---

1. Abû Sulaymân al-Mantiqî al-Sajistânî, *Siwan al-Hikma wa Thalâth Rasâ'il*, ed. by A. Badawî, (Tehran, 1974), p. 155; see also Ibn al-'Arabî, *Kitâb al-Fanâ' fî'l-Mushâhada*, (Haydar Abad, Dâ'irat al-Ma'ârif al-'Uthmâniyya, 1361 AH), pp. 2ff.
2. See Mark 6:4; also Ibn Hazm, *Risâla fî Fadl al-Andalus*, p. 166.

IBN HAZM

KITĀB AL-AKHLĀQ WA'L-SIYAR FĪ MUDĀWĀT AL-NUFŪS

CHAPTER IV

Introduction

In the name of Allah the most merciful and clement: [O Allah I implore your assistance, O Allah bless Muhammad and his family and grant them peace.]

Abû Muhammad 'Alî Ibn Ahmad Ibn Sa'îd Ibn Hazm [the Andalusian jurist]. Allah may be blessed with him has said:

1. Praise be to Allah for His great gifts. May Allah bless [our master] Muhammad, His servant, the seal of His Prophets and Messengers; may He grant them eternal blessings. I rely on Him for any ability and strength I may have, and I seek His aid and protection against all the various terrors and ills of this world. And may He deliver me from all horror and suffering in the next world.

2. Now, I have gathered together in this book numerous ideas which Allah, the provider of intellect, has enabled me to profit from as day succeeded day, [and year succeeded year] and circumstances altered, permitting me to understand the vicissitudes of fate and to control its fluctuations, to the extent that I have devoted the larger part of my life to it. I have chosen to master these problems by study and contemplation, rather than throw myself into the various sensual pleasures which attract most souls on this earth, and rather than amass unnecessary wealth. I have gathered together all my observations into this book in the hope that the Almighty may allow it to benefit whichever of His servants He wishes who has access to [is capable of understanding] my book, in the matters over which I have slaved, devoting all my efforts to them and reflecting at length upon them. I hope that it will be well received, and I present it with good intentions and blessings [with a good heart].

This book will benefit a person more than financial treasures and the possession of property, if he meditates upon it, and if Allah enables him to make good use of it. As for myself, my hope in this enterprise is to win the greatest reward from Allah, since my intention is to help His servants, to remedy whatever is corrupt in their character, and to heal the sickness of their souls. I beseech the assistance of Allah [Almighty, we wish only for God, the best of defenders].

I

Section dealing with the Treatment to be given to Souls, and the Reform of Vicious Characters.

3. The pleasure which a prudent man has from his own good sense, a scholar from his knowledge, a wise man from his wisdom, the pleasure of anyone who works hard in ways pleasing to Almighty God, is greater than the pleasure which a gourmet has from his food, a drinking man from his tipple, a lover from the act of love, a conqueror from his conquest, a reveller from his amusements [the player from his game] or a commander from giving orders. The proof of this is that the wise man, the prudent man, the scholar,[1] the practising Muslim and all those that we have mentioned are capable of enjoying these pleasures as much as the man who indulges in them. They have the same feelings, desires as those who hasten to satisfy them. But they have deliberately refrained and turned away from them, preferring to seek after moral excellence. None can judge these two [kinds of pleasure] except someone who has known both, not someone who has known one and not the other.

4. [As things happen one after the other] If you look deeply into worldly matters you will become melancholy and will end by reflecting upon the ephemeral nature of everything here below, and the fact that truth lies only in striving for the hereafter, since every ambition to which you might cling will end in tears; either the goal is snatched from you, or you have to give the attempt up before you reach it. One of these two endings is inevitable except in the search for God the Almighty and Powerful. Then the result is always joy, both immediate and eternal. The immediate joy is because you stop worrying about the things which usually worry people; this leads to an increase in the respect paid to you by friends and enemies alike. The eternal joy is the joy of Paradise.

5. I have tried to find one goal which everyone would agree to be excellent and worthy of being striven after. I have

---

1. The French translation changes the order of this list unnecessarily.

found one only: to be free from anxiety. When I reflected upon it, I realized that not only do all agree in valuing it and desiring it, but I also perceived that, despite their many different passions and aspirations and preoccupations and desires, they never make the slightest gesture unless it is to dispel anxiety, they never utter a single word unless it is designed to drive anxiety far away. One man loses his way, another comes close to going wrong, finally another is successful - but he is a rare man, and success is rare, [O, all-knowing God].

Dispelling anxiety is a goal upon which all nations agree - from the time when the Almighty created the world until the day when this world will pass away and be followed by the Day of Judgment - and their actions are directed to this goal alone. In the case of every other objective there will always be some people who do not desire it.

For example, some people are not religious and do not take eternity into account.

There are some who by nature and inclination prefer obscurity to fame [the obscurity of satisfied passion].

There are some people of evil nature who are not striving for good, for peace [loyalty] or for justice.

There are some who have no interest in amassing a fortune, preferring abstinence to ownership; this was the case with many of the Prophets. God's peace be upon them - and those who followed their example, ascetics and philosophers. There are some who by nature dislike sensual pleasures and scorn those who seek after them, such as those men we have just mentioned, and who prefer to lose a fortune rather than gain one. Some prefer ignorance to knowledge, in fact most of the people that you see in the street are like this. These are the objectives of people who have no other aim in life. Nobody in the whole world, from the time of its creation until its end, would deliberately choose anxiety, and would not desire to drive it far away.

6. When I had arrived at this great piece of wisdom, when I had discovered this amazing secret, when Allah the Almighty had opened the eyes of my mind [spirit] to see this great treasure, I began to search for the way which would truly enable me to dispel anxiety, that precious goal desired

by every kind of person, whether ignorant or scholarly, good or evil. I found it in one place alone, in the action of turning towards God the Almighty and powerful, in pious works performed with an eye to eternity.

7. Thus the only reason that someone chases after riches is to dispel the anguish of poverty. The only reason that someone seeks fame is to dispel the anxiety of seeing someone else outdo him. The only reason that someone chases after pleasures is to dispel the anxiety of missing them. The only reason that someone chases after knowledge is to dispel the anxiety of being ignorant about something.

People enjoy listening to other people's conversation and gossip only because it dispels the anxiety of being alone and isolated. People eat, drink, make love, wear clothes, play games, build a shelter, mount a horse, go for a walk, only in order to avoid the reverse of all these actions and every other kind of anxiety.

8. In all the actions listed here, anyone who pauses to reflect will see that anxieties will inevitably occur, such as problems which arise in the course of the action, the impossibility of performing the impossible, the fleeting nature of any achievements, and the inability to enjoy something because of some difficulty. There are also bad consequences which arise from every success: fear of one's rival, attacks by the jealous, theft by the covetous, loss to an enemy, not to mention criticism, sin and such things. On the other hand, I have found that actions performed with an eye on eternity are free from * every kind of * fault, free from every stain, and a true means of dispelling anxiety. I have found that the man who is striving for eternity may be sorely tested by bad fortune on his way but does not worry; on the contrary, he is glad, because the trial to which he is subjected gives rise to hope, which aids him in his endeavour and sets him the more firmly on the path towards his true desire. I have found that, when he finds his way blocked by an obstacle, he does not worry, because it is not his fault, and he did not choose the actions that he will have to answer for. I have seen such a man be glad, when others have wished evil upon him, and be glad when he has undergone some trial, and be glad when he has suffered on his chosen path, and be glad, always [living]

in a permanent state of joy while others are permanently the opposite. You should therefore understand that there is only one objective to strive for, it is to dispel anxiety; and only one path leads to this, and that is the service of the most high God. Everything else is misguided and absurd.

9. Do not use your energy except for a cause more noble than yourself. Such a cause cannot be found except in * Almighty * God Himself: to preach the truth, to defend womanhood, to repel humiliation which your creator has not imposed upon you, to help the oppressed. Anyone who uses his energy for the sake of the vanities of the world is like someone who exchanges gemstones for gravel.

10. There is no nobility in anyone who lacks faith.

11. The wise man knows that the only fitting price for his soul is a place in Paradise.

12. Satan sets his traps, under the cover of finding fault with hypocrisy. It can happen that someone refrains from doing a good deed for fear of being thought a hypocrite. [If Satan whispers such an idea in your ear, take no notice; that will frustrate him.]

II

Important Chapter about the Mind and about Repose

Do not listen to what other people say. Listen only to the words of the Creator. That is the way to a completely sound mind and to perfect repose.

13. Anyone who believes himself safe from all criticism and reproach is out of his mind.

14. Anyone who studies deeply and disciplines his soul not to rest until it has found the truth, even if it is painful at first, will take more pleasure in criticism than in praise. Indeed, if he hears people praise him, even if it is well-deserved, he will become proud, and his virtue will be corrupted.

If he hears people praise him and the praise is undeserved, he will be pleased, but wrongly so, and this is a serious fault. On the other hand, if he hears people criticize him and it is deserved, he might be led to correct the behaviour that led to it. This criticism would be a piece of considerable good luck that only a fool would ignore. If someone is criticized unjustly and he controls himself, he will gain merit by his meekness and patience. Furthermore, all the good works ever done by his critic will be credited to him, and he will gain the benefit of them on Judgment Day when they will stand him in very good stead when he needs them, although they were not the result of his own efforts. And this is a supreme piece of good luck which it would be mad to disdain. If he does not hear people's praise, what they say or do not say makes no difference to him. But it is a different matter with their criticism, he wins either way, whether he hears their criticism or does not hear it.

15. If it were not for the words of the Prophet (may Allah be pleased with him) about "good praise" which "brings to believers the express good news of the happiness which has been promised", it might have been a sign of wisdom to prefer being criticized even unjustly to being praised with good reason. But these words were spoken. The promised happiness "will always arise from merit, not from absence of merit;

it will reward only the object of praise, not merely the fact that praises were uttered".

16. There is no difference between the virtues and the vices, between acts of devotion and acts of rebellion, except in as far as the soul feels attracted or repelled. Happy the man whose soul finds pleasure in virtue and good deeds, fleeing vice and rebellion. And unhappy the man whose soul finds pleasure in vice and rebellion, fleeing virtue and good deeds. This is nothing less than the sacred order of things ordained by the providence of Almighty Allah.

17. Anyone who strives after eternity is on the side of the angels. Anyone who strives after evil is on the side of the demons. Anyone who seeks fame and victory is on the side of the tigers. Anyone who seeks sensual pleasures is on the side of the [dumb] beasts. Anyone who seeks money for its own sake, not for spending on pious obligations and praise-worthy acts of charity, is too base, too vile to be compared with any beast. He resembles rather the waters which gather in caves in inaccessible places: no animal profits at all from them, [except now and then a bird; then the wind and the sun dry up what is left. And the same thing happens to posses-sions which are not consecrated to pious works].

18. A wise man has no satisfaction in a quality which sets him below tigers, dumb beasts and inanimate objects. He rejoices only in his progress in that virtue by which Allah dis-tinguishes him from these same tigers, dumb beasts and inanimate objects: this is the virtue of intelligence which he shares with the angels.

19. Anyone who feels proud of courage which is not applied in its normal direction, the service of the Almighty God, let him understand that the tiger is braver than him, that the lion, the wolf and the elephant are braver than him.

20. Anyone who glories in his own physical strength, let it be known to him that the mule, the ox and the elephant are physically stronger than him.

21. Anyone who glories in his ability to carry heavy weights, let it be known to him that the donkey can carry greater weights.

22. Anyone who glories in his ability to run, let it be known to him that the dog and the hare are faster runners

than he.

23. Anyone who glories in the sound of his own voice, let it be known to him that many of the birds have sweeter voices than he, and the sound of flutes is more exquisite and charming than the sound of his voice.

How can anyone take pride or satisfaction in qualities in which these animals are superior?

24. But a man whose intellect is strong, whose knowledge is extensive and whose deeds are good, he should rejoice because only the angels and the best of men are superior to him in these matters.

25. Allah says *"Anyone who fears the majesty of God, and controls himself against passion, he shall have Paradise for his refuge."* [79:40] These words encapsulate all virtue: to control oneself against passion means in fact to turn away from one's natural tendency towards anger and lust, things which are both under the dictates of passion. Then all that is left for the soul to use is the intellect which God has given it, the good sense which distinguishes it from the beasts, from insects or vermin and from tigers.

26. "Never lose your temper," as Allah's Prophet (peace be upon him) said to a man asking his advice, and, as he also said commanding him, "Do as you would be done by", together encapsulate the whole of virtue. Indeed, the fact that the Prophet forbade all anger implies that although the soul has been given the ability to be angry, it should refrain from this passion, and the [Prophet's] commandment to do as you would be done by implies that souls should turn away from the strong force of greed and lust and should uphold the authority or the means of justice which springs from the rationality which is part of the reasonable soul.

27. I have seen the majority of people - except those whom God the Almighty has protected, and they are few - throw themselves into the miseries, the worries and fatigues of this world, and pile up a mountain of sin which will mean that they enter hellfire in the Hereafter and will have no advantage from the perfidious intentions which they nurse so carefully, such as wishing for an inflation of prices which would bring disaster upon children, and the innocent, or wishing the worst trials upon those they hate. They know

very well that these bad intentions will not necessarily bring about what they desire or guarantee its advent, and if they clarified and improved their intentions they would hasten the repose of their spirits. They would then have the time to devote themselves to their own business and would thus profit a great deal in addition to the return of their souls to God, and all this without having at all hastened or delayed the realization of their desires. Is there any worse deception than the attitude which we warn against here, and is there any greater happiness than the one which we are promoting?

28. When we contemplate the duration of the universe, we see it limited to the present moment, which is nothing but the point which separates two infinities of time. The past and the future are as meaningless as if they did not exist. Is anyone more misguided than the man who barters an eternal future for a moment which passes quicker than the blink of an eye?

29. When a man is asleep, he leaves the world and forgets all joy and all sorrow. If he kept his spirit in the same state on waking, he would know perfect happiness.

30. A man who harms his family and neighbours is viler than them. Anyone who returns evil for evil is as bad as them. Anyone who refrains from returning evil is their master, their superior and the most virtuous among them.

III

Section Dealing with Knowledge

31. If knowledge had no other merit than to make the ignorant fear and respect you, and scholars love and honour you, this would be good enough reason to seek after it. Let alone all its other merits in this world and the next!

32. If ignorance had no other fault than to make the ignorant man jealous of knowledgeable men and jubilant at seeing more people like himself, this by itself would be reason enough to oblige us to flee it. Let alone the other bad results of this evil in this world and the next!

33. If knowledge and the action of devoting oneself to it had no purpose except to free the man who seeks it from the exhausting anxieties and many worries which afflict the mind, that alone would certainly be enough to drive us to seek knowledge. But what should we say of the other benefits too numerous to list, the least of which are the abovementioned, and all of which accrue to the knowledgeable man. In search of benefits as small as these the petty kings have worn themselves out in seeking distraction from their anxieties in games of chess, dicing, wine, song, hunting expeditions and other pastimes which bring nothing but harm in this world and the next and absolutely no benefit.

34. If the scholar who has spent long peaceful hours [at his studies] stopped to think how his knowledge has protected him against humiliation at the hands of the ignorant, and against anxiety about unknown truths, and what joy it has brought him by enabling him to solve problems which others find insoluble, he would certainly increase his expressions of gratitude to Allah and rejoice more in the knowledge that he has and desire even more to add to it.

35. Anyone who spends his time studying something inferior, abandoning higher studies of which he is capable, is like someone who sows corn in a field capable of growing wheat, or who plants bushes in a soil which could support palm trees and olives.

36. To spread knowledge among those incapable of understanding it would be as harmful as giving honey and

sugary confections to someone with a fever, or giving musk and amber to someone with a migraine caused by an excess of bile.

37. A man who is a miser with his knowledge is worse than a man who is a miser with his money, for the money-miser is afraid of using up what he possesses but the knowledge-miser is being mean with something which does not get used up and is not lost when it is given away.

38. Anyone who has a natural inclination towards a branch of knowledge, even if it is inferior to other branches, should not abandon it, or he would be like someone who plants coconuts in al-Andalus or olive trees in India where neither would produce fruit.

39. The most noble branches of knowledge are those which bring you close to the Creator and help you to be pleasing to Him.

40. When you compare yourself with others in matters of wealth, position, and health, you should look at people less favoured than yourself. When you compare yourself with others in matters of religion, knowledge and virtue, look at people who are better than yourself.

41. The mysterious branches of knowledge are like a strong drug which benefits a strong body but damages a weak one. In the same way, the esoteric branches of knowledge enrich a strong mind and refine it, purifying it of its flaws, but destroy a weak mind.

42. If a madman threw himself as deeply into good sense as he throws himself into madness, he would surely be wiser than al-Hasan al Basrî,[1] Plato of Athens[2] and Vuzurgmihr the

---

1. Al-Hasan al Basrî (100 AH, 718 AD) is a great Muslim traditionalist and Sufi ascetic. In the history of Islam he looms large for his literary writings and moral sayings. See Ibn Khallikân, *Wafayât* (Cairo, Bulaq) vol. 1, p. 227. He was born and lived in Basra, southern Iraq.
2. Plato, the famous Greek philosopher, d. 347 BC, disciple of Socrates, visited Egypt and lived there for one year and learned before Egyptian wise men in 'Ayn Shams. Jamâl al Dîn Abû al-Hasan al-Qaftî, *Târikh al-Hukamâ'*, ed. by Julius Lippert (Leipzig, 1903) p. 16, also Abû Sulaymân al-Mantiqî al-Sijistânî, *Siwan al-Hikma wa Thalâth Rasâ'il*, ed. by A. Badawî, Tehran, 1974) pp. 84; 128FF.

Persian.[1]

43. Intelligence has its limits; it is useless unless it is based on the guidance of religion or on good fortune in this world.

44. Do not harm your soul by experimenting with corrupt views in order to demonstrate their corruption to someone who has consulted you, otherwise you will lose your soul. If you shield yourself from acting in a detestable way, any criticism that can be thrown at you by a man of corrupt beliefs because you disagree with him is better than his respect and better than the bad effect on both of you if you committed these detestable acts.

45. Guard against taking pleasure in any way that will harm your soul and is not required of you by the religious law nor by virtue.

46. Knowledge no longer exists if one has ignored the attributes of the Almighty Great Creator.

47. There is no worse calamity for knowledge and for scholars than when outsiders intrude. They are ignorant and think that they are knowledgeable; they ruin everything and believe that they are helping.

48. Anyone who is seeking happiness in the Hereafter, wisdom in this world, the best way to behave, the sum of all moral qualities, the practice of all the virtues, should take as his model Muhammad, the Prophet of God - God grant him blessings and peace - and emulate as far as possible the Prophet's morals and behaviour. May God help us to take him as an example, by His grace, amen [amen]!

49. The ignorant have annoyed me on two occasions in my lifetime. First, when they spoke of things they did not know, at a time when I was equally ignorant; the second time when they kept silent in my presence [in the days when I had learnt something]. In the same way they were always silent about matters which would have benefited them to speak about, and spoke about matters which brought them no benefit.

---

1. Vuzurgmihr was the minister of the ancient Persian king Khusrau Nushirwan, and his son's tutor. He is famous for his wise sayings, which are often quoted in Arabic sources, and he is said to have been the first to translate the Indian text *Kalila wa Dimna* into the Persian language.

50. Scholars have brought me pleasure on two occasions in my lifetime: first, they taught me when I was ignorant; the second time was when they conversed with me after I had been taught.

51. One of the merits of religious knowledge and asceticism in this world is that Almighty God does not put it within reach of anyone except those who are worthy of it and deserve it. One of the disadvantages of the great things of this world, wealth and fame, is that they mostly fall to the lot of people who are unworthy of them and do not deserve them.

52. Anyone who is seeking after virtue should keep company with the virtuous and should take no companion with him on his way except the noblest friend, one of those people who is sympathetic, charitable, truthful, sociable, patient, trustworthy, loyal, magnanimous, pure in conscience and a true friend.

53. Anyone who is seeking fame, fortune and pleasure will keep company only with people who resemble mad dogs and sly foxes: they will take for their travelling companions only people [inimical to his belief] who are cunning and depraved in nature.

54. The usefulness of the knowledge [of good] in the practice of virtue is considerable: anyone who knows the beauty of virtue will practise it, though it may be rarely. Knowing the ugliness of vice, he will avoid it, though it may be rarely. The man with knowledge of the good will listen to soundly-based praise and desire it for himself. He will listen to talk of evil and desire to avoid it. From this premise it necessarily follows that knowledge has a part in every virtue, and ignorance has a part in every vice. A man who has had no instruction in the knowledge [of good] will not practise virtue unless he has an extremely pure nature, a virtuous constitution. It is the particular state of the Prophets (peace and the blessings of God be upon them!) for God has taught them virtue in its entirety, without them having learnt it from men.

55. It is true that I have seen among the common people some who, by their excellent behaviour and morals, were not surpassed by any wise man, any scholarly, self-controlled

man. But this is very rare. And I have seen men who have studied the different branches of knowledge, who have a good knowledge of the messages of the Prophets - peace be upon them - and the advice of the philosophers and who nevertheless surpass the most wicked in their bad behaviour, their depravity, both internal and external. * These are the worst of all creatures.* This is very common and I therefore perceive that these two [moral attitudes] are a favour which is granted or withheld by Allah the Almighty.

IV

Section dealing with Morals and Behaviour

56. Take care to have the reputation of being a man of good intention. Beware of gaining the reputation of being devious or people will avoid you more and more and you will finish by being harmed or even lost.

57. Train yourself to think about the things that frighten you. If they do come to pass, you will not be so worried by them. You will not lose anything by growing accustomed to the thought of them, and your pleasure will be greater or even doubled if something nice or unexpected happens.

58. When worries multiply, they will all fall to the ground. [A way out will be found.]

59. A deceitful man may occasionally keep his word to a lucky man, and a faithful man may occasionally betray an unlucky man.[1] Happy is he who in this world is not obliged by fate to put his friends to the test.

60. Do not worry about a man who wishes you ill. If fortune favours you he is lost and your luck will protect you. If fortune does not favour you then anyone can harm you.

61. Blessed is the man who knows his own faults better than others know them.

62. Patience in the face of others' insolence is of three kinds: patience with someone who has power over you when you have none over him; patience with someone you have power over when he has none over you; finally patience with someone when neither of you has power over the other. The first kind is humiliating and degrading; it is not a virtue. The advice for someone who is afraid of such an intolerable situation would be to abandon everything and run away. The second kind is a virtue, it is charitable, it is the true meekness which characterizes virtuous souls. The third sort consists of two kinds. The insolence may arise from a misunderstanding or from fear, and the one at fault may realize the ugliness of his act and regret it. To be patient with him would be a virtue

---

1. French translation is too free here. It misunderstands the Arabic word *majdûd* as *mahdûd*.

and an obligation; this is true magnanimity. But with a person who overestimates his own value and is proud and arrogant and feels no regret for his action, to tolerate this is humiliating, it encourages the wrongdoer in his wrongdoing, because he will act even more violently and it would be stupid to respond in the same way. The wisest course of action is to let him know that you could fight back but that you are refraining from doing so because he is beneath contempt and unworthy of your attention. No more is necessary. As for the insolent behaviour of the lower classes, the only remedy is to punish it.

63. Anyone who mingles with the crowd is never short of worries to pain him, or sins to regret on the day when he will return to God, or anger to give him a pain in the liver [heart],[1] or humiliation to make him hang his head. Then what shall I say about someone who is intimate with people and always in their company? Solitude is where you will find dignity, repose, happiness and security. You should treat company like a fire: warm yourself but do not fall in. ["You may draw near but without going right in."]

64. If the company of people had only the two following faults, that would be enough to keep us away: the first is letting out vital secrets during a friendly meeting, secrets which would otherwise never have been revealed. The second is showing off, putting our immortality in mortal peril. There is no other escape from these two trials than to withdraw into absolute solitude, far from people altogether.

65. Do not put off to tomorrow what you can do today. If you recognise this obligation you will make haste to do today

---

1. Ibn Hazm's text states clearly that he has been told that the spleen is the seat of both good and bad temper. He may have this idea from reading the works of Ibn Qutayba (died 276 AH, 889 AD), who reported it from Wahb Ibn Munabbih, who in his turn ascribed it to the Torah. God created man from the four elements water, earth, fire and air; wet, dry, hot and cold. God then gave him a mind in his head, covetousness in his kidneys, anger in his liver, determination in his heart, fear and terror in his lungs, emotions, laughter and tears in his spleen, his happiness and sadness in his face, and in the human body he made 360 joints. This is a medical matter which may be true but it is for doctors to say. See Abû Muhammad Abd Allah Ibn Muslim Ibn Qutayba, 'Uyûn al Akhbâr, (Cairo, al-Mu'asasa al-Misriya al-'Ama lil Ta'lif n.d.) vol. 2, p. 62.

even very small preparations for tomorrow, for if a small number of tasks are left to mount up they become a great number. In fact they may become too many to do and the whole enterprise will be wrecked.

66. Do not despise any of the actions that you hope to see counted in your favour on the Day of Resurrection. By doing them now, even in small measure, these actions will eventually outweigh the number of your sins which would otherwise add up to sufficient reason to throw you into hellfire.

67. With depression, poverty, misfortune and fear, the pain is only felt by the sufferer. People looking at them from the outside have no idea what they are like. On the other hand, with false judgment, shame and sin, only the onlooker sees how horrible they are! The person who is sunk deep in them does not perceive this.

68. Security, health and wealth are only appreciated by a person who does not have them. Anyone who has them does not appreciate them. On the other hand, a sound judgment and virtue, working towards eternity, their value is known only to those who share in them. Anyone who has no share in them has no knowledge of what they are like.

69. The first person to break with a deceiver is the one whom the deceiver has deceived. The first person to detest a false witness is the person whom the false witness supported. The first person to despise an adulterous woman is the man who caused her to commit adultery.

70. As far as we know, nothing can be degraded and then resume its natural state without great trouble and difficulty. What can we say about the man whose head is poisoned by intoxication every night. Indeed, a mind which drives its master towards its own deprivation every night must be a mind condemned.

71. The highway [or a long journey] is fatiguing, a quiet retreat is restorative. Too much wealth makes for greed. A small fortune makes for contentment.

72. The plans of an intelligent man may go wrong. The plans of a stupid man never go right.

73. Nothing is more harmful to a governor than to be surrounded by a great number of unemployed people. A prudent ruler knows how to keep them busy without being

unfair to them, otherwise they will overwhelm him with petty matters.

Anyone who invites his enemies to come close to him is suicidal.

74. Anyone who sees an important person too often regards him as less eminent and less important.

75. Parading, putting on, for example, a severe and discontented air, this is the veil with which ignorant people who have risen in the world try to cover their ignorance.

76. A wise man should not delude himself about a friendship which started when he was in power, because everyone was his friend then.

77. The best person to help you in your affairs is someone with equal interest in their success. Do not get anyone to help you who would be just as well off elsewhere.

78. Do not respond to talk which is brought by someone on the part of a third person, unless you are sure that the latter did say it, because the one who brought lies to you will go away carrying the truth [the unpleasant truth which you will have told him and which he will hawk around].

79. Put your trust in a pious man, even if the religion that he practises is a different one from your own. Do not put your trust in anyone who scorns sacred things, even if he claims to belong to your own religion. As for a man who defies the commandments of the Almighty, do not ever trust him with anything you care greatly about.

80. I have noticed that people are more generous with their opinions than with their pennies. In my long study of this matter, this has never been disproved in spite of countless observations. Since I cannot understand the cause of this, I suppose it must be innate in human nature.

81. It is the height of injustice to deny to a habitual wrongdoer the opportunity of doing an occasional good deed.

82. When you get rid of one enemy you see a great many others advancing.

83. I have never seen anything more lifelike than the shadow-theatre with its little actors mounted on wooden handles that are turned rapidly so that some disappear and oth-

ers appear.[1]

84. For a long time I have been thinking about death. I had certain dear friends, as closely bound to me by the bonds of sincere affection as the soul is bound to the body. After they died, some of them appeared to me in dreams. Others did not. While one of the latter was still alive, we had each promised to visit the other in a dream after we had died, if at all possible. But I have not seen him at all since he preceded me into the other world. I do not know whether he has forgotten or been engaged.

85. The oblivion of the soul who forgets the state it was in in the world of temptation [its first abode] while waiting for the resurrection of the body [to enter the body] is like the oblivion of someone who has fallen into mud and has sunk [all his promises] together with everything which he knew before and which was familiar to him. I have also reflected for a long time about this matter, and it seems to me that there is another possible explanation in addition to the one just mentioned. I have studied a sleeping person at the moment when his soul leaves his body, and his senses sharpen to the point of being able to see the unseen; the soul forgets completely, absolutely, the state which it was in just a moment before falling asleep, although it was so recent.

The soul knows other states in which it is endowed with memory and feelings, it can be pleased, it can be hurt. The joys of sleep are felt even during the sleep, for the sleeper feels happy, he dreams, he is afraid, he is sad even in his sleep.

86. The soul is not happy except in the company of a soul. The body is heavy and wearying. This is proved by the haste with which one buries the body of a loved one when the soul has departed from it, and by the sorrow caused by the disappearance of the soul although the corpse is still there.

87. I have never seen Satan use a worse trick, or an uglier or a more foolish one, than when he puts two phrases onto the tongues of those who follow him. The first is when some-

---

1. This is an important historical reference to shadow-theatres in al-Andalus in the time of Ibn Hazm. c.f. Ibn Hazm, *al-Fisal*, vol. 1, p. 110 and vol. 5, p. 6; also al-Tâhir Makkî's note on the above passage.

one excuses his own evil deed by alleging that someone has done the same to him. The second is when someone makes light of doing evil today because he did evil yesterday, or he does wrong in one sense because he has already done it in another. These two phrases excuse and facilitate evil-doing; they bring it into the arena of what is acceptable, tolerable and not to be criticized.

88. Be mistrustful if you are able to be sufficiently careful and cautious, but if you cannot check on them you will have to trust people. This will bring you peace of mind.

89. The definition of generosity, the supreme objective of generosity, is to give away the entire surplus of your possessions in charitable works. The best charitable work is to bring relief to a neighbour in need, a poor relation, a man who has lost his own possessions and is close to ruin. Anyone who holds on to his superfluous money without spending it in one of these ways is an example of miserliness. And he should be praised or criticized in proportion to whether he is more or less generous in this way. Anything given to causes which are not these charitable ones is squandered, and the action is blameworthy. It is virtuous to give to someone in greater need part of what you need to keep alive; this is a nobler act of self sacrifice than plain generosity is. To keep what you need is neither praiseworthy nor blameworthy but simply fair. To carry out one's obligations is a duty; to give away surplus food is generosity. To forget yourself and to give away food as long as you will not starve yourself is a virtue. To hinder anyone from performing his duty is against the Law. To refuse to give away the leftovers of our food is greedy and extremely miserly. To refuse to deprive yourself in order to give away part of the food which you need is excusable. To deprive yourself of food, and to deprive your family to any extent, is ignoble, vile and criminal. To be generous with property which you have acquired by unfair means is to aggravate the evil already committed, and it should be rewarded by criticism, not praise, since you are in fact giving away someone else's property, not your own. To give people their rightful part of your possessions is not generosity; it is a duty.

90. The definition of courage is to fight to the death in

defence of religion, in defence of womanhood, of ill treated neighbours, of the oppressed who seek protection, or in defence of a lost fortune, honour which has been attacked, and other rights, against all adversaries, whether they be few or many. To do less than this would be cowardliness and weakness. To use up one's courage fighting for the vanities of the world would be stupid recklessness. But it is even more stupid to devote your courage to fighting against right and duty, either in your own interest or for others. And even more stupid than all these, there are men whom I have seen who do not know to what cause to devote themselves; sometimes they fight Zayd on Amr's account, and sometimes they fight Amr on Zayd's account, sometimes both in the same day, exposing themselves needlessly to danger, hurtling towards hellfire or running towards dishonour. About such people the Messenger of Allah (peace be upon him) has warned: "There will come a time for men when the one who kills will not know why he has killed, and his victim will not know why he has been killed."

91. The definition of continence is to turn away one's glance and all one's organs of sense from forbidden objects. Everything other than this is debauchery. Anyone who goes further, and forbids himself what the Almighty has made lawful, is weak and powerless.

92. The definition of justice is to give spontaneously what is due and to know how to take what is your right. The definition of injustice is to take one's due and not to give others their due. The definition of nobility of soul is to give spontaneously and with a good heart what is due to others, and to allow them their rights willingly; this is also a virtue. All generosity is noble and virtuous, but not every noble act and every virtue is generous. Virtue is a more general term; generosity is more specific. Magnanimity is a virtue without being generosity. Virtue is a general prescription to which one adds a specific action.

93. One hour of neglect can undo a year of pious effort.

94. In the course of affairs, a mistake made by an individual is better than a just policy followed by the whole assembly of Muslims if they are not grouped under the leadership of one man. This is because the individual's mistake can be

put right, but the correct views of the Muslim assembly will lead them to ignore something that may have been wrong, and they will be lost because of it.

95. In times of civil war, the blossom does not set fruit.

96. I myself had faults, and I tried continually to correct them, by discipline, by studying the words of the Prophets (may they be blessed) and also the words of the most virtuous sages among the ancients who are more advanced in morality and self-discipline, until God helped me overcome most of my faults, thanks to his guidance and grace.

It is an act of perfect virtue, of self-discipline, a sign that one controls the truth, to confess such faults in order that one day someone may learn from them, if God wills.

97. One of my faults was that I tended to an extreme of self-satisfaction when I was in the right and an extreme of bad temper when I was in the wrong. Ever seeking to cure myself of this, I decided that I would never again display any irritation in my remarks, my actions or my discussions. I renounced every kind of triumph that is not permitted, and I suffered under the heavy burden of this decision. I had enough patience to bear a dreadful affliction which nearly made me sick and an invalid. But I was not capable of overcoming my passion always to be in the right. It almost seemed that I did not really think this a fault, that I did not really think I should give up this attitude.

98. Another fault I had was an ungovernable propensity for sarcasm. What I decided to do about this was to refrain from anything that might irritate the person I was talking to. But I did allow myself to crack jokes, feeling that not to do so would have been narrow-minded and almost arrogant.

99. Another fault: extreme pride. My mind wrangled with my soul, knowing my defects, and argued so long and so successfully that my pride vanished completely, leaving no trace, thanks be to God. Moreover, I set myself to despise myself absolutely and to be a model of humility.

100. Another of my defects was that I suffered from trembling caused by my youthfulness and the weakness of my limbs. I forced myself to make it stop, and it disappeared.

101. Another fault: a love of great fame and glory. To deal with this defect I decided to renounce everything which is

forbidden by religion, God helping with the rest, since if the
soul remains under the control of reason even its irritability
can become a virtue and be regarded as a praiseworthy disposition.

102. I used to feel extreme repugnance for the company
of women on any occasion, and this made me difficult to get
on with. I seem to have been struggling for ever against this
immoderate feeling, which I know to be bad from the problems it has caused me. God help me.

103. I had two faults which the Almighty has kept private
and helped me to fight and overcome by His goodness. One
has completely disappeared, all praise to Him for this. In this
case, good luck seems to have been on my side: as soon as
this fault rears its head I hasten to stifle it. But the other fault
has tormented me for a long time. When its waves came
sweeping over me, my veins would throb and this fault
would be on the point of reappearing; but God has allowed
me to hold it back by one of the manifestations of His goodness and it has now disappeared.

104. I used to persist in bearing extreme grudges; I have
been enabled to conceal and hide this with the help of the
Almighty and to avoid the manifestation of all its effects. But
I have never been able to stamp it out completely, nor have I
ever found it possible to make friends with anyone who has
acted in a truly hostile way towards me.

105. Mistrust itself is regarded by some as an absolute
fault. This is not so, unless it leads the person who feels it to
commit deeds not allowed by religion, or to adopt behaviour
which is unsocial. In other cases mistrust can be steadfastness, and steadfastness is a virtue.

106. As for the reproach made to me by ignorant adversaries who say that I put no value on anyone who disagrees
with me when I believe that I am in the right, and that I
would never act in concert with the ones I contradict even if
they amounted to the entire human population on the face of
the earth, and that I place no value on conforming with the
people of my country in many of the customs or costume
which they have adopted for no particular reason[1] - this inde-

---

1. Nothing in the French translation about costume.

pendence is a quality which I regard as one of my most important virtues. There is nothing equal to it, and, upon my life, if I did not possess it (God forbid), it would be this that I most longed for, and hoped for, and prayed for to God Almighty. In fact, my advice to all who may hear my words is to behave in the same way. There is no benefit to be had from copying other people if their actions are vain and pointless. By so doing one annoys the Almighty, and disappoints one's mind [deludes oneself], causes suffering to one's soul and body, and takes upon one's shoulders an unnecessary yoke.

107. A man who knows nothing of the truth has reproached me for not caring about wrongs done to me, or even about wrongs done to my friends, so that I do not even get annoyed if they are wronged in my presence.

108. My reply would be that anyone who described me like that was speaking too hastily and needs to be more precise. When one speaks hastily one slips into using language that makes the bad not so bad and the good not so good: for example, "So-and-so is sleeping with his sister," would be an abominable thing to say and would horrify everyone who heard it, but if you explained that it is a matter of "his sister in Islam", it would be clear that it was the hasty speaking that created the indecent and ugly aspect of the matter.

109. For myself, if I pretended not to feel hurt when I am attacked by someone, I should not be telling the truth, for it is natural to feel hurt in such a case, it is only human. But I have forced myself to show neither anger nor bad temper nor fury. If I manage to hold back an angry answer by preparing myself in advance, then I do so, thanks to the strength and power of Almighty God. But if I have no time to prepare myself, I restrict myself to retaliating with cutting phrases, but not insults, and I attempt to say only what is true, and to express myself without anger or cruelty. I detest doing even this, except when it is absolutely necessary, for example when I wish to punish someone who is determined to attack me, or when I wish to stop the spread of a false rumour, for most people love to pass on, to anyone who will listen, hateful tidbits of gossip (which they attribute to a third person), and nothing will stop them so effectively as this course of action. It stops them touting around calumnies which they attribute

to others, and which serve no purpose except to corrupt consciences and to spread slander only.

110. Furthermore, as for the man who is wronging me, there are two possibilities and two only. Either he is lying or he is telling the truth. If he is lying, then God will surely make haste to allow me to refute him by his own tongue, for this man will go the way of all liars and will draw attention to my merit by falsely imputing bad things to me - for, late or soon, this will become clear to most of those who listen to him. If he is telling the truth, there are three possibilities and only one can be true. Perhaps I had been his associate in some business and had confided in him as one does with someone one relies on and trusts, and he would then be the most despicable sneak: I hardly need say more about such base villainy. Or, perhaps he may be criticizing in me something which he regards as a fault and which in fact is not. His ignorance is enough to make this obvious; it is he who should be accused, and not the one whom he has criticized. Or, finally, he may be accusing me of a fault which I really do have. Having perceived one of my faults, he has let his tongue wag about it. If he is telling the truth, I deserve more blame than he does. In that case, I should be angry with myself, not with my critic, who is justified in his criticism.

111. As for my friends, I have not forbidden myself to defend them. But I do it gently, contenting myself with persuading the person who has slandered them in my presence to repent, urging him to reproach himself, to apologize, to feel ashamed, to take back what he said. I achieve this by following the method which consists of blaming the slanderers and telling them that it would be better to mind their own business and put their own houses in order rather than track down the faults of others; I go on to recall the merits of my friend, reproaching the critic for limiting himself to recalling his faults without mentioning his virtues, and saying to him, "He would never speak like that about you. He has a more generous spirit than you, and that is what you would not accept," or something similar. As for attacking the speaker, annoying him, irritating him, making him angry, in this way pushing him to increase the insults to my friend which I so dislike, this would make me guilty towards my friend

because it would expose him to coarse and repeated insults which would be spread to the ears of those who had not heard them before and would give rise to further slander. Perhaps this would make me just as guilty towards myself, which would not suit my friend, because I should suffer insult and injury. For myself, I would not want my friend to defend me beyond the limits that I have outlined. If he goes further, and goes to the point of injuring the one who is insulting me, he will push him to increase his attacks, to go even further, to attack him, or even my father, my mother and his own parents, depending on how insolent and impudent the one who started it is. They might even come to blows, which, for my part, I would consider as my friend's fault, and I should scorn him, because he had brought this upon me; I certainly would not be grateful to him. On the contrary I should be extremely cross with him. God help us!

112. A man of prejudice who never stops to think has accused me of squandering my fortune. This is more hasty talk, which I would explain as follows: I only squander the portion which it would be against my religion to keep or would cast aspersion on my honour or would fatigue me. I consider that what I avoid of these three evils, however small, far outweighs the amount of fortune lost, even if it amounted to everything that the sun shines on.

113. The best gift that God can give his servant is to endow him with justice and a love of justice, with truth and a love of truth [equity] above all else. To stamp out my evil tendencies, to do everything which is good according to religion and to the world, I have done only what I could. There is no strength and power except in God the Almighty. On the other hand, a man who has a natural tendency towards injustice and who finds it easy to act unjustly, a man who has a tendency to transgress and enjoys doing it, let him despair of ever improving or of amending his nature. Let him realize that he will not succeed, either in religion or in good conduct.

114. As for vanity, envy, falsehood and treachery, I have absolutely no experience of them from my nature. It seems that I have no merit for avoiding them since all my being spurns them. Thanks for this be rendered to God, Lord of the Worlds.

115. One of the defects of the love of renown is that it cancels out the value of good deeds, if the man performing them likes them to be spoken of. This makes him almost impious because he is working for something other than for God. This defect removes all the value from virtues because the man affected by it is hardly trying at all to do good for the sake of good, but for love of renown.

116. There is no worse blame than that of a man who praises a quality in you that you do not have, thereby drawing attention to its absence.

117. There is no better praise than that of a man who reproaches you for a fault that you do not have, thereby drawing attention to your merit, and he gives you your revenge on him by exposing himself to rebuttal and the reproach of having slandered you.

118. If one knew one's imperfections one would be perfect. Since no creature is exempt from faults, happy the man whose defects are few and unimportant.

119. The thing that happens most often is something unexpected. Steadfastness consists of preparing yourself for as much as can be foreseen. Glory be to the One who has so arranged it in order to show to mankind man's powerlessness and his need for his Creator, the Almighty.

V

Section dealing with Friends, Close Friends, and the Exchange of Advice

120. Anyone who criticizes you cares about your friendship. Anyone who makes light of your faults cares nothing about you.

121. Criticizing a friend is like melting an ingot: it will either become refined or it will disappear.

122. A friend who conceals a secret which concerns you is more disloyal towards you than one who tells a secret of yours. For the one who tells your secret is simply betraying you, but the one who conceals one from you is betraying you and also mistrusting you.

123. Do not try to be friends with those who scorn you. You will gain nothing from it but deception and shame.

124. Do not scorn those who try to be friends with you; to do so is a form of injustice and it would be failing to respond to their kindness, and this is bad.

125. Anyone who is forced to mix with men should on no account tell his companion everything that passes through his mind. When he leaves him, he must always behave as if he were a desperate enemy. When he wakes up each morning he should always expect his friends to betray him and do evil, expect them to behave exactly like his sworn enemies. If nothing of the sort happens, he should praise God; if it does, then at least he will be prepared and the shock will be less. For myself, I tell you that I had a friend who had sworn friendship, sincere pure friendship, for bad times or good, for richer or poorer, in anger and in satisfaction. This friend changed in his attitude towards me, in a most hateful way, after twelve years of perfect friendship, and for an absolutely futile reason which I would never have believed could influence such a man. He has never been reconciled with me since, and this has made me very sad for many years.

However, one should not do bad things and follow the example of wicked men and traitors.

126. On the contrary, we should learn from this example

the path that we should take. It is perilous and difficult to follow and a man would do well to advance as carefully as the pintailed grouse, more cautiously than the magpie, until he turns off the road trodden by mankind and makes his way towards his Lord. This road leads to victory, so we are told by religion and also by the world. The man who follows it will keep the pure intention of healthy souls who are true to their promises, men without guile and trickery. He will possess the virtues of the elect, the character of the virtuous. And, moreover, he will feel as safe as the worst deceivers, as free from care as the evil-doers, as the most wicked and cunning people.

127. You should keep any secret that is confided to you, and not reveal it to any friend or stranger, even the man closest to you, if you are at all able to keep it. You should be true to everyone who trusts you, and do not yourself trust anyone in affairs which you want to succeed except when absolutely necessary, and even then you should stop and think again and make a personal effort and draw strength from God.

128. Be generous with your superfluous possessions and strength to help others, whether they ask you or not, and to help anyone who needs you and whom you are able to help, even if he does not expressly come to you for help.

129. Do not expect any help in return from anyone except God the Almighty and Great. As you go on your way always remember that the first person you help will be the first to do you harm and turn against you. Indeed, because of their profound jealousy, men of bad character detest those that help them when they see that the latter are better off.

130. [In your social life] treat every human being as graciously as you can. If someone comes to you with defects and problems such as arise in the normal course of life, do not let them know that you do not like them. In this way you shall live in peace and quiet.

131. When you give advice, do not give it only on condition that it will be taken. Do not intercede only on condition that your intercession is accepted; do not make a gift only on condition that you will be recompensed. Do it only in order to practise virtue, and to do what you should do when giving

advice, interceding, or being generous.

132. The definition of friendship: [it is the middle point] between two extremes.[1] What makes one friend sad makes the other sad too. What makes one happy makes the other happy too. Any relationship less than this is not friendship. Anyone who answers to this description is a friend. A man may be the friend of someone who is not his friend for a man can love someone who hates him. This is the case above all with fathers and their sons, brother and brother, husband and wife, and all those in whom friendship has become burning love. Not every friend is a counsellor although every consellor, by giving advice, shows himself to be a friend.

133. The definition of advice is that the man giving it feels bad about what harms his friend, whether the latter feels good or bad about it, and he feels happy about what is good for him, whether his friend is happy or unhappy about it. This is the added factor which a counsellor has which goes beyond the limit of simple friendship.

134. The highest aim of friendship, and there is nothing higher than this, is to have all things in common, one's own person, one's belongings, without any constraint, and to prefer one's friend to every other being. If I had not known Muzaffar and Mubarak, the two masters of Valencia, I should have thought that such a sentiment had disappeared in our times. But I have never seen any two other men draw so deeply on all the joys of friendship, despite events which would have separated other men.

135. There is no virtue which so much resembles a vice as the faculty of having many friends and acquaintances. But it is really a perfect virtue, made up of various qualities, since friends are only gained by tolerance, generosity, patience, loyalty, signs of affection, shared feelings, and moderation. It

1. Nada Tomiche comments on this point by saying that this phrase is fairly obscure at first sight, so much so that Asín, *Los Caracteres* has refrained from translating it. It alludes to the theory of Plato and Aristotle taken up by Cicero and adopted by Ibn Hazm: virtue is a happy medium between excess and defect; see below § 295 and note 1, where Ibn Hazm tells us which are the two extremes of which friendship is the happy medium (see also § 308); they are: excessive attachment and excessive hatred.

is important to protect one's friends, teach them what one knows, and to win them over by every kind of praiseworthy action.

We do not mean mercenaries, or those who follow us in our days of glory. They are the thieves of the title of friendship, they deceive friendship. You think that they are friends and they are not. The proof is that they abandon you when fortune abandons you. Nor do we mean those who make friends for a particular purpose, nor do we mean drinking companions, nor those who gang together to commit crimes, or villany, to attack people's honour, to satisfy their unhealthy curiosity or for any other useless objective. These are not friends at all. The proof is that they speak evil of each other, and that they disperse as soon as the evil interests which brought them together are finished. We only mean to speak of those pure friends who unite only in the love of God, either to help each other to make some real virtue triumph or to taste the pleasures of the only true kind of friendship.

If one commits the fault of having too many friends, there is the difficulty of keeping them all happy, the dangers of associating with them, the duties which fall on us when they are subjected to trials (for if you betray them or let them down, you will be criticized and blamed; but if on the other hand you are true to them, you will harm yourself to the extent that you could lose your own life, and this choice is the only one acceptable to the virtuous man if he wishes to be true to his friendship); if one thinks of the worries which we have from the misfortunes which come upon them or which come upon us because of them: death, separation, betrayal of one among them, one will see that the joy brought by these friends is outweighed by the painful sadness which they cause.

136. There is nothing among the vices which is so like a virtue as the desire to be praised. Indeed, if someone sings our praises in our presence, we would be silly to believe it, knowing everything that the Tradition has taught us about flatterers. However, praise may be useful in encouraging someone to do fewer bad things and more good things. It

may lead the person who hears it to desire to have a character similar to the one who has been praised. Thus I feel that
the following anecdote has the ring of truth: one of the great
rulers of the world met one of those people who spread evil
wherever they go and who are said to have done evil things,
and he received him with praise. He had heard his praises
sung everywhere, he said; on every side people spoke of
nothing but his good deeds and his generosity. After this the
criminal could not possibly do wrong!

137. Certain kinds of advice are difficult to distinguish
from slander for anyone who hears a man criticising someone
else unjustly or unfairly and conceals it from the person who
is the object of this unjust and wicked statement, by doing
this so unjust and to be blamed. Moreover, if he breaks it to
him bluntly, he may bring more trouble upon the spiteful
critic than the latter really deserved. This would be unfair to
him, for it is not fair to punish ill-doers beyond the measure
of their unjust deed. It is difficult for anyone except a very
intelligent man to cope with this situation.

138. The solution to be adopted by the intelligent man in
such a situation is to protect the victim against the slanderer,
and no more, not inform him what the latter said; this is to
prevent him going to the slanderer and getting into more
trouble. As for sly tricks, one should protect the person
threatened from the trap which threatens him, as discreetly
as possible, without giving away the name of the trickster,
and do all one can to protect the victim, but nothing more
than that.

139. Giving information consists of reporting to someone
something one has heard which in no way harms the person
one tells it to, strength is from God.

140. Advice can be given twice. The first time is as pre-
scribed as a religious duty. The second time is a reminder
and a warning. If you repeat the advice a third time it
becomes a remonstrance and a reprimand. After that you
have to slap and punch and perhaps try even more serious
methods which may cause harm and damage. Certainly, it is
only in questions of religious practice that it is permissible to
repeat advice incessantly, whether the listener accepts it or

gets irritated, whether the adviser suffers from it or not. When you give advice, give it softly, do not shout it out; use hints, do not speak openly unless you are advising someone who is determined not to understand. Then explanations would be essential. Do not give advice only on condition that it is followed. Otherwise you are a tyrant, not an adviser; you are demanding obedience, you are not allowing religious feeling and brotherly spirit their due. Neither reason nor friendship gives you the right to insist. It is rather the right that a ruler has over his subjects or a master over his slaves.

141. Do not ask of your friend more than you yourself are prepared to give. To ask for more is to abuse his friendship. Do not gain except when there is a possibility of losing. Do not take power unless you know how to set it aside again. Otherwise you will harm yourself and your behaviour will be detestable.

142. If you find excuses for selfish and greedy men and shut your eyes to their faults, you are not displaying humanity or virtue. On the contrary, it is a base and feeble thing to do which encourages them to continue in their bad attitudes, it applauds and supports them in their wicked actions. Such indulgence would only be humane when displayed towards the just who are quick to pardon and to act unselfishly. In that case it is an obligation for a good man to behave in the same way towards them, above all if they have an urgent need of such tolerance, and if it is more necessary for them.

143. One might retort, "According to what you say, we should stop being tolerant, we should stop turning a blind eye when it is a question of our friends. Friends, enemies, strangers would all be treated exactly the same; this cannot be right." Our reply would be - and may God help us succeed - nothing but encouragement towards tolerance and unselfishness.

144. You should turn a blind eye not on [the faults of] the greedy but only on [those of] a true friend. If you wish to know how you should act in this matter, how you can keep on the path of truth: if there is a situation where one of two friends needs to be unselfish for the other's sake, each of the two friends should examine the problem and see which of

them is in the most urgent need, the most pressing circumstances. Friendship and humanity then impose on the other
the obligation to be unselfish. If he does not, he is greedy,
avid, and deserves no indulgence since he is acting neither
like a friend nor like a brother.

If the two find themselves in equal need, in equal straits,
true friendship would require that they race each other to be
the more unselfish. If they behave like this, they are both
friends. If one of them hastens to be unselfish and the other
does not, and if this is what usually happens, the second is
not a friend and there is no need to be friendly towards him.
But if he would hasten to sacrifice himself in other circumstances then this is a pair of true friends.

145. If there is someone in need whom you wish to help,
whether the initiative came from him or from you, do no
more than he expects of you, not what you might personally
wish to do. If you overstep the mark, you will deserve not
thanks but blame from him and from others, and you will
attract hostility, not friendship.

146. Do not repeat to your friend things that will make
him unhappy and which it would not benefit him to know.
That would be the action of a fool. Do not hide from him anything that would cause him loss not to know. That would be
the action of a wicked person.

147. Do not be pleased if someone praises you for qualities which you do not have; on the contrary, be very sorry
because it will bring to public attention that you lack them.
To sing such praises is to mock and poke fun, and only an
idiot or an imbecile would be pleased. Do not be sorry if
someone criticizes you for a fault that you do not have; on the
contrary, you should be pleased because your merit will be
brought to public attention.

148. On the other hand, you should be pleased to possess
a praiseworthy quality, whether anyone actually praises you
for it or not, and you should be sorry to have a blameworthy
fault, whether anyone actually criticizes you for it or not.

149. Anyone who hears bad things said about the wife of
his friend must on no account tell him, particularly if the person who said them was a slanderer or libeller or notorious

gossip, one of those people who try to draw attention away from their own faults by increasing the number of people like themselves; this often happens. As a general rule, it is best to stick to the truth. Now, in this case, you cannot know whether the statements are true or false, but you do know that it is a grave sin against your religion to hold such opinions. However, if you perceive that the same thing is being said from several sides, that the statements originate from several gossips, not just one, or if you are able to verify that the statement is well founded, even if you cannot put your friend in a position to observe what you have observed, then you should tell him everything, privately and tactfully. You should say something like "There are many women..." or "Look after your house, teach your family, avoid this, mind that..." If he takes your advice and is put on his guard, he will have profited from the chance. If you notice that he takes no precautions and does not worry about anything, you must control yourself, not say a word, and remain friends, for the fact that he has not believed what you have told him does not oblige you to break with him. But if, having been in a position to observe some definite proof, you are able to put your friend in a position to see some identical proof, it is your duty to tell him and to make him face the whole truth. If he changes his attitude, that is good. But if he will not change his attitude, you should shun his friendship, because this would be a vile man with no virtue and no noble aspirations.

150. The fact that a man enters a house secretly is proof enough that he means ill. The same is true of a woman who enters a man's house secretly. It would be stupid to require further proof. You should run from such a woman or at least separate. Anyone who kept her with him would be a virtual go-between.

151. Men can be divided into seven categories according to certain traits of their characters. Some praise you to your face and criticize you behind your back. This is the characteristic feature of hypocrites and slanderers; it is common, mostly among men. Others criticize you to your face and behind your back. This is characteristic of slanderers who are powerful and insolent. Some men flatter you to your face and

behind your back. This is the mark of flatterers and social climbers. Others again criticize you to your face and praise you behind your back. This is characteristic of fools and imbeciles. Virtuous people take care neither to praise nor to criticize you in your presence. Either they praise you in your absence, or they refrain from criticizing you. Slanderers who are not hypocrites or ignorant say nothing to your face and criticize you in your absence. As for those who want a quiet life, they take care that they neither praise you nor criticize you, whether you are present or absent. We have seen these different types of individual for ourselves, and we have tested the categories and found them to be true.

152. When you give advice, find a private place and speak gently. Do not say that somebody else has said the criticisms that you address to your companion, that would be to speak ill. If you phrase your advice bluntly, you will annoy and discourage. "Speak to him courteously," the Almighty has said: *"And speak unto him a gentle word."* [Qur'an 20:44] And the Prophet - peace be upon him - said: "Do not discourage him." If you are advising someone, and you insist on seeing your advice taken, you are doing wrong since you could be mistaken and you would be insisting on him accepting your error and rejecting the truth.

153. Everything has its use. Thus, I have profited greatly from mixing with the ignorant. This has inspired my inward self, it has sparked off my spirit, it has sharpened my mind, it has driven me to action. It has given rise to written works of some value. If the ignorant had not roused something deep within myself, if they had not woken something that lay hatching in me, I should not have thrown myself into writing these works.

154. Do not bind yourself to a friend by taking a wife from his family; do not sign a contract with him. We have never known these two acts to result in anything but rupture, where ignorant people would expect the ties of friendship to be strengthened. Not so, and the reason is that the two acts force each party to press his own interests, and there are few people who would forget their own interests to the advantage of others. When there is a clash of individual interests, quar-

rels result, and quarrels bring about an alteration in affections. The firmest alliance is one between two people who are already related, because the fact that they are already related forces them to bear the union, even if they are very unhappy, since they are joined by an unbreakable tie, that of their common origin, which nature obliges them to defend and protect.

VI

Section dealing with the different kinds of Love

155. I have been asked to focus on what there is to say about love, and the different kinds of love. All the different kinds of love belong to the same family. Love is characterized by longing for the loved one, horror of separation, hope of having one's love reciprocated. It has been suggested that the sentiment varies according to its object. But the object varies only according to the lover's desires, according to whether they are on the increase, the decrease, or are vanishing altogether. Thus, love felt for God Almighty is perfect love; that which unites beings in the quest for the same ideal, the love of a father, a son, parents, a friend, a sovereign, a wife, a benefactor, a person in whom one has placed one's hopes, a lover, all is generically the same, all is love, but there are different species as I have just listed, differing by the amount of love inspired by what the loved one is able to give of itself. Thus love can take different forms: we have seen men die broken-hearted because of their sons exactly as a lover may have his heart broken by his loved one. We have heard of a man who burnt with such fear of God, with such love, that he died of it. We know that a man can be as jealous of his prince and of his friend as of his wife, as jealous of them as a lover is of his mistress.

156. The least that the lover can desire of the loved one is to win her esteem, her attention, to approach her - not daring to expect more. This is how far those aspire who love each other in God Almighty.

157. The next stage is when desire grows as time is spent together, in conversation, and interest is shown by one to another. This is the level of the love of a man towards his prince, his friend or his own brother.

158 But the height of what a lover may wish from the loved one is to take her in his arms when he desires her. That is why we see a man who is passionately fond of his wife trying different positions in making love, and different places, so as to feel that he possesses her more completely. It is in

this category that we should put caresses and kisses. Some of these desires may arise in a father towards his child and may drive him to [express them] in kisses and caresses.

159. Everything that we have just mentioned is uniquely the function of [extreme] desire. When for some reason, the desire for some object is suppressed, the soul is driven towards a different object of desire.

160. Thus we find that the man who believes in the possibility of seeing God Almighty longs for it, has a great yearning for it and will never be satisfied with anything less since it is that which he desires. On the other hand, a man who does not believe in it does not aspire to this ecstasy and does not wish for it, having no desire for it. He is content to bow to divine will and to go to the mosque. He has no other ambition.

161. We have observed that a man who is legally able to marry his close relatives is not satisfied with favours which would satisfy someone who is not permitted to marry them. His love does not stop at the same point as the love of a man who is forbidden by law to love them. Those, such as Magians or Jews, who are permitted to marry their own daughters or nieces, do not curb their love at the same point as a Muslim does. On the contrary, they feel the same love to their daughter or their niece as a Muslim does to a woman that he will sleep with. One never sees a Muslim desiring his close relatives in this way, even if they are more beautiful than the sun itself, even if he is the most debauched and the most amorous of men. And if, very exceptionally, it should happen, it would be only among the impious, who do not feel the constraint of religion, and who allow themselves every lustful thought, and who find every gate of desire open to them. It cannot be guaranteed that a Muslim might not love his cousin so excessively that his love became a passion and overstepped the affection which he bore towards his daughter and his niece, even if the cousin was not so beautiful as they. In fact he might desire favours from his cousin which he would never expect from his daughter or his niece. On the other hand, a Christian will treat his cousin with equal respect, for he is not permitted to desire her. But [unlike a

Muslim] he does not have to restrain himself with anyone who shared a wet nurse with him, since he may desire her without offending the laws of his religion.

162. We now see the truth of what we said earlier: love in all its manifestations forms one single generic family, but its species vary according to the different objects of its desire.

163. Having said this, human nature is the same everywhere but different customs and religious beliefs have created apparent differences.

164. We do not say that desire has an influence only on love. We would say that it is the cause of all kinds of cares, even those which concern one's fortune and social position. Thus it may be observed that a man who sees the death of his neighbour, or of his maternal uncle, his friend, his cousin, his great-uncle, his nephew, his maternal grandfather or his grandson, having no claim on their property, does not fret because it has escaped him, however large and considerable their fortunes might be, because he had no expectation of them. But as soon as a distant member of his father's family dies, or one of his remotest clients, he begins to covet their belongings. And with the coveting comes crowding in anxiety, regret, anger and great sorrow if some tiny part of their fortune escapes him.

165. It is the same with one's position in society: a man who belongs to the lowest social class does not fret if he is not consulted when someone else is given charge of the affairs of the land. He does not fret if someone else is promoted or demoted. But as soon as he begins to feel an ambition to better himself, it provokes so much worry, anxiety and anger that it could make him lose his soul, his world and his position in the hereafter [lose his soul here and in the hereafter]. Thus covetousness is the cause of all humiliation and every kind of anxiety. It is a wicked and despicable kind of behaviour.

166. The opposite of covetousness is disinterest. This is a virtuous quality which combines courage, generosity, justice and intelligence. A disinterested man is truly intelligent because he understands the vanity of covetousness and prefers disinterest. His courage gives birth to a greatness of

spirit which makes him disinterested. His natural generosity stops him fretting about property which is lost to him. His equitable nature makes him love reserve and moderation in his desires. Thus disinterest is composed of these four qualities, just as covetousness, its opposite, is composed of the four opposite faults, that is, cowardice, greed, injustice and ignorance.

Greed is a kind of covetousness which would like to possess everything; it is insatiable and ever increasing in its demands. If there were no such thing as covetousness, nobody would ever humiliate himself to anybody else. Abû Bakr ibn Abû al-Fayyâd has told me that 'Uthmân Ibn Muhâmis [died 356 AH; 966 AD] inscribed upon the door of his house in Ecija [in Seville] "'Uthmân covets nothing".

Other species of this kind

167. A man made unhappy by the presence of a person he detests is like a man made unhappy by the absence of the person he loves. There is nothing to choose between them.

168. When a lover wishes to forget, he is sure to be able to do so. This wish is always granted.

169. If you treat the person you live with with respect, he will treat you with respect.

170. The man who is happy in love is the one who is racked by a passion for one whom he can keep locked away and with whom he may be united without incurring the wrath of God or the criticism of his fellow-men. All is well when the two lovers agree in loving each other. For love to run its course freely, it is essential that the two do not feel bored, for that is a bad feeling which gives rise to hatred. Perfect love would be if destiny forgot the two lovers while they were enjoying each other. But where could that happen except in Paradise? Only there can love be sure of shelter, for that is the home of everlasting stability. Otherwise, in the world, such feelings are not protected from misfortunes, and we go through life without ever tasting pleasure to the full.

171. When jealousy dies, you may be sure that love has

also died.

172. Jealousy is a virtuous feeling which is made of courage and justice; truly, a just man hates to infringe the sacred rights of others, and hates to see others infringe his own sacred rights. When courage is inborn in a person, it gives rise to a grandeur of spirit which abhors injustice.

173. A man whose fortunes I have followed during these times told me once that he himself had never known jealousy until he was racked by love. Only then did he feel jealous. This man was corrupt by nature, he was a bad character, but nevertheless he was perspicacious and generous.

174. There are five stages in the growth of love: the first is to think someone pleasant, that is, someone thinks of someone else as being nice or is charmed by their character. This is part of making friends. Then there is admiration; that is the desire to be near the person that one admires. Then there is close friendship when you miss the other one terribly when they are absent. Then there is amorous affection when you are completely obsessed with the loved one. In the special vocabulary of love this is called *'ishq*, "the slavery of love". Finally, there is passion, when one can no longer sleep, eat or drink. This can make you ill to the point of delirium or even death. Beyond this there is absolutely no place where love ends.

A note

175. We used to think that passion was found more often among lively and emotional women. But our experience has shown that this is not the case. Passion is found most often among calm women, as long as their calmness is not the placidity of stupidity.

VII

Section dealing with the different kinds of Physical Beauty

When I was asked to examine this matter, this is how I responded:

176. **Gracefulness** consists of delicate features, supple movements, graceful gestures, a soul in harmony with the form which fate has given it, even where there is no visible beauty.

177. **Allure** is the beauty of each feature regarded separately. But someone whose features are beautiful when considered separately can still appear cold and be without piquantness, charm, seductiveness or grace.

178. **Seductiveness** is the aura of the visible parts; it also goes by the name of elegance and attractiveness.

179. **Charm** is a certain something which has no other name to explain it. It is the soul which perceives it, and everyone knows what it is as soon as they see it. It is like a veil covering the face, a shining light which draws all hearts to it so that all agree that it is beautiful, even if it is not accompanied by beautiful features. Anyone who sees it is seduced, charmed, enslaved, and yet if you looked at each feature separately you would find nothing special. It might be said that there is a certain unknown something which you see when you look into the soul. This is the supreme kind of beauty. However, tastes do differ. Some prefer seductiveness, others prefer gracefulness. But I have never met anyone who preferred allure as such.

180. We call beauty piquant when there is a combination of some of these qualities.

VIII

Section dealing with Practical Morality

181. Fickleness, which is a fault, consists of switching from one way of life which is forced and senseless, to another way of life which is equally forced and senseless from one absurd state to an equally absurd state for no good reason.

182. But a man who will adopt habits which suit his capabilities and his needs, and who will reject everything that is of no use to him [will be drawing on] one of the best sources of good sense and wisdom.

183. The Prophet (Allah grant him blessing and greeting), the model of all goodness, whose character was praised by God, in whom God gathered together the most diverse and perfect virtues, and whom He kept from sin - the Prophet was in the habit of visiting the sick, accompanied by his friends. They went to the boundaries of Medina on foot, wearing neither boots nor sandals, hat nor turban. He wore clothes woven from the hair of wild beasts when he had them, or he might equally likely be wearing embroidered cloth if he had it, never wearing anything unnecessary and never forgetting anything necessary, content with what he had and doing without whatever he did not have. Sometimes he went barefoot, sometimes he wore boots. Sometimes he would ride a fine mule or he would ride a horse bareback or a camel or a donkey, with a friend riding behind him. Sometimes he ate dates without bread, sometimes dry bread, sometimes he ate roast lamb, fresh melon, or halwa, taking as much as he needed and sharing out the surplus, or leaving what he did not need and not forcing himself to take more than he needed. He was never angry when he found himself alone fighting for a cause, and he let nothing prevent him from anger when it was a question of God, the Almighty.

184. The perseverance which consists of keeping one's word and the perseverance which is nothing but obstinacy are so alike that they can only be told apart by someone who knows what different characters are like. The difference between the two kinds of perseverance is that obstinacy clings to error. Its actions are the actions of someone who per-

sists in doing what he has decided upon when he knows that he is wrong, or when he does not know for sure whether he is right or wrong. Such obstinacy is wrong. The opposite of obstinacy is fairness. As for the kind of perseverance which consists of keeping one's word, its actions are the actions of someone who is right, or who believes himself to be right, not having seen any reason not to believe this. This quality is worthy of praise, and its opposite is inconstancy. Only the first of the two kinds of perseverance [obstinacy] is wrong, because it makes you lose the habit of thinking about a matter once it has been decided, and you stop wondering whether the decision is right or wrong.

185. Good sense is defined as the practice of obedience to God and the practice of piety and the virtues. This definition implies avoidance of rebellion and vices. God has stated this clearly more than once in His holy book (the Qur'an), emphasizing that anyone who disobeys Him is acting unreasonably. Speaking of certain people, the Almighty has said, *"They will say: if we had listened, if we had understood, we would not be among the damned"*, [67:10] and He has confirmed their words as true by saying, *"They have recognized their own sins, so misfortune be to the damned."* [67:11]

186. Stupidity is defined as the practice of disobedience to God and the practice of vices.

187. As for going wild, throwing stones at people, not knowing what one is saying, that is lunacy and excess of bile.

188. Stupidity is the opposite of good sense, as we have shown above; and there is no middle point between good sense and stupidity unless it is ineptitude.

189. The definition of ineptitude is to work and speak in a way that neither serves religion nor the world nor a healthy morality. This is neither disobedience to God nor obedience, it does not bring anybody else to such acts, it is neither a virtue nor a harmful vice. It consists only of drivelling and rambling about doing pointless things. According to whether these actions are frequent or rare, the person should be treated as more or less inept. Moreover he may be inept in one matter, sensible in another, stupid in a third.

190. The opposite of madness is the ability to discern and the ability to make free use of the sciences and technical

knowledge. It is what the ancients called the "faculty of reasoning". There is no middle point between these two extremes.

191. As for the art of conducting one's affairs and flattering people by means that might win their good will and save a situation, such as false dealing, perversion or any other bad practices, and as for the tricks which allow one to amass a fortune or to increase one's reputation or to achieve glory by means of a crime or every kind of base behaviour, these are not the works of good sense. Indeed, even those people who avowed that they had lost their senses and whose words God confirmed as true when He said that they had lost their senses, knew very well how to conduct their worldly affairs, build up their fortunes, flatter their rulers and protect their own standing. This characteristic is called astuteness, and the opposite of it is intelligence and honesty.

192. However if, in order to achieve these same ends, someone acted with reserve and dignity, this would be firmness. Its opposite is weakness or wasting.

193. To be serious, to know how to put each word in the right place, to preserve moderation in the way that you conduct your life, to show courtesy towards anyone who comes to you, that is called steadiness and is the opposite of ineptitude.

194. The virtue of keeping one's word is made up of fairness, generosity and courage. Because a trustworthy man thinks it unfair to deceive anyone who has put his trust in him or anyone who has done him a good deed, he acts with fairness. Because he wishes to help to repair the injustices of fate as quickly as possible, he acts with generosity. Because he has decided to bear without flinching all the likely consequences of his fidelity, he is courageous.

195. The virtues have four roots which form all virtue. They are: fairness or justice, intelligence, courage and generosity.

196. The vices have four roots which are the basis of all faults and which are the opposite of the constituents of the virtues. They are: unfairness, ignorance, cowardice and greed.

197. Honesty and temperance are two kinds of fairness

and generosity.

Here are some lines of my poetry dealing with morals. Abu Muhammad Ali Ibn Ahmad says:

> The spirit is the foundation,
>   morals build the fortress upon it.
> If the spirit does not adorn itself with
>   knowledge it will surely find itself
>   in distress.
> An ignorant person is surely blind
>   and does not see where he is going.
> If knowledge is not paired with justice
>   it is deceitful.
> If justice is not paired with generosity
>   it is oppressive.
> Generosity depends on courage.
>   Cowardice is deceitful.
> Keep yourself in check if you are jealous.
>   A jealous person has never yet
>   committed adultery.
> All these virtues are sublimated in piety.
>   Truth spreads light when it is spoken.
> It is from the roots of Good that spring vows
>   [that bring us nearer God].

And here are some other lines of poetry in my style:

> The reins which control all the virtues are
>   justice, intelligence, generosity and
>   strength.
> The other virtues are composed of these four.
>   Anyone who possesses them is at the
>   head of his people.
> Likewise it is in the head that one finds
>   the qualities of good sense that enable
>   one to resolve all difficulties.[1]

---

1. This poem appears towards the end of the book in Makki's edition [pp. 239F].

198. Disinterest as a human quality is a virtue which is made up of courage and generosity. The same is true of patience.

199. Magnanimity is one kind of courage. It does not have an opposite.

200. Moderation is a virtue which is made up of generosity and fairness.

201. Ruthlessness arises from covetousness, and covetousness arises from envy. Envy arises from desire, and desire arises from injustice, greed and ignorance.

202. Ruthlessness gives rise to great vices, such as servility, theft, anger, adultery, murder, passions and fear of poverty.

203. To beg for something that belongs to someone else stems from a tendency which is midway between ruthlessness and covetousness.

204. If we make a distinction between ruthlessness and covetousness, it is only because ruthlessness reveals the covetousness that is hidden in the soul.

205. The art of dealing with people is a quality composed of magnanimity and patience.

206. Truthfulness is composed of justice and courage.

207. Anyone who comes to you with lies will go away with truths; that is to say, anyone who repeats to you lies which he attributes to a third person will make you beside yourself with rage; you will respond to him, and your response is the truth that he will carry away. Therefore be careful not to behave like this, and only answer when you are certain about the provenance of the lies.

208. There is nothing worse than falsehood. For how do you regard a vice which has as one of its varieties disbelief or impiety itself? For all disbelief is falsehood. Falsehood is the genus and disbelief is one of its species. Falsehood arises from wickedness, cowardice and ignorance. Truly, cowardice debases the soul. A liar has a vile soul which is far from achieving a greatness worthy of praise.

209. If we categorize people by their way of speaking - and, remember, it is speech that distinguishes mankind from donkeys, dogs and vermin - we can divide them into three groups: the first kind do not worry about what they pass on,

they say everything that comes into their heads, without keeping to the truth or correcting mistakes, and this is the case with the majority of people. Another group speak in order to defend their own fixed opinions, or to protest against what they believe to be false, without trying to establish the truth, merely holding their ground. This is frequently the case, but it is not so serious as the first group. The third group makes use of language in the way God intended and this is more precious than red sulphur.

210. Endless anxiety awaits the man who is goaded or irritated by justice.

211. Two kinds of people live a life without care: one kind are extremely worthy of praise, the other kind are extremely worthy of criticism. The two kinds are those who care nothing for the pleasures of this world, and those who care nothing for *hayâ'*, modesty.

212. To distance ourselves from the vanities of the world it should suffice to remember that every night every man alive, in his sleep, forgets everything that worried him during the day, all his fears, all his hopes. He no longer remembers his children or his parents, glory or obscurity, high social responsibilities or unemployment, poverty or riches, nor catastrophes. Such a lesson should be sufficient for a thoughtful person.

213. One of the most marvellous arrangements in God's world is that he made the things that are most necessary also the most easily attainable, as can be seen in the case of water and the thing which is even more necessary. (i.e. air) And the less essential a thing is, the rarer it is, as can be seen in the case of sapphires and things which are even less useful.

214. With all his worries, a man is like someone walking across a desert. Every time that he crosses a certain area, he sees other areas opening up in front of him. Likewise, every time that a man gets something done, he finds other tasks piling up.

215. That man was right who said that the good have a hard time in this world. But the man who said that the good are at rest was also right. The good do suffer from all the evil that they see spread over everything, dominating it, and all the appearances of justice which rear up between true justice

and themselves. But their calmness comes from [their indifference to] all the vanities of this world which so worry the rest of mankind.

216. Take care not to agree with a wicked speaker, not to help your contemporaries by doing anything which might harm you in this world or the next - however little - for you will reap nothing but regret, at a time when regret will not help you at all. The man you helped will not thank you. On the contrary, he will rejoice at your misfortune, or, at least - you may be certain - he will be indifferent to the bad results [of your action] and your sad ending. But guard against contradicting the speaker and opposing your contemporaries to the extent that you harm yourself in this world or the next, however little. You will reap only loss, hostility and enmity. You may even allow yourself to take sides, and you may suffer considerable trials which will be of no benefit [to you] whatsoever.

217. If you have to choose between annoying people or annoying the Almighty, and if there is no way out except either to run away from the right or to run away from the people, you should choose to annoy the people and run away from them, but do not annoy your God, do not run away from justice.

218. You should imitate the Prophet - peace be upon him - when he preached to the ignorant, the sinful and the wicked. Anyone who preaches drily and cheerlessly is doing wrong and is not applying the Prophet's method. Such preaching would usually only drive his audience to persist in their wicked ways, from obstinacy, anger and rage against the insolent sermonizer. He would then have done bad with his talk, not good. But a man who exhorts in a friendly fashion, with a smile and with gentleness, putting on the appearance of offering advice and seeming to be speaking of a third person when he criticizes the faults of the one he is speaking to, then his words reach farther and have more effect. But if they are not well received, he should go on to exhort or to appeal to the man's sense of shame, but only in private. And if [his advice] is still not taken, he should speak in the presence of someone who will make the sinner change. This is the practice which God ordains when He commands the use of "cour-

teous terms". The Prophet used not to address his listeners directly; instead, he would say to them "What are they thinking of, the people who do such a thing?..." Peace be upon him! He praised gentleness, commended us to be tolerant and not to argue. He varied his sermons so as not to be boring. And God has said, *"If you are harsh, and hardhearted, they would have scattered from about you."* [Qur'an 3:159.] Severity and hardness should not be used except to inflict the punishments ordained by God. A man who has been given special authority to inflict such punishment must not be gentle.

219. Something which can also have a good effect in a sermon is to praise, in the presence of a wrongdoer, somebody who has acted differently. This is an incitement to behave better. I know no other benefit of the love of praise: a person who hears another being praised models himself on him. It is for this reason that we should tell stories of virtue and vice, so that anyone who hears them may turn away from the wicked deed that he hears that others have done and accomplish the good deeds that he hears that others have done, so learning from history.

220. I have considered everything that lives beneath the skies, I have reflected long upon it, and I have observed that everything that exists, whether animate or inanimate, has a natural tendency to build itself up by divesting the other species of their characteristics and investing them with his own. Thus, a virtuous man hopes that all mankind will become virtuous and the sinner hopes that all mankind will become sinful. One may observe that everybody who recalls a past action of their own which they incite others to imitate says, "I always do such and such"; someone with a doctrine wishes that everybody would agree with him. This phenomenon can also be seen among the elements: when some become stronger than the others, they change them to their own substance: you can see how trees are formed, and how plants and trees are nourished by transforming water and the moisture in the soil into their own substance. For this may glory be given to Him who created and organized all things, there is no other God but He.

221. One of the most astonishing manifestations of God's power is that [despite] the great number of creatures that

exist, you never see one so alike another that there is no difference between them. I asked a man who was very old and had reached his eighties whether he had ever seen in the past any form which resembled somebody nowadays to the point of being identical. "No," he replied, "on the contrary, every form has something distinctive about it." The same is true of everything that exists in the world. Whoever makes a study of various objects and of the bodies they make up, whoever makes a long and frequent examination of them, knows this, and is able to discern the differences and to distinguish one object from another thanks to the nuances which the soul can perceive but words cannot express. Glory then to the Almighty, the Omniscient, whose power is infinite.

222. A curious thing in this world is to see people allow themselves to be dominated by perverse hopes which will bring them nothing but trouble in the short term and anxiety and sin in the long term. For example, one person will hope for a rise in the price of foodstuffs, a rise which might be fatal for some people. Some people hope for things which involve damage for other people. But, even if one has a certain interest in something happening, the fact that one hopes for it does not make it happen before its time, and nothing will happen that God has not decided. If he had wished for the good and the prosperity of other people, he would have speeded his own reward, achieved peace of mind and virtue, without fatiguing himself at all. Be amazed at the useless corruption of these characters!

IX

Section dealing with the treatment of corrupt character

223. A man who is subject to pride should think of his faults. If he is proud of his virtues, he should seek out what is mean in his character. And if his faults are so well hidden from him that he thinks he has none, let him know that his misfortune will last for ever, that he is the worst of men, that he has the worst faults of all and is the least perceptive.

224. In the first place, he is weak in mind and ignorant. No fault is worse than these two, for a wise man is one who sees his own faults, fights against them and tries to overcome them. A fool ignores them because he has little knowledge and discernment and his thoughts are feeble, possibly because he takes his faults to be good qualities, and there is nothing on earth worse than this.

225. There are many who boast of having committed adultery, homosexuality [acts of child abuse], theft, and other sins, and are proud of these stains and of the aptitudes that they deployed in these shameful acts.

226. Know well that nobody upon earth is free of all faults except the Prophets, may God bless them.

227. A man who does not see his own faults is a fallen being; he comes to be so from baseness, turpitude, stupidity and feebleness of intelligence, lack of discernment and understanding, to such a point that he is no different from vile men and it is not possible to drop lower into degradation than he has. Let him save his soul by seeking out his own faults and turning attention upon them instead of his pride and the faults of others, the doing of which harms him neither in this world or the next.

228. I do not know of any benefit to be drawn from hearing about the faults of other people except that he who hears about them may learn the lesson, avoid them and seek to cure himself of them with God's assistance and might.

229. To speak of the faults of others is a serious shame which is absolutely not acceptable. One should avoid doing it

except when one wishes to advise someone whom one fears to see fall into the clutches of the person one is criticising or when one only wishes to reprimand a boastful person, which should be done to his face and not behind his back.

230. Then you should say to the boastful man, "Turn round and look at yourself. When you have perceived your own faults you will have found the cure for your pride. Do not compare yourself with someone who has more faults than you do *so that you find it easy to commit faults and to imitate wicked people* [Do not allow yourself to commit vile things and to imitate wicked people]. We have already criticized people who imitate good actions slavishly, what should we say of people who imitate evil actions slavishly? On the contrary, you should compare yourself with someone who is more virtuous than you, then your pride will fade away. Then you will be cured of this hateful disease which gave birth in you to scorn of other people when there are doubtless better people than you among them. If you scorn them with no cause, they will have cause to scorn you, for the Almighty says [*"To condone an evil is to commit the same evil."*] (Qur'an 42:40) "The reward of an evil is an evil like it." So you will expose yourself to scorn, even to deserved disdain, and the anger of God and the loss of every trace of virtue that there may have been in you.

231. If you are proud of your intelligence, remember all the bad thoughts that come into your mind, the deceitful hopes which assail you, then you will realize how feeble your intelligence is.

232. If you are proud of your personal ideas remember your mistakes, keep them in your memory, do not forget them: think of all the times you have believed yourself right and you have been proved wrong, all the times that someone else has been right and you have been wrong. If you do this, you will see that in most cases you have been wrong about as often as right. The score will come out about equal. But it is more likely that your mistakes will be more numerous because this is the case with every human being except the Prophets, the peace of God be upon them!

233. If you are proud of your good works, remember your times of rebellion, your faults, your life in all its aspects. Ah,

by God, then you will find that they outnumber your good works and it will make your good deeds forgotten. So you should worry about this for a long time and replace your pride with self disdain.

234. If you are proud of your knowledge, you should know that it is no credit to you, it is a pure gift that God has granted you. Do not receive it in a way that would anger the Almighty because He might wipe it from your memory by subjecting you to an illness which would make you forget all that you have learned and stored in your memory. I have been told that this happened to 'Abd al-Malik ibn Tarif [d. 400 AH, 1009 AD], who was a scholar, intelligent, moderate, exact in his researches, who had been allotted by fate such a prodigious memory that virtually nothing reached his ears that had to be said to him twice. Now he undertook a journey by ship and experienced such a terrible storm at sea that he lost the memory of most of what he had learnt and suffered considerable upset to his mind. He never recovered his full intelligence. I myself have been struck by illness. When I got up from it I had forgotten all my knowledge except for a few ideas of little value. I did not recover it until several years later.

235. You should also know that there are many people greedy for knowledge, who devote themselves to reading, to study and to research but do not reap any benefit from it. A scholar should realize that it is enough to pursue knowledge, many others will rank higher than him. Knowledge is truly a gift from God. So what place is there for pride? One can only feel humble, give thanks to God Almighty and beg Him to increase His gifts and beseech Him not to withhold them.

236. You should also remember that everything that remains hidden from you, everything that you do not know of the different branches of knowledge, the aspects that you have specialized in, and that you are proud to have penetrated [nevertheless what you do not know] is greater than what you do know. You should therefore replace your pride with scorn and self disdain, that would be better. Think of those who are more knowledgeable than you - you will find that there are many of them - and may your spirit be humble in your own sight.

237. You should also remember that you may be deceived by knowledge, for if you do not put into practice what you know your knowledge will be a testimony against you and it would have been better for you if you had never been a scholar. For you should remember that an ignorant man is wiser than you, he is in a better position, he is more excusable. May your pride then completely disappear.

238. Moreover, the knowledge that you are so proud of having penetrated is perhaps one of the less important branches of knowledge, of no great value, such as poetry or suchlike. You should then remember the man whose branch of study is more noble than yours on the scale of this world and the next, and your soul should become humble in your own sight.

239. If you are proud of your courage, remember those who are more valiant than you. Then examine what you do with your courage that God has granted you. If you waste it in rebellion against God, you are a fool for you are losing your soul by committing acts of no value to it. If you use your courage in obedience to God, you are spoiling it by your pride. You should also remember that your courage will fall away as you grow old and if you live so long you will become dependent, as weak as a baby.

240. It is true that I have never seen less pride than among the brave, and to my mind that proves the purity, greatness and majesty of their spirits.

241. If you are vain because you are strong remember those who may rise against you, your peers, your equals, men who may be perverse, feeble and vile. But you should remember that they are equal to you in the strength you possess even if you would be ashamed to be like them because of their extreme baseness, the ignominy of their souls, their morals, their origins. You should despise any honours which make you the colleague of such men as I have just described, even if you owned the whole world and you had no opponent[1] - something that is far from likely, since no one has

---

1. French translation "and there were no Caliph above you". The word *mukhâlif* is translated "Caliph". In the Arabic text used by the French translation the word appears as *Khalîfa*, but in a footnote the translator writes that

ever heard tell of one man owning the whole inhabited world, even when it was still small and of limited dimensions compared with the uninhabited areas. And just think how tiny it is compared with the celestial sphere that surrounds the universe!

242. Remember what was said by Ibn al Sammâk [Abû al-'Abbâs Muhammad Ibn Subayh, d. 183 AH; 799 AD] to al-Rashîd when the latter asked to be brought a cup of drinking-water: "Commander of the faithful, if this drink were refused you, how much would you offer to get it?" "My entire kingdom," replied al-Rashîd. "Commander of the faithful," continued the other, "if you found that you could not pass water from your body, how much would you sacrifice to be able to do so?" "My entire kingdom." "O Lord of Believers, how can you boast of a kingdom which is not worth as much as a little urine and a few mouthfuls of water?"[2] Ibn al-Sammâk was right, Allah grant him peace.

243. If you were king of all the Muslims, you should remember that the king of Sudan, a disreputable black man, an ignorant man who does not cover his private parts, has a larger kingdom than yours. If you say "I have taken it by right", [no], upon my life, you have not taken it by right if it is a source of arrogance in you and you do not use your position to bring justice. You should be ashamed of your position; it is a state of turpitude, not a state to feel proud of.

244. If you take pride in your wealth, that is the worst degree of pride. Think of all the vile and debauched men who are richer than you and do not take pride in something in which they outdo you. You should realize that it is stupid to take pride in possessions; riches are burdens which bring no benefit until you dispose of them and spend them according to the law. Wealth is also ephemeral and fleeing. It can escape, and you can find it again anywhere, perhaps in someone else's hands, perhaps in the hands of your enemy.[3] To

LQQ [p. 67] has *mukhâlif*, which agrees with the edition of al-Tâhir Makkî (p. 207). I believe that the latter reading is correct and also more fitting in the context.

2. See Ibn Khallikân, *Wafayât*, vol. 2, p. 296.

3. This passage reminds us of Plato's words: "Do not amass gold and silver because the [future] husbands of your [widowed] wives, who will gloat over your demise and ridicule you, will inherit it, while the guilty conscience

take pride in your wealth is stupid, to put your trust in good fortune is a trap and a weakness.

245. If you take pride in your beauty, think of the harm it gives rise to, which we would be ashamed to put into words. You yourself will be ashamed of it when your beauty disappears with age. But in saying this we have said enough.

246. If the praises heaped on you by your friends make you vain, think of the criticism that your enemies direct at you. Then your pride will melt away. And if you have no enemies then there is no good in you at all, for there is nothing lower on the scale of values than the man who has no enemies. That position is reserved for people who have not received from God a single favour worth envying (God preserve us from being in this position!) If you think that your faults are slight, imagine someone else looking at them and think what he would say about them. Then you will feel shame and will know the measure of your faults, if you have the slightest discernment.

247. If you study the laws that regulate human nature and the development of different characters according to the mixture of elements rooted in their souls, you will surely become convinced that you have no merit from your own virtues, that they are only gifts from the Almighty, which, if He had granted them to another, would have made him just like you, and you will realize that, left to your own devices, you would collapse and die. You should replace the pride that you take in your virtues with acts of grace towards the One who gave them to you, and with the fear of losing them, for even the most admirable characters can be altered by illness, poverty, fear, anger or the decrepitude of old age. Show compassion towards those who lack the gifts that you have received, and do not risk losing them by seeking to raise yourself above the One who gave them by claiming merit for yourself or rights in what He has granted you, or by thinking that you can dispense with His protection, for without it you would perish at once and for ever.

---

remains yours alone." [See *Mukhtâr min Kalâm al-Hukamâ' al-Arba'a al Akâbir* in Dimitri Gutas, Greek wisdom literature in Arabic translation, A study of the *Graeco-Arabic Gnomologia*, (New Haven, American oriental society, 1975) p. 129.

248. [For example,] I once suffered a severe illness that caused enlargement of the spleen. I became anguished, peevish, impatient and touchy, and I reproached myself for this, not being willing to face the fact that my character had changed. I was extremely surprised that I had lost my good characteristics. In this way I had good proof that the spleen is the centre of good temper, and that when it is diseased bad temper is the result.

249. If you take pride in your ancestry, that is even worse than everything we have mentioned so far, since it is pride in something that has no real usefulness for you in this world or the next. Just ask yourself whether your ancestry protects you against hunger, or dishonour, or whether it does you any good in the next world.

250. Next, consider those who are equally well descended, or even better, those who are descended from the Prophets [peace be upon them] or their successors, from the virtuous Companions of Muhammad or from scholars; then remember those who are descended from non-Arab kings, the Khosrau[1] and Caesars, those who are descended from the Tubba' and the various kings of Islam. Consider what remains of them and what has survived. Observe those who boast of their ancestry as you do of yours, and you will find that most of them are as ignoble as dogs. You will find that they are low, extremely vile, unreliable; you will find that they are adorned with the very worst characteristics.

251. Therefore you should not boast of something in which such people are your equals or even superior to you. The ancestors which make you so proud may have been debauched, drunken, licentious, frivolous and stupid. Circumstances allowed them to become despots and tyrants; they left an infamous record which will perpetuate their shame for ever. Their crime is immense and their repentance shall be immense on the day of the Last Judgment. Since this is the case, remember that you are taking pride in something that shares in vice, ignominy, shame and dishonour; it is not something to be admired.

---

1. Khosrau or Chosroes is a designation of the ancient Persian kings in general.

252. If you are proud of your descent from virtuous ancestors, how empty their virtue will leave your hands if you yourself are not virtuous! How little pride your ancestors will have in you in this world and the next if you do no good! All men are children of Adam whom God created by His own hand, giving him Paradise for a dwelling place and letting His angels bow down before him. But how little is the advantage they have from this since all the vices dwell in mankind and all the wicked impious people in the world are among their number.

253. When the wise man considers that the virtues of his ancestors do not bring him any closer to his Lord the Almighty and do not win him any favour which he could not have gained by luck in a competition or by his own virtue, not by his wealth, what sense is there in taking pride in a descent which is of no use to him? Someone who feels proud of it, is he not like someone who feels proud of his neighbour's wealth, or a third person's glory, or another's horse because it once wore a bridle that had been his property? It is, as people say, "like a eunuch who takes pride in his father's potency."

254. If your pride leads you to boast, you will be doubly guilty, because your intelligence will have shown that it is incapable of controlling your pride.

255. This would be true if you had good reason to boast, so imagine what it is like if you have no good reason. Noah's son, Abraham's father, and Abu Lahab, the uncle of the Prophet - may God grant him blessings, as also to Noah and Abraham - these were the closest relations of God's most virtuous creatures out of all the sons of Adam. To achieve nobility it would have been enough to follow in their footsteps. But they drew no benefit from it.

256. Among those who have been born illegitimate, some have risen to the highest positions in control of the world's affairs, for example Ziyâd [Ibn Abihi d. 53 AH; 672 AD] and Abû Muslim al-Khurasânî [d.129 AH; 746 AD]. There have been others who have attained supreme virtue, like those whom we respect too highly to name them in this context. We come nearer to God if we love them and model our lives on their glorious achievements.

257. If you take pride in your physical strength, remember that the mule, the donkey, and the bull are stronger than you, and better suited to carrying heavy loads. If you feel vain about the lightness of your running style, remember that the dog and the hare surpass you in this field. It is extremely curious that rational beings feel proud of something in which they are surpassed by dumb animals.

258. You should know that a man who has pride or a feeling of superiority buried deep in his soul should measure how well he tolerates anxieties, adversity, pain, toil or the worries and misfortunes which plague him. If he realizes that he tolerates them with a bad grace, he should remember that all those who are subjected to trials, those who are starving and have nothing to eat for example, all those who suffer patiently, they have more merit than he does, despite their weaker understanding. However, if he finds that he is capable of endurance, let him remember that this makes him no more exceptional than those we have just mentioned; he may be inferior to them, or their equal, but he is not their superior.

259. Next, let him consider his conduct. Does he act fairly or unfairly when he makes use of the gifts which God has granted him, money, power, slaves, health or fame? If he finds that he has failed in his obligation to feel grateful towards the Almighty Benefactor, if he finds that he is at the extreme edge of fairness, bordering on injustice, he should remember that people who are just and grateful and honest have been more favoured than he and are more virtuous than he. If he considers that he does love justice let him remember that a just man is far from proud because he knows the real importance of things, the real value of characters, and he loves the happy medium which is the balance between two bad extremes. It follows that if he feels proud, he cannot be a just man; on the contrary, he must incline towards one of these bad extremes.

260. You should remember that if you oppress or maltreat beings whose fate has been entrusted to you by God as slaves or subjects, this shows that you have an ignoble soul, a vile spirit, a weak intelligence. Indeed, a wise man with his noble spirit, his elevated thoughts, fights only against people as strong as himself, his peers in potency; but to attack those

who cannot defend themselves is the sign of a vile nature, a depraved soul and character, it shows you to be incapable and dishonorable. A man who behaved like this would descend to the level of someone who was pleased to have killed a rat, to have exterminated a flea or to have squashed a louse. There is nothing more base or vile.

261. Remember that it is harder to tame the self than to tame wild beasts. In fact, when wild beasts are shut inside cages ordered for them by kings, they cannot harm you. But the self, even if it were put in a prison, could not be guaranteed to do you no harm.

262. Pride is like a tree trunk; its branches are complacency, presumptuousness, haughtiness, arrogance and superiority. These terms refer to concepts that are very similar to each other and hard for most people to tell apart. A proud man becomes proud because of an obvious merit: one man may be vain about his own scholarship, and be haughty and scornful towards others; another may be vain about his deeds and believe himself to be eminent and superior. One man is proud of his own judgment and becomes arrogant; another is self-satsified and becomes complacent. Another, full of his own reputation and high standing, becomes self-important and haughty.

263. The lowest degree of pride is when you refrain from laughing when laughter is not out of place; you avoid quick movements and responses except when it is unavoidable in daily life. However, such a fault is not very serious. To behave in this way in order to get on with one's work and to avoid timewasting nonsense would even be a praiseworthy virtue. But these people only behave like this out of disdain for others and from pride in themselves, and so they deserve only blame, for deeds are of value according to the intentions of the doer, and every being shall be rewarded according to what he intended to do.[1]

264. Next, a more serious case is when you are not clever enough to keep pride within its rightful limits, when your spirit is too weak, and you reach the point of showing dis-

---

1. This is a part of a *hadith* reported by 'Umar Ibn al-Khattâb and related by al-Bukhari and Muslim.

dain and scorn towards other people by your words and
deeds. Then, going even further, when your sense and your
spirit are even weaker, you reach the point of desiring to
harm people with words and with blows, to give them
orders, to commit abuses, to tyrannise them and to exact
where possible, obedience and submission from them. When
he is unable to do this, the proud man sings his own praises
and contents himself with criticizing other people and mocking them.

265. Pride can also exist for no good reason and where
there is no merit in the proud person; this is the strangest
thing about it. The popular phrase for it is *"Mutamandil discernment"*.[1] It is often found in women or in men whose spirit
is rather effeminate. It is the pride of someone who has absolutely no good quality: neither knowledge, nor courage, nor
high social standing, nor noble descent, nor fortune, which
might give him abusive authority. And, what is more, such a
man knows that he is a nonentity in every way, for even the
idiot that has stones thrown at him knows this. The only person who can deceive himself is one who has a small part of
some good qualities. For example, a man who is endowed
with a little brain might imagine himself to have reached the
extreme limits of intelligence; someone with a little scientific
knowledge might imagine himself to be a perfect expert.
Someone whose genealogy has [obscure] bad origins and
whose ancestors were not even great tyrants is more infatuat-
ed with himself than if he were the son of the [mighty]
Pharaoh of the forces.[2] If he has some value as a warrior he
thinks he can put 'Alî [Ibn Abî Tâlib] to flight, capture al
Zubayr [Ibn al-'Awwâm] and slay Khâlid [Ibn al-Walîd]. If he
is at all notorious, he holds Alexander the Great in small
esteem. If he is capable of gaining a little money and to
obtain a little more than the absolute necessities of life, he is
as proud of it as if he had got hold of the sun by its horns.

---

1. The French translation has *Mutamandil*. Makkî supplies a long footnote
about the colloquial term current among the Andalusians. He thinks that it
may go back to classial Arabic *Taraka* - "abandon, leave, forget", (pp. 220F).

But we feel that it may mean "talking too much about something one
lacks", as a miser might speak of generosity etc.

2. This is a Qur'anic expression, [Qur'an 89:10].

However, pride among such men, even if they are admirable
fellows, is not common. However, it is common among those
who have not an iota of knowledge, nobility, fortune, reputation or courage. They are dragged along by others, and they
trample on those who are weaker than themselves. Although
they are perfectly aware that they themselves are lacking in
all good qualities and have none whatsoever, they are still
haughty and insolent.

266. I took the opportunity of asking one such man - gently and tactfully - what was the cause of his sense of superiority and his disdain of others. The only answer I could get
was this: "I am a free man", he said, "I am nobody's slave."

I replied "Most people that one meets share this same
quality with you. Like you, they are free men, except for a
certain number of slaves who are more generous than you
and who give orders to you and to many other free men." I
could not get anything else out of him.

267. I returned to consideration of their case, going into
the matter deeply. I thought about it for years on end, trying
to find the reasons which drove them to a pride that was so
unjustified. I searched the recesses of their souls incessantly,
on the basis of what their words reflected of their situation
and their intentions. I came to the conclusion that they imagined themselves to have a superior intelligence and perception and a good sense of judgment. [They believed that] if
fate had allowed them to make use of these talents, they
would have had immense possibilities, they would have
known how to direct powerful kingdoms and their merit
would have appeared superior to that of other men. If they
had had a fortune they would have been very good at spending it. And this is the angle by which vanity has taken possession of them and pride has penetrated their souls.

268. Here one might make curious digressions and [point
out] certain paradoxes. It is a fact that no virtue except that
of intelligence and perception allows one to believe that one
is a past master in it, and the more one is completely sure
that one has attained perfection in it, the more one lacks it.

This is so much the case that one will see a raving lunatic
or an inveterate sot making fun of a sane man. A mentally
deficient person will mock men who are wise, virtuous and

knowledgeable. Little boys shout after grown men. Men who are stupid and insolent disdain men who are intelligent and reserved. Even the weakest women think that the spirit and opinions of great men lack vigour. In sum, the weaker the intelligence the more the man imagines himself well endowed and in possession of excellent powers of perception. This is not at all the case with other qualities: someone who has none of them knows that he lacks them. Error only arises in a man who has a small portion, even if it is tiny, because he then imagines, if he has limited powers of perception, that he possesses this quality to the highest degree.

269. The cures for pride among such people are poverty and obscurity; there is nothing more effective, for if not awed they are bad and a considerable nuisance to other men. You find them doing nothing but discrediting people, attacking their reputations, mocking at everybody, scorning all rights and permitting themselves every indiscretion. They go to the limit, to the point of risking injury to themselves, and entering into dispute, they even come to blows and punches for the most futile cause that presents itself.

270. It can happen that pride lies hidden in the depths of a man's heart and does not appear until he meets with some success or acquires some fortune and his good sense can neither control nor conceal this feeling.

271. Something that I have seen that is very curious, among certain weak creatures, is that they are so dominated by a deep love for their grandchild or their wife that they describe them in public as extremely intelligent. They go as far as to say, "She is more intelligent than me and I regard her advice as a blessing." They praise her beauty, her charm, her vivacity - this often happens with very feeble men - and do it so much and so well that if they wished to find her a husband they need say nothing more in order to make someone desire her from their description. Such behaviour is only found among souls which are weak and lacking in all self-esteem.

272. Take care not to boast, because nobody will believe you, even if you are telling the truth. On the contrary, they will take everything that you have said when boasting about yourself and use it as the basis of their criticism of you.

273. Take care not to praise someone to his face; this would be to behave like a vile flatterer.

274. Also take care not to criticise anyone, either to his face or behind his back. You have enough to do correcting your own behaviour.

275. Take care not to pretend to be poor. You will not gain anything except to be treated as a liar or to be scorned by anyone who listens to you. You will have no benefit from it except that you will fail to recognize the gifts you have from the Lord, and if you complain about it to anyone they will have no pity on you.

276. You should also take care not to display your wealth for all that you will achieve is that those who hear you will covet what you possess.

277. Be content to offer thanks to the Almighty, to confide your needs to Him, and to take no notice of those who are inferior to Him. In this way you will keep your dignity, and those who envy you will leave you alone.

278. A wise man is one who does not neglect the duties imposed upon him by his intelligence.

279. Anyone who tempts others with his riches has no choice but to share them out - and there would be no end to this - or to refuse them which would make him seem mean and would attract universal hostility. If you wish to give something to somebody, do it of your own initiative and before he asks for it; this is more noble, more disinterested and more worthy of praise.

280. Something peculiar about envy is when you hear a jealous person say, when someone has done original work in some branch of science, "What a silly person! Nobody has ever put forward that hypothesis before and nobody has ever believed that." But if the same person hears someone expound an idea which is not new, he exclaims, "What a silly person! This is not a new idea!" This sort of person is harmful because he is bent on obstructing the path of knowledge and turning people away from it in order to increase the number of his own sort, the ignorant.

281. The wisdom of the wise man brings him no profit in the eyes of a wicked man; the latter thinks that he is as wicked as himself. Thus I have seen vile creatures imagine in

their vile souls that everybody was like themselves; they would never believe that it was possible, in one way or another, not to have their faults. There is no character more corrupt, there is none more remote from being virtuous and good. Anyone who is in this state cannot hope to be cured at all. Allah helps us in all matters.

282. Justice is a fortress in which all who are frightened take refuge. In fact, if a tyrant feels oppressed, does he not call for justice and scorn and condemn injustice? But you never see the opposite, someone condemning justice. Therefore a man who is equitable by nature can rest at peace in this impregnable fortress.

283. Scorn is a variety of treachery, for someone can be disloyal towards you without scorning you, but if he scorns you he is betraying the impartiality he should show towards you. Therefore every scornful man is disloyal, but not every disloyal man is scornful.

284. If you scorn a thing it shows that you scorn the man who possesses it.

285. There are two circumstances in which it is good to do something which would otherwise be bad: it is when one wishes to reproach someone or to present excuses to someone. In these two cases, it is permissible to list past benefits and to recall gifts. In all cases except these two it would be in the worst possible taste.

286. We should not criticise someone who has a natural tendency towards a vice - even if it were the worst possible fault, the greatest of vices - as long as he does not let it appear in anything he says or does. He would almost deserve more commendation than someone who naturally inclines towards virtue, for it takes a strong and virtuous mind to control a corrupt natural inclination.

287. To attack a man's conjugal honour is worse than to attack his life.

288. To a well-born man, honour is dearer than gold. A well-born man should use his gold to protect his body, his body to protect his soul, his soul to protect his honour, and his honour to defend his religion. But he must never sacrifice his religion in defence of anything whatsoever.

289. To attack a man's honour is less serious than to steal

from his property. The proof of this is that almost nobody, not even the most virtuous, can say that he has never attacked anyone's honour, though it may have been only rarely. But to have stolen someone's property, whether on a small scale or a large scale, is definitely the deed of a vile person and far from virtue.

290. Drawing analogies between different situations is mostly deceptive and it can be quite false. This form of argument is not acceptable in problems which concern religion.

291. A man who blindly follows another slavishly is asking to be cheated out of his own thoughts when he would consider it the greatest of crimes to be cheated out of his money. He is equally wrong in both cases.

292. A man who considers it hateful to be tricked out of his fortune, and regards it as the worst of crimes, must have an ignoble character, a mean spirit, and a soul worthy of disdain.

293. Anyone who does not know where to find virtue should rely on the commandments of God and His Prophet - peace of Allah be upon him. All the virtues are contained in these commandments.

294. It is possible to bring about something dangerous by trying to guard against it. It is possible to let out a secret by trying too hard to keep it. Sometimes it is better to avoid a subject than to raise doubts by dwelling on it. In each of these cases the harm comes from overdoing it and going beyond the boundaries of the happy medium.

295. Virtue is the medium between the two extremes [the "too much" and the "too little"]. These two extremes are to be criticised - and virtue, lying between them, is to be praised - except when it is a question of intelligence, and then there can be no excess.

296. It is better to sin by being too strict than by being too soft.

297. It is astonishing to see that virtue is regarded as lovely but difficult, and vice as awful but easy to commit.

298. A person who wishes to be fair should put himself in his adversary's position. He will then see the unfairness of his own behaviour.

299. The definition of strictness consists of being able to

distinguish a friend from an enemy. The height of stupidity and weakness is the inability to distinguish one's enemy from one's friend.

300. Do not deliver your enemy to an oppressor, and do not oppress him yourself. Treat him as you would treat your friend, except for trusting him. Be careful not to mix with him or to help him rise socially; that would be the behaviour of a fool. Anyone who treats his enemy as equal to his friend in closeness and in promoting his position only succeeds in making people avoid his friendship and they find it just as easy to be his enemies. He will only win the disrespect of his enemy by handing him his vulnerable places, and he will lose his friend, since the latter will join the ranks of his adversaries.

301. The greatest of good deeds is to refrain from punishing your enemy and from handing him over to an oppressor. As for mixing with him, that is the mark of fools who will soon be lost.

302. The worst evil is to oppress your friend. As for keeping him away from yourself, that would be the action of a man without spirit and destined for misfortune.

303. Magnanimity consists not of mingling with our enemies but of showing mercy to them while still not trusting them.

304. How many men have we not seen take pride in their possessions and so be lost! Guard against this attitude, it is really harmful and completely useless. How many men we have seen lost because of something they said. But we have never heard of anyone being lost because he kept silent. Therefore you should speak only to please your Creator; and if you fear that what you say will be abused, then keep silent.

305. I have rarely seen a lost opportunity ever reoccur.

306. A man undergoes many trials during his life, but the worst are those inflicted by his fellow man. The harm done by man to man is worse than the harm done by furious beasts and poisoned vipers for you can protect yourself against animals, but you cannot protect yourself at all against the human race.

307. Hypocrisy is the thing which is most widespread among people and it is amazing to see that, despite this, peo-

ple only like those who treat them hypocritically.

308. If we said that characters are round like a globe because their extremes meet, we should not be far from the truth. Indeed we see that the consequences of the two extremes are alike and a person cries for joy as much as he cries for sorrow; too much love makes one commit as many successive faults as excessive hatred does, and can cause estrangement if the loved one lacks patience and fairness.

309. If a man is dominated by a natural passion, then, however firm and sensible he is in other ways, he can be overcome if you attack this weak point.

310. An over-suspicious mind learns to tell lies: since he often needs to excuse himself by lying he is practised in it and finds it easy.

311. The most impartial witness against a man who is given to sincerity is his face; it clouds over as soon as he tells a lie or is about to do so.

312. The most implacable witness against a liar is his own tongue; it gets twisted and contradicts itself.

313. It is a greater catastrophe to have an unfaithful friend than to lose him.

314. Those who show most horror when speaking out loud of shameful acts are those who are most apt to commit them. This can clearly be seen in the insolence offered by guttersnipes and the insults of vile men who have reached the nadir of vileness in practising vile professions. For example, those men and women who earn their living by playing the flute, sweeping out farmyards, working as servants in abattoirs, those who frequent the [drinking houses] brothel authorized as meeting places of people of the lowest class or stable boys. Nobody abuses them more than they abuse themselves. More than anybody else they cry scandal when they wallow in it in the first place and have acquired the worst of reputations by it.

315. Meetings make grudges melt away.[1] One would think that when glances meet, hearts grow peaceful. Do not torture yourself if your friend meets your enemy, for the meeting will lessen the latter's hatred towards you.

---

1. This is a part of *hadith*.

316. The worst misfortunes that can come upon men are fear, anxiety, sickness and poverty. But the thing that makes the soul suffer most cruelly is the anxiety of losing what one loves and to see something happen that one hates. After this comes sickness, then fear, then poverty. The proof of this is that people would willingly accept poverty if this kept fear at bay and would sacrifice a fortune to feel safe. People would willingly accept fear and poverty to avoid the pains of illness. For a man quests ardently after health and does not count what he spends to recover it when he fears death. When his end is certain he would like to be able to give his entire fortune to be saved and cured. Fear is bearable when it drives off anxiety, for a man seeks with all his soul to drive away anxiety. The worst of all illnesses is pain that persists in one organ, always the same.

317. But to a well born spirit, humiliation is less bearable than all the misfortunes we have described. On the other hand, it is the one that knavish spirits fear the least.[1]

---

1. It should be noted that Ibn Hazm's stanza on morality in Makkî's text (pp.239F) has been placed elsewhere according to the order of the French translation (see p.66 and F.N.1).

X

Section dealing with Curious Particularities of the Characteristics of the Soul

318. A wise man should not judge by appearances when a sniveller cries for mercy, pretends that he is oppressed, complains, twists and turns and laments. With a man who behaves like this I have become certain that he was the oppressor who went over the limit and committed excessive abuses. And likewise I have seen a man bearing an injustice speak calmly without complaining and only displaying a little anxiety. At first glance, without further examination, you would have taken him for the oppressor. In cases such as this it is important to establish the facts, fight resolutely against our inclination to take sides, not incline towards or against such attitudes as we have described, and seek to be impartial to all, as we are obliged to by justice.

319. A curious thing about human nature is that carelessness is bad when it is good to know how to make use of it sometimes. This can only be explained by the fact that a man who is naturally inclined to carelessness, makes use of it when he should be vigilant. It is absentmindedness with no sense of reality. His carelessness belongs under the heading of ignorance and that is why it is bad. On the other hand, a spirit which is vigilant by nature only makes use of carelessness for a good purpose when he should not study or research deeply into a subject. To pretend to ignore something in this case means to understand reality, to refuse to act precipitously, to use moderation and to prevent the worst happening. Thus it is praiseworthy to know how to pretend not to be listening, and bad to be naturally inattentive.

320. The same could be said about admitting one is afraid or concealing the fact. To make it obvious that one is troubled as soon as one begins to have difficulties is bad, because it means that you cannot control yourself and your display of emotion serves no useful purpose. Indeed, divine law counsels against it; it stops you doing what has to be done and to make the necessary arrangements in view of the events

which one foresees and which may be more terrible than the present situation which has given rise to this fear.

321. Now, given that it is wrong to let your fear be seen, the opposite is good, that is, to display patience, because that means you are in control of yourself, you have turned away from useless actions and towards actions which are profitable and useful both immediately and in the future.

322. As for hiding your patience, that is wrong too, since it would look as if you were unfeeling, hardhearted and lacking in mercy. These faults are found only among wicked people, vicious natures, cruel and vile souls.

323. All this being very ugly, the opposite, which consists of concealing the fact that you are troubled, is praiseworthy because it is a mark of pity, gentleness, charity and compassion.

324. Thus one can say that the happy medium, for a man, is to have a sensitive soul but an impassive body, that is to say that neither on his face or in his comportment should there be any sign that he is troubled.

If a man whose own judgment is poor only knew what harm his false calculations had brought upon him so far, he would find success in the future if he stopped relying on his own judgment, Allah guide us.

XI

Section dealing with a Man's Desire to Know, What you Should Tell Him and Not Tell Him, and How to be Praised and Renowned.

325. These are longings from which hardly anyone is exempt, except a man whose thoughts are completely vile or one who has trained himself by a perfect system of discipline and has completely tamed the power of his angry soul. In order to cure the avid desire that the soul feels to seize information that one wants to conceal from it or to see an object that one wants to hide from him, you should think of all the things of the same kind which escape him in places where he has not been, let alone the most distant areas of the earth. If the person worries about them he is completely mad and totally lacking in reason. [On the other hand] if he is not worried about these other things, is the thing hidden from him not the same as these things that do not worry him, absolutely identical in fact? He should multiply the arguments directed against his passion, and he should speak to his soul with the voice of reason, "O my soul, if you did not know that there was something there being hidden from you, do you think that you would worry about getting to know it?" There is no doubt that the answer would be "No." Then he should say to his soul, "Act as if you did not know that there was something there being hidden from you. Then you can relax and you will be able to drive away your anxiety and calm your painful agitation and your hateful greed." These are numerous victories, considerable gains, and noble ambitions to which a wise man aspires and which only someone totally lacking disdains.

326. As for the man who has the ambition and the obsession to spread his fame to every country and to be remembered throughout the centuries, let him reflect and say to his soul: "O my soul, if you were gloriously famous in all the countries of the world, for all eternity and to the end of time, but if I was not told about it and if I knew nothing about it, do you think I would be happy or satisfied about it, yes or

no?" There is no doubt that the answer would be "No", for any other answer would be impossible. Having convinced himself of this truth, the man must understand that when he is dead he will have no possibility of knowing whether he is famous or not. Moreover he would not know while he was still alive if nobody told him.

327. He should also consider two important points. First, that there have been in earlier times a great number of virtuous Prophets and Messengers of God - God grant them His blessing - of whom nobody on the surface of the earth remembers the name, nor any trace, nor any memory, nor their history, nor the slightest thing about them.

328. Secondly, there have been, among the good and virtuous men who were the companions of the Prophets in ancient times, ascetics, philosophers, scholars, excellent men, kings of nations which have disappeared, founders of cities which are now deserted, courtesans of princes whose history has also not come down to us. Nobody knows anything about them nowadays and nobody has the slightest knowledge that they existed. Has that fact harmed any of them that were virtuous? Has it diminished their merit, destroyed their good deeds, has it lowered them in the eyes of their Almighty Creator? Let me tell anyone who did not already know it that there does not exist anywhere in the world the smallest scrap of information about any of the earthly sovereigns or the ancient generations who preceded men's historical knowledge, which begins with the kings of Israel. And everything that we know of the history of the sovereigns of Greece and of Persia does not go back further than two thousand years. Where is the remembrance of the men who peopled the earth before them? Is it not, in fact, totally wiped out, disappeared, vanished, forgotten?

This is why the Almighty has spoken of *"Messengers of whom We have not told you the history at all"* [Qur'an 4:164] and God also said: *"Many centuries in between,"* [Qur'an 25:38] and God also said: *"Those who came after and who are known only to God"* [Qur'an 14:9]. Even if the memory of a man persists for a short period of time, would that in itself make him any different from those who lived in olden times in nations that have disappeared and of which the memory also persisted a short while before being completely lost?

329. We should also think of those who were famous for their good deeds or their bad deeds; did their fame raise them one single degree in the sight of God? Did it win them a reward that they had not already won by their actions during their life?

330. Since this is so, the desire to be famous is nothing but the desire for something absolutely senseless and useless. On the contrary, a wise man should aspire only to multiply his virtues and his good deeds, which make the one who applies himself to them merit a good reputation, praise, commendation and a praiseworthy reputation which will bring him nearer to his Creator and will be useful in remembering him to the Almighty. He will keep himself in this beneficial state and will never be lost for all eternity; assistance is from God.

331. Gratitude towards a benefactor is a necessary obligation. To fulfil it, you should at least render to him the good that he has done you, and more. Afterwards you should show interest in his affairs, protect him as much as possible, keep faithfully to promises that you have made him, in his life or after his death, and to his relations, both distant and close. Thus you should continue to show affection to him, to give him advice. You should make his good qualities known truthfully and you should conceal his faults. [These obligations lie upon you] for the rest of your life and should be handed down to your descendants and to those you love.

332. However, it is no part of gratitude to assist someone in committing a sin and not to advise him in the cases where he is doing himself harm in this world and the next. On the contrary, anyone who helps his benefactor to do evil is deceiving him, denying his benefactions, acting unjustly in his respect and failing to recognize his goodness. Moreover, the goodness and benefactions of God towards each one of His creatures are much more considerable, more longstanding, more salutary than those of any other benefactor. Indeed, it is the Almighty who has opened our eyes to see, who has pierced our ears to hear, it is He who has granted us the other excellent senses and has endowed us with speech and discernment, two benefits by grace of which we have been

made able to hear His words. He has subjected to our service everything which exists in the skies and upon the earth - stars and elements - and has placed none of His creatures above us, except only His holy angels, the inhabitants of the heavens. What are the gifts of men compared with these! Anyone who imagines that he is thanking a benefactor by helping him to do evil, or by taking his side when he should not, would be denying the gifts of the greatest of his benefactors, whose gifts he would be failing to recognize. He would not be rendering thanks to Him to whom all thanks truly belong, he would not be praising Him who is the essence of praiseworthiness, that is to say, Allah the Almighty.

Anyone who steps between his benefactor and evil, leading him back to the bitter truth, would be showing true gratitude and would be fulfilling perfectly his obligation towards him. Praises be to God at first and at last and in all circumstances!

XII

On the Way to Attend Study-Sessions

333. If you attend a study-session, behave only like someone who wishes to increase his knowledge and to win greater
recompense from God. Do not behave like someone who is
content with what he has, who is looking for some fault to
criticise or a curious detail to hawk around. This would be
the behaviour of vile men who never succeed in their studies.

If you come to it with good intentions, you will always
obtain the best results. Otherwise, to stay at home would be
less tiring for your body, more worthy of your moral conduct
and more salutary for your religious life.

334. If you do attend under the conditions that we have
indicated, take care to adopt one of these three attitudes -
and there cannot be a fourth: [First,] you may keep quiet in
the silence of ignorance. Thus you will obtain the reward of
your intention in attending the study-session, praise for your
reserve, dignity in your behaviour and the friendship of
those you mix with.

335. [Secondly,] if you do not behave like this, ask the
questions which someone would ask who wished to learn.
Then you will obtain, in addition to the four advantages just
mentioned, a fifth, which is to increase your knowledge.
What characterizes the questions asked by someone who
wishes to learn is that he only asks about the points he does
not know, not those he does know. To ask about what one
already knows is a proof of ineptitude and a weak spirit, it is
only palaver and a useless waste of time for oneself and for
others. By doing this you will only provoke dislike and it will
only be pure verbiage. So do not play games, it is a bad fault.

If the person you are asking replies satisfactorily, stop
questioning. If his reply is not satisfactory, or if you do not
understand it, say to him, "I do not understand", and ask
him to elaborate. If he does not explain himself more clearly,
if he keeps silent or if he repeats what he said before without
adding anything, keep silent, otherwise you will only bring
upon yourself trouble and dislike, without obtaining the
desired enlightenment.

[Thirdly,] you can riposte as a scholar would, that is to say that you can reply to the arguments advanced in a way that refutes them clearly. If you are not capable of replying in this way, if you are able only to repeat yourself or to reply using arguments which your adversary will not find convincing, do not insist for you will not gain by your repetitions any extra result or any information. You will only succeed in annoying yourself and starting a hostility between the two of you which could have serious consequences.

337. Guard against the questions that a prejudiced man would ask or the ripostes of a show-off who is bent on being right without knowing anything about the matter. These two attitudes are bad: they witness to absence of piety, a great tendency to verbiage, a weakness of spirit and considerable vanity. Let us commend the matter to God who is our best support.

338. If certain statements are put to you verbally, or if you come across a written text, guard against reacting violently, which will bring about excesses in language, before you have assured yourself by irrefutable proof that the ideas expressed are erroneous.

Neither should you accept them with the enthusiasm of someone who is credulous and convinced until you have assured yourself of their veracity by an irrefutable proof. In the two cases, you would be shutting your eyes and turning away from knowing the truth. On the contrary, consider what is being put to you as one would who is neither against it nor for it, one who wants to understand, to the best of his ability, what he has heard and read in order to increase his knowledge, to adopt the new ideas if they are good or reject them if they are erroneous. It is certain that if you behave like this you will be generally rewarded, greatly praised and your merit will be recognized.

339. A man who is content with the small fortune that he has and does not envy your opulence is as rich as you, even if you are a Croesus. If this man resists the bait of gain to which you have succumbed, he will be much richer than you.

340. Anyone who rises above the things of this world to which you kneel is mightier than you.

341. It is a pious duty for Muslims to teach the good and

to practise it. Anyone who does both these things at once is doing two virtuous deeds to perfection. But a person who contents himself with teaching the good without practising it is acting well by teaching and acting badly by failing to put his teaching into practice, so mingling a good with a bad deed. This case is preferable to that of the person who would not teach the good any more than he would practise it. Such a man, although not virtuous, is more worthy of imitation, he is less blameworthy than someone who forbids the teaching of good and opposing anyone who practises it.

342. If it was only a man completely without sin who had the right to forbid evil, if it was only the man of perfect virtue who could teach the good, nobody yet would have forbidden evil or ordained the good since [the death of] the Prophet - peace be upon him. This should be enough to make clear to you the corruption, wickedness and opprobrium of anyone who might think this.

343. Abu Muhammad - may God be satisfied with him - said, "Here someone contradicted, protesting, 'When al-Hasan [al-Basrî] - may God be satisfied with him - forbade something [bad], he never did it himself, and when he ordained something [good], he himself put his orders firmly into practice. Wisdom requires that we do the same, for it has been said that: nothing is more odious than to preach something and not practise it, or to preach against an action and then to do it.'"

344. Abû Muhammad replied, "The person who said that was lying. There is something more ugly, that is, not to preach good and not to preach against evil and also to allow oneself to act badly and not to do good."

345. Abû Muhammad added: Abû al-Aswad al-Du'alî said this: Do not forbid a vice that you are given to yourself, for great shame will fall on you. Start with yourself and forbid yourself your own misdeeds. If you stop devoting yourself to them you will become a wise man. Then your sermons will be accepted, people will take their example from your knowledge and your teaching will be profitable.

346. Abû Muhammad continued: Abû al-Aswad wished to condemn only someone who has done a deed after forbidding it to others: such a deed would be doubly bad for hav-

ing been committed by the very person who forbade it. The poet was quite right for this is what the Almighty said, "*Will you command people to do good and forget to do it yourself?*" [Qur'an 2:44]. It cannot be believed that Abû al-Aswad wanted to express any other idea. As for thinking that he did not want to be condemned for a bad deed, God protect him from that! That would have been to act like a wicked man.

347. Here is a true story about al-Hasan: When he heard someone say that only a person who did no evil had the right to forbid evil, he replied, "Satan would like us to believe that, and then nobody could forbid evil or ordain good."

Abû Muhammad continued: "Al-Hasan was right, and that is what we said before."

348. May God grant that we may count among the number of those whom He permits to do good and to practise it, and among the number of those who see the straight road, for no one is without faults; someone who perceived his own weaknesses will forget those of others. May God permit us to die in the *Sunna* [law] of Muhammad. Amen, O Lord of the Worlds!

[The book is finished, with the grace of God,
His help and His good will. May God
bless our master Muhammad, his
family and his companions,
grant them life eternal,
and may God be pleased
with Ahmad [Muhammad],
messenger of God!]

BIBLIOGRAPHY

Arabic Sources

Abû Hayyân al-Tawhidî, *al-Imtâ' wa'l Mu'ânasa*, ed. by Ahmad Amîn and Ahmad al-Zîn, vol. 2, (Beirut, Dâr Maktabat al-Haya, n.d.).

Abû Zahra, Muhammad, *Ibn Hazm Hayâtu wa 'Asru Arâ'u wa Fiqhu*, (Cairo, Dâr al-Fikr al-'Arabî, 1954).

Al-Afghânî, Sa'id, *Ibn Hazm al-Andalusi wa Risâla fî'l-Mufadâla Bayna al-Sahâba*, (Beirut, Dâr al-Fikr, 1969).

----- *Mulakhkhas Ibtâl al-Qiyâs wa'l Ra'y wa'l-Istihsân wa'l-Taqlîd wa'l Ta'lîl*, (Damascus, 1960).

----- *Nazarât fî'l-Lugha 'Inda Ibn Hazm al-Andalusi*, (Beirut, Dâr al-Fikr, 1969).

al-'Amiri, *al-I'lam Bimanâqib al-Islam*, ed. by Ahmad A. Ghurâb, (Cairo, Dâr al-Kitâb al-'Arabî, 1967).

al-Ash'ari, Abû al-Hasan, *al-Ibâna 'An Usûl al-Diyâna*, ed. by Fawqiyya Husayn Mahmûd, (Cairo, Dâr al-Ansâr, 1397 AH; 1977 AD).

Badawî, 'Abd Al-Rahmân, *al-Akhlâq al-Nazariyya*, (Kuwait, Wakâlat al-Matbû'at, 1975).

----- *Dirâsât wa Nusûs fî'l Falsafa wa'l 'Ulûm 'Ind al-'Arab*, (Beirut, al-Mu'asasa al-'Arabiyya lil Dirâsât, 1981).

----- (ed.) *Rasâ'il Falsafiyya*, (Beirut, Dâr al-'Afâq al-Jadîda, n.d.).

al-Bunî, Ahmad Ibn 'Alî, *Shams al-Ma'ârif al-Kubrâ*, 4 vols., (Cairo, Subayh, n.d.).

Al-Dhahabî, Abû 'Abd Allah Shams al-Dîn, *Siyar al-Nubalâ*, ed. by Sa'id al-Afghânî, (Beirut, Dâr al-Fikr, 1969).

----- *Tadhkirat al-Huffâz*, part 2, vol. 3, (Hyderabad, Dâr al-Ma'ârif al-'Uthmâniyya, 1958).

Farrûkh, 'Umar, *Ibn Hazm al-Kabîr*, (Beirut, Dâr Lebanon lil-Tibâ'a wa'l-Nashr, 1980).

al-Ghazzâlî, Abû Hâmid, *Ihyâ 'Ulûm al-Din*, vol. 8, (Beirut, Dâr al-Kitâb al-'Arabî, n.d.).

Al-Hajrî, Taha, *Ibn Hazm sûra Andalusiyya*, (Cairo, Dâr al-Fikr al-'Arabî, 1954).

Himâya, Mahmûd 'Alî, *Ibn Hazm wa Manhaju fî Dirâsât al-Adyân*, (Cairo, Dâr al-Ma'ârif, 1983).

al-Humaydî, Abû 'Abd Allah Muhammad Ibn Fattûh, *Judhwat al-Muqtabas fî Dhikr Wulât al-Andalus*, (Cairo, al-Dâr al-Misriyya li'l-Ta'lif wa'l-Tarjama, 1966).

Ibn al-Abbâr, Muhammad Ibn 'Abd Allah, *al-Hulla al-Siyrâ*, ed. by Husayn Mûnis, 2 vols., (Cairo, Matba't Lajnat al-Ta'lif wa'l-Tarjama wa'l-Nashr, 1963).

Ibn 'Abd al-Barr, Abû 'Umar Yûsuf Ibn 'Abd Allah, *Bahjat al-Majâlis wa Uns Mujâlis*, ed. by Muhammad Mursî al-Khulî and 'Abd Al-Qadîr al-Qit, vol. 1, (Cairo, al-Dâr al-Misriyya, n.d.).

Ibn 'Abd Rabbihi, *al-'Iqd al-Farîd*, dâr. 1, (Cairo, al-Maktaba al-Tujariyya, n.d.).

Ibn Abi al-Hadid, *Sharh Nahj al-Balâgha*, ed. by Muhammad Abû al-Fadl Ibrahim, vol. 11, 12, (Cairo, al-Halabi, 1387 AH; 1967 AD).

Ibn al-'Arabî, Muhyi al-Din, *Fusûs al-Hikam*, ed. by Abû al-'Ila 'Afifi, (Beirut, Dâr al-Kitâb al-'Arabî, n.d.), pp. 214ff.

----- *Kitâb al-Fanâ' fî'l-Mushâhada*, (Haydar Abad, Da'irat al-Ma'ârif al-'Uthmâniyya, 1361 AH).

----- *al-Futûhât al-Makkiyya*, vol. 1, (Beirut, Dâr Sadir, n.d.).

----- *Rasâ'il, Risâla Ila al-Imâm Fakhr al-Din al-Râzî*, (Haydarabad, Deccan, Dâ'irat al-Ma'ârif al-'Uthmâniyya, 1367 AH; 1948 AD).

Ibn al-Azraq, Abû 'Abd Allah, *Badâi' al-Silk fî Tabâi' al-Mulk*, ed. by 'Alî Sâmî al-Nashshâr, vol. 2, (Iraq, Kutub al-Turâth, 1978).

Ibn Bashkuwâl, Abû al-Qâsim Khalaf, *al-Sila*, 2 parts, (Cairo, al-Dâr al-Misriyya lil Ta'lif wa'l-Tarjama, 1966.)

Ibn Bassâm, Abû al-Hasan, *'Alî, al-Dhakhîra fî Mahâsin Ahl al-Jazira*, ed. by Ihsân 'Abbâs, part 1, vols. 1, 2, (Libya, Tunisia, al-Dâr al-'Arabiyya lil Kitâb, 1398 AH; 1978 AD)

Ibn al-Bayhaqi, Ibrahim, *al-Mahâsin wa'l Masâwi'*, (Beirut, Dâr Sâdir, 1390 AH; 1970 AD).

Ibn Fâtik, Abû al-Wafâ' al-Mubashshir, *Mukhtâr al-Hikam wa Mahâsin al-Kalim*, ed. by 'Abd Al-Rahmân Badawî, (Madrid, Matba'at al-Ma'had al-Misrî lil Dirâsât al-Islâmiyya, 1377 AH; 1958 AD)

Ibn Hajar, Abû al-Fadl Ahmad, *Lisân al-Mizân*, vol. 4, (Beirut, al-A'lami, 1971).

Ibn Hazm, 'Alî Ibn Ahmad, *al-Akhlâq wa'l-Siyar fî Mudâwât al-Nufûs*, ed. by al-Tâhir Ahmad Makkî, (Cairo, Dâr al-Ma'ârif, 1401 AH; 1981 AD).

----- *Fadâ'il al-Andalus wa Ahliha*, ed. by Salâh al-Dîn al-Munajjid, (Beirut, Dâr al-Kitâb al-Jadîd, 1397 AH; 1968 AD)

----- *al-Fisal fī'l-Milal wa'l-Ahwâ' wa'l-Nihal*, 5 vols., (Cairo, Subayh, 1384 AH; 1964 AD).

----- *al-Fisal*, al-Sulaymâaniyya Codex, Râghib Bâsha Library in Turkey, numbered 815 and 816.

----- *Al-Ihkâm fî Usûl al-Ahkâm*, ed. by Ahmad Shâkir, re-printed and published by Zakariyya 'Alî Yûsuf, 8 vols. in 2 parts, (Cairo, Dâr al-I'tisâm, n.d.).

----- *Jamharat Ansâb al-'Arab*, ed. by 'Abd al-Salâm Hârûn, (Cairo, Dâr al-Ma'ârif, 1962).

----- *Jawâmi' al-Sîra al-Nabawiyya*, (Cairo, Maktabat al-Turâth al-Islâmi, 1982).

----- *Naqt al-'Arûs fî Tawârikh al-Khulafâ'* ed. by Shawqî Dayf, (Cairo, Cairo University, Majallat Kulliyyat al-Adab, December 1951).

----- *Al-Radd 'Alâ Ibn al-Nighrîla al-Yahûdi wa Rasâ'il Ukhra, al-Majmû'a al-Thaniya*, ed. by Ihsân 'Abbâs, (Cairo, Dâr al-Urûba, 1960).

----- *Rasâ'il Ibn Hazm al-Andalusi al-Majmû'a al-Ulâ*, e.d by Ihsân 'Abbâs, (Cairo, al-Khanji/Baghdad, al-Muthanna, 1954).

----- *Rasâ'il Ibn Hazm al-Andalusi, Risâla fî Marâtib al-'Ulûm*, ed. by Ihsân 'Abbâs, vol. 4, (Beirut, al-Mu'asasa al-Misriyya lil Dirâsât wa'l Nashr, 1983); see also Chejne, Ibn Hazm.

----- *Risâla Fî Fadl al-Andalus* in al-Maqqarî, *Nafh al-Tîb*, ed. by Ihsân 'Abbas, vol. 1, (Beirut, Dâr Sâdir, 1968).

----- *Risâla fî'l-Mufadâla Bayna al-Sahâba*, ed. by Sa'îd al-Afghânî, (Beirut, Dâr al-Fikr, 1969).

----- *Al-Taqrîb li Hadd al-Mantiq wa'l-Madkhal Ilayhi Bi'l-Alfâz al-'Ammiyya wa'l-Amthila al-Fiqhiyya*, ed. by Ihsan 'Abbas, (Beirut, Dâr al-Haya, 1959).

----- *Tawq al-Hamâma*, trans. into English by A. J. Arberry under the title *The Ring of the Dove*, (see Arberry).

----- *Tawq al-Hamâma*, ed. by al-Tâhir Ahmad Makkî, (Cairo, Dâr al-Ma'ârif, 1400 AH; 1980 AD)

----- *Al-Usûl wa'l-Furu'*, ed. by Muhammad 'Atif al-'Irâqî et al., 2 vols., (Cairo, Dâr al-Nahda al-'Arabiyya, 1978).

Ibn 'Idhâri, Ahmad Ibn 'Idhâri, *al-Bayân al-Mughrib fî Akhbâr al-Andalus wa'l-Maghrib*, ed. by G. S. Colin and E. Provençal, vols. 1,2,3,4, (Leiden, E. J. Brill, 1951).

Ibn Ishâq, Muhammad, *Sirat Rasûl Allah*, see Guillaume.

Ibn Kathîr, Abû al-Fidâ', *Mukhtasar Tafsîr*, ed. by Muhammad 'Alî al-Sâbûnî, 3 vols., (Beirut, Dâr al-Qur'an al-Karim, 1402 A.H.; 1981 A.D.).

----- *Shamâ'il al-Rasûl*, ed. by Mustafa 'Abd Al-Wâhid, (Beirut, Dâr al-Ma'rifa, 1386 AH; 1967 AD).

Ibn Khaldûn, 'Abd Al-Rahmân, *Muqaddima*, ed. by 'Alî 'Abd al-Wâhid Wâfî, vols. 1,2,3, (Cairo, Dâr Nahdat Misr, third edition, n.d.).

Ibn al-Khatîb, Lisân al-Dîn, *al-Ihâta fî Akhbâr Gharnata*, ed. by Muhammad 'Abd Allah 'Inân, vols. 1,4, (Cairo, al-Khanji, 1397 AH; 1977 AD).

Ibn Manzûr, Muhammad Ibn al-Mukarram, *Lisân al-'Arab al-Muhît*, vol. 10, (Beirut, Dâr Beirut, 1388 AH; 1968 AD).

Ibn Miskawayh, Abû 'Alî Ahmad Ibn Muhammad, *Tahdhîb al-Akhlâq*, (Beirut, Dâr Maktabat al-Haya, n.d.). English translation by Constantine Kzrayk under the title *"The Refinement of Character"*, see Kzrayk.

Ibn Qutayba, *'Uyûn al-Akhbâr*, vol. 2, (Cairo, Dâr al-Kutub, 1343 AH).

Ibn Rushd, Abû al-Walîd, *Talkhîs al-Khatâba*, ed. by Muhammad Salîm Salîm, (Cairo, al-Majlis al-A'lâ lil Shi'ûn al-Islâmiyya, 1387 AH; 1967 AD).

Ibrâhîm, Zakariyya, *Ibn Hazm al-Andalusi al-Mufakkir al-Zâhiri al-Mawsûi*, (Cairo, al-Dâr al-Misriyya lil Ta'lif wa'l-Tarjama, 1966).

Ikhwân al-Safâ, *Rasâ'il*, vol. 2, (Beirut, Dâr Beirut, 1376 AH; 1957 A.D.).

Imru' al-Qays, *Diwân*, ed. by Muhammad Abû Al-Fadl Ibrâhâm, (Cairo, Dâr al-Ma'ârif, 1958).

'Inân Muhammad 'Abd Allah, *Duwal al-Tawâ'if mundh Qiyâmiha Hattâ al-Fathal-Murâbiti*, (Cairo, al-Khanji, 1389 AH; 1969 AD).

al-Jâhiz, Abû 'Uthman 'Amru Ibn Bahr, *al-Bayân wa'l Tabîn*, ed. by 'Abd al-Salâm Hârûn, vol. 1, (Cairo, Lajnat al-Ta'lif, 1369 AH).

----- *Majmû'at Rasâ'il*, (Beirut, Dâr al-Nahda al-Hadîtha, 1972).

al-Kâshânî, *al-Haqâ'iq Fî Mahâsin al-Akhlâq*, ed. by Ibrâhîm al-Mabanjî, (Beirut, Dâr al-Kitâb al-'Arabî, 1399 AH; 1979 AD)

Khalîfa, 'Abd al-Karîm, *Ibn Hazm al-Andalusi Hayâtu wa Adabu*, (Beirut, al-Dâr al-'Arabiyya/'Amman, Maktabat al-Aqsa, n.d.).

Khalîfa, Hajjî, *Kashf al-Zunûn*, vol. 2, (Tehran, al-Maktaba al-Islamiyya, 1387.)

al-Makkî, Abû Tâlib Muhammad Ibn Abû al-Hasan, Qûut al-Qulüb, 2 vols., (Beirut, Dâr Sâdir, n.d.).

Makkî, al-Tâhir Ahmad, *Dirâsât Andalusiyya fî'l-Adab wa'l-Târikh wa'l-Falsafa*, (Cairo, Dâr al-Ma'ârif, 1980).

----- *Dirâsât 'An Ibn Hazm wa Kitâbu Tawq al-Hamâma*, (Cairo, Dâr al-Ma'ârif, 1401 AH; 1981 AD).

al-Maqdisî, Ahmad Ibn 'Abd Al-Rahmân Ibn Qudâma, *Mukhtasar Minhâj al-Qâsidîn*, ed. by Shu'ayb al-Arna'ut and 'Abd al-Qadîr al-Arna'ut, (Damascus, 1398 AH).

Al-Maqqarî, Ahmad Ibn Muhammad, *Nafh al-Tîb Min Ghusn al-Andalus al-Ratîb wa Dhikr Wazîriha Lisân al-Dîn Ibn al-Khatîb*, ed. by Ihsân 'Abbâs, vols., 1,2,3,4, (Beirut, Dâr Sâdir, 1968).

Al-Marrâakushî, Muhyî al-Dîn Ibn Muhammad 'Abd al-Wâhid, *al-Mu'jib fî Talkhîs Akhbâr al-Maghrib*, ed. by Dozy, 1st edition, (Leiden, E. J. Brill, 1881), 2nd edition, (Amsterdam, Oriental Press, 1968).

al-Muhâsibî, *al-Ri'âya li Huqûq Allah*, ed. by M. Smith, (London, 1940).

Muqâtil Ibn Sulaymân, *al-Ashbâh wa'l Nazâ'ir fî'l Qur'an al-Karim*, ed. by 'Abd Allah Shihâta, (Cairo, Dâr al-Ma'ârif, n.d.).

al-Nubâhî, *Târikh Qudât al-Andalus*, (Beirut, al-Maktaba al-Tujariyya lil-Tibâ'a wa'l Nashr, n.d.).

Nwyia, Paul (ed.), *Nusûs Sûfiyya Ghayr Manshûra, Tafsîr Ibn 'Atâ'* (Beirut, Dâr al-Mashriq, 1973).

Nykl, A. R., *Mukhtârât min al-Shi'r al-Andalusi,* (Beirut, Dâr al-'Ilm lil Malain, 1949).

al-Qirawânî, 'Abd Al-Karîm al-Nahshali, *al-Mumti' fî 'Ilm al-Shi'r,* ed. by M. al-Ka'bi, (Libya and Tunis, 1398 AH; 1978 AD)

al-Râzî, Ibn Abîi Hâtim, *Adab al-Shâfi'i wa Manâqibuh,* ed. by 'Abd al-Ghanîi 'Abd al-Khâliq, (Syria, Maktabat al-Turâth, 1372 AH; 1953 AD).

----- *al-Tîbb al-Rûhânî,* in Badawî, *Rasâ'il Falsafiyya.*

Sâ'id, Ibn Ahmad Ibn Sâ'id, *Tabaqât al-Umam,* introduced by al-Sayyid Ahmad Bahr al-'Ulûm, (Baghdad, al-Najaf, al-Maktaba al-Haydariyya, 1967).

al-Sajistânî, Abû Sulaymân al-Mantiqî, *Siwân al-Hikma wa Thalâth Rasâ'il,* ed. by A. Badawî, (Tehran, 1974).

al-Sakûnî, Abû 'Alî 'Amr, *'Uyûn al-Munazarât,* ed. by Sa'd Ghurâb, (Tunis, Tunis University Press, 1976).

Al-Shâfi'i, Muhammad Ibn Idrîs, *al-Risâla,* (Cairo, al-Halabi, 1403 AH; 1983 AD).

Al-Shahrastânî, Muhammad Ibn 'Abd Al-Karîm, *al-Milal wa'l-Nihal,* 5 vols., in the margin of Ibn Hazm's *al-Fisal,* (Cairo, Subayh, 1964).

al-Shak'a, Mustafa, *Islâm Bilâ Madhâhib,* (Cairo, al-Halabi, 1977).

Al-Tabarî, 'Alî Ibn Rabban, *al-Dîn wa'l-Dawla fî Ithbât Nubuwwat al-Nabiyy Muhammad Salla Allahu 'Alayhi wa Sallam,* ed. by 'Adel Nuwihad, (Beirut, Dâr al-Afâq al-Jadîda, 1979).

Al-Tabarî, Ibn Jarîr, *Jamî' al-Bayân fî Tafsîr al-Qur'an*, vols. 8 and 29, (Beirut, Dâr al-Ma'rifa, 1392 AH; 1972 AD).

al-Tibrizî, Muhammad Ibn 'Abd Allah al-Khatîb, *Mishkât al-Masâbih*, ed. by M. N. al-Albânî, (Beirut, al-Maktab al-Islami, 1399 AH; 1979 AD).

al-Tustarî, Sahl Ibn 'Abd Allah, *al-Mu'ârada wa'l Radd 'Alâ Ahl al-Firaq wa Ahl al-Da'âwa fî'l Ahwâl*, ed. by Muhammad Kamâl Ja'far, (Cairo, Dâr al-Insân, 1400 AH; 1980 AD).

'Uways, 'Abd Al-Halîm, *Ibn Hazm al-Andalusi wa Juhûdu fî'l-Bahth al-Târikhi wa'l-Hadâri*, (Cairo, Dâr al-I'tisâm, 1979).

Yâqût, Ibn 'Abd Allah al-Hamawî, *Irshâd al-Arib*, vols. 12,17, (Beirut, Dâr al-Mustashriq, 1922).

Other Sources:

Ackrill, J. L., *Aristotle the Philosopher*, (Oxford, Oxford University Press, 1981.)

Alfonsi, Petrus, *The Disciplina Clericalis*, translated and edited by Eberhard Hermes, translated into English by P. R. Quarrie, (London and Henley, Routledge and Kegan Paul Ltd, 1977).

Arberry, A. J., *The Ring of the Dove*, (Great Britain, Burleigh Press, 1953), see Ibn Hazm.

Aristotle, *The Nicomachean Ethics*, translated by J. E. C. Welldon, (London, Macmillan and Co., 1892).

Asín Palacios, Miguel, *Abenházam de Cordoba y su historia critica de las ideas religiosas*, 5 vols., (Madrid, Real Academia de la Historia, 1929-1932).

Boigues, Pons, *Dos obras importantisimas de Aben Hazam "en Homenaje a Menendez y Pelayo"*, (Madrid, 1899).

Chejne, Anwar G., *Ibn Hazm [Risâla fî Marâtib al-'Ulûm]*, (A study and translation, Chicago, Kazi Publications, 1982).

Dozy, Reinhart, *Spanish Islam*, trans. by F. G. Stokes, (Pakistan, Karimsons, 1978).

Gibb, H. A. R., *Arabic Literature, An Introduction*, (Oxford, Oxford University Press, 1974).

Gilson, E., *Reason and Revelation in the Middle Ages*, (New York, 1938).

Goldstein, David, *Hebrew Poems From Spain*, (London, Routledge and Kegan Paul, 1965).

Goldziher, Ignaz, *The Zahiris, Their Doctrine and Their History*, trans. and ed. by Wolfgang Behn, (Leiden, E. J. Brill, 1971).

Guillaume, A., *The Life of Muhammad*, A translation of Ibn Ishaq's *Sirat Rasul Allah*, (Oxford, Oxford University Press, 1978).

Ibn Daud, Abraham, *The Book of Tradition (Sefer Ha-Qabbalah)*, trans. and ed. by Gerson D. Cohen, (Philadelphia, The Jewish Publication Society of America, 1967).

Ibn Hazm, *al-Akhlâq wa'l Siyar*, Introduction, Edition critique, Remarques par Eva Riad, (Sweden, Uppsala, 1980).

Ibn Iskandar, Kai Ka'us, *A Mirror for Princes (The Qabus Nama)*, translated from the Persian by R. Levy, (London, The Cresset Press, 1951).

Imamuddin, S. M., *Some Aspects of the Socio-Economic and*

Cultural History of Muslim Spain (711-1492 AD), (Leiden, E. J. Brill, 1965).

Kzrayk, Constantine, *The Refinement of Character*, (Beirut, American University, 1966), see Ibn Miskawayh.

Levy, R., *The Social Structure of Islam*, (Cambridge, Cambridge University Press, 1969).

Mingana, A. (Trans.), *The Apology of Timothy the Patriarch before the Caliph al-Mahdi*, (Cambridge, Heffer and Sons Ltd, 1928).

Nicholson, Reynold A., *Literary History of the Arabs*, (Cambridge, Cambridge University Press, 1930).

Rosenthal, Franz, *The Classical Heritage in Islam*, (U.S.A., University of California Press, 1975).

----- *The Muslim Concept of Freedom*, (Leiden, E. J. Brill, 1960).

Sell, Edward, *Islam in Spain*, (Vepery, Madras, Diocesan Press, 1929).

Sharif, M., (ed.), *A History of Muslim Philosophy*, vol.1,2, (Germany, Allgaüer Heimatverlag GMbH, Kempten, 1963).

Spinoza, *Risâla fi'l-Lâhût wa'l-Siyâsa*, trans. by Hasan Hanafi and Fu'ad Zakariyya, (Cairo, al-Hay'a al-Misriyya al-'Amma lil Ta'lif wa'l-Nashr, 1971).

al-Turki, 'Abd al-Majid, *Polémiques entre Ibn Hazm et Baqi sur les principes de la loi musulmane: essai sur le littéralisme zahirite et la finalité malikite*, (Alger: Etudes et Documents, 1973).

-----   *Theologiens et juristes de l'Espagne musulmane; aspects polémiques*, (Paris, Editions G.P., Maisonneuve et Larose, 1982).

Wolfson, Harry Austryn, *The Philosophy of the Kalam*, (U.S.A., Harvard University Press, 1976).

Wüstenfeld, F., *Die Geschichtschreiber der Araber und ihre Werke*, (Gottingen, 1882).

Encyclopaedias, Dictionaries, Articles and unpublished materials:

Abû Layla, M., "An Introduction to the Life and Work of Ibn Hazm" (I), *The Islamic Quarterly*, vol. 29, number 2, (London, The Islamic Cultural Centre, 1405 AH; 1985 AD), pp.75-101.

-----   "An Introduction to the Life and Work of Ibn Hazm" (II), *The Islamic Quarterly*, vol. 29, number 3, (London, The Islamic Cultural Centre, 1405 AH; 1985 AD).

-----   *Faith meets Faith*, edited by Gavin D'Costa, (London, B.F.S.S. R.E. Centre, 1988).

-----   "Ibn 'Abd al-Warith al-Andalusi al-Mukhtari: al-Haqiqi li Braille", *al-Muslimoon, The Muslim International Weekly*, vol. 1, number 32, (London, 1985), p.19.

-----   "Ibn Hazm's influence on Christian thinking in Research", *The Islamic Quarterly*, vol. 31, number 2, (London, The Islamic Cultural Centre, 1407 AH; 1987 AD), pp.103-115.

-----   *"The Muslim View of Christianity with Special Reference to the Work of Ibn Hazm"*, unpublished PhD thesis, Exeter University, (England, 1404 AH; 1983 AD).

Albornoz, Sanchez, *Ibn Hazm Qima Aspaniyya*, see Makki.

Algermissen, P. Ernst, *"Die Pentateuchzitate Ibn Hazm's Ein Beitrag zur Geschichte der Arabischen Bibelubersetzungen"*, unpublished PhD thesis, Munster, 1933.

Ben Adereth, Salomo ben Abraham, *Sein Leben und Seine Schriften*, (his answer to Ibn Hazm al-Andalusi), (J. Perles, Breslau, Schletter, 1863), pp.1-27.

Cross, F. L., (ed.), *The Oxford Dictionary of the Christian Church*, (London, Oxford University Press, 1961).

De Vaux, Carra, "Akhlak" in M.Th. Houtsma et al, (ed.) *The Encyclopaedia of Islam*, first edition, vols. 1,2,3, (Leiden, E. J. Brill/London, Luzac and Co., 1927).

Goldziher, Ignaz, "Ibn Hazm" in James Hastings (ed.), *The Encyclopaedia of Religion and Ethics*, vol. 7, (Edinburgh, T. & T. Clark, 1908).

----- *"Proben Muhammedanischer Polemik gegen den Talmud"*, (Jeschurun, vol. 8, (Lemberg, 1872), pp.76-104.

Guthrie, D., et al, *New Bible Commentary*, third edition, (Oxford, Oxford University Press, 1985).

Hourani, George F., *Reason and Revelation in Ibn Hazm's Ethical Thought, in Islamic Philosophical Theology*, ed. by Parviz Marewedge, (U.S.A., State University of New York Press, 1979), pp.142-164.

Al-Kittânî, Muhammad Ibrâhîm, *Hall Aththara Ibn Hazm fi'l-Fikr al-Masîhî*, [Majallat al-Bayyina al-Maghribiyya, no. 1], (Morocco, 1962), pp.68-87.

----- *Shadharât min Kitâb al-Siyâsa li Ibn Hazm*, (Morocco, Majallat Tatwan, number fifteen, 1960).

Lane, Edward William, *An Arabic-English Lexicon*, Part 2, (Beirut, Lebanon, Librairie du Liban, 1968).

Margoliouth, D. S., "Old and New Testament in Moham-madanism" in James Hastings (ed.) *The Encyclopaedia of Religion and Ethics*, vol. 9, pp. 480-483.

Palencia, Angel Gonzales, *al-Shi'r al-Andalusi wa Ta'thiru fi'l Shi'r al-Urubbi*, (The Modern Spanish Journal, first year, number 2, January 1935)

Perlmann, M., "Ibn Hazm on the Equialence of Proofs", *The Jewish Quarterly Review*, vol. 40, 1949), pp. 280f.

Rif'at, N., *Ibn Hazm on Jews and Judaism*, PhD thesis, (England, Exeter University, 1988).

Schreiner, M., "Beitrage Zu Geschichte der Theologischen Bewegun in Islam", (*Zeitschr. D. Deutschen Morgenld Gessellsch.*, vols. 52 and 53), (1899).

Wenham, J. W., "Moses and the Pentateuch", in Guthrie, et al, *New Bible Commentary*, pp. 41-43.

Young, Edward J., "History of the Literary Criticism of the Pentateuch", in Guthrie, *New Bible Commentary*, pp. 34-40.